Almut E. I. Bettels
Traditionelle Baukunst
Traditional Architecture
in China

Almut E. I. Bettels

Traditionelle Baukunst
Traditional Architecture
in China

Mit Fotografien von
With photographs by
Li Yuxiang

Benteli Verlag

Die Deutsche Bibliothek CIP-Einheitsaufnahme

Bettels, Almut:
Traditionelle Baukunst in China = Traditional architecture in China /
Almut Bettels. – Wabern : Benteli, 2002
   ISBN 3-7165-1264-8

Benteli Verlags AG
Seftigenstrasse 310, CH 3084 Wabern/Bern
Tel. (+41) 031 960 84 84; Fax (+41) 031 961 74 14
info@benteliverlag.ch; www.benteliverlag.ch

© 2002 Almut E. I. Bettels, Hildesheim; Benteli Verlags AG, Wabern/Bern
© 2002 Fotografien/Photographs: Li Yuxiang, Jiangsu Art Publishing House, Nanjing
Weitere Bildrechte siehe Abbildungsnachweise/for additional photographic copyright
see Illustration acknowledgements

Englische Übersetzung/English Translation: Almut E. I. Bettels; Lektorat/copy editing: Michael Robinson
Gestaltung/Design: Almut E. I. Bettels
Satz und Reproduktion/Type setting and repro: Lithoscan, Braunschweig
Druck/Printing: Brillant Offset GmbH, Hamburg

Printed in Germany

ISBN 3-7165-1264-8

Inhaltsverzeichnis

Einführung	8
Die Höfe im Stil der Höhlen in Shanxi	12
Der Stil der versenkten Höhlen	12
An das Ufer angelehnte Höhlen	18
Höfe im Stil der freistehenden Höhlen	20
Die Pfahlbauten (ganlan) und ihre Abkömmlinge	34
Die Pfahlbauten in Yunnan	34
Die überhängenden Häuser (diaojiaolou) der Tujia	40
Die Baukunst des Dong-Volkes	56
Die reitenden Stockwerke (qilou) in Jiangnan	74
Anmerkungen zu den Grundlagen der traditionellen Baukunst	84
Anmerkungen zum fengshui	88
Baustile	116
Die traditionellen Freilichthöfe im siheyuan-Stil in Beijing	122
Hierarchie der Residenzen	129
Traditionelle Höfe in Shanxi	134
Traditionelle chinesische Baukunst und ihre Variationen in Anhui	160
Zur Geschichte der alten Dörfer in Süd-Anhui	165
Anlage und Dekoration der Höfe	170
Kennzeichen der Hofanlagen in der Ming- und Qing-Zeit	178
Der östliche Geist in der traditionellen Baukunst	190
Erdgestampfte Festungsbauten in Fujian	202
Die Erdgebäude (tulou)	202
Die Fünf-Phönix-Gebäude (wufenglou)	210
Die Erdschlösser (tubao)	212
Das Erdschloß Anzhenbao	216
Festungen (diaofang) und Wachtürme (diaolou) in Sichuan	222
Die Rote Backsteinbaukunst in Fujian	226
Register	236
Bibliographie	239
Abbildungsnachweise	240

Contents

Introduction	8
The cave style courtyards in Shanxi	12
The sunken cave style	12
Draw alongside caves	18
Courtyards in the style of standalone caves	20
The stilt houses (ganlan) and their offspring	34
The stilt houses in Yunnan	34
The overhanging houses (diaojiaolou) of the Tujia	40
The Dong people's architecture	56
The riding storeys (qilou) in Jiangnan	74
Notes on the principles of traditional architecture	84
Notes on fengshui	88
Architectural styles	117
Traditional open air courtyards in the siheyuan style in Beijing	122
Hierarchy of the residences	129
Traditional courtyards in Shanxi	134
Traditional Chinese architecture and its special features in Anhui	160
On the history of the old villages in South Anhui	165
Layout and decoration of the courtyards	170
Characteristics of the courtyards in the Ming and Qing time	178
The Eastern mind in traditional architecture	190
The rammed earth fortresses in Fujian	202
The rammed earth buildings (tulou)	202
The Five-Phoenix-Buildings (wufenglou)	210
The earth castles (tubao)	212
The earth castle named Anzhenbao	216
Fortresses (diaofang) and Watchtowers (diaolou) in Sichuan	222
The Red-Brick-Architecture in Fujian	226
Index	236
Bibliography	239
Illustration acknowledgements	240

Zeittafel		Chronicle table	
Neolithikum	ca. 6000 – 200 v. Chr.	Neolithic period	ca. 6000 – 200 BC
Xia-Dynastie	21.–16. Jh. v. Chr.	Xia Dynasty	21.–16. C. BC
Shang-Dynastie	16.–11. Jh. v. Chr.	Shang Dynasty	16.–11. C. BC
Zhou-Dynastie	11. Jh. – 221 v. Chr.	Zhou Dynasty	11. C. – 221 BC
Westliche Zhou-Dynastie	11. Jh. – 771 v. Chr.	Western Zhou Dynasty	11. C. – 771 BC
Östliche Zhou-Dynastie	770 – 256 v. Chr.	Eastern Zhou Dynasty	770 – 256 BC
Chunqiu-Periode	770 – 476 v. Chr.	Spring/Autumn Period	770 – 476 BC
Zhanguo-Periode	475 – 221 v. Chr.	Warring States Period	475 – 221 BC
Qin-Dynastie	221 – 207 v. Chr.	Qin Dynasty	221 – 207 BC
Han-Dynastie	206 v. Chr. – 220 n. Chr.	Han Dynasty	206 BC – 220 AD
Westliche Han-Dynastie	206 v. Chr. – 220 n. Chr.	Western Dynasty	206 BC – 220 AD
Östliche Han-Dynastie	25 v. Chr. – 220 n. Chr.	Eastern Han Dynasty	25 BC – 220 AD
Die Drei Reiche	220 – 280 n. Chr.	The Three Kingdoms	220 – 280 AD
Wei-Dynastie	220 – 265 n. Chr.	Wei Dynasty	220 – 265 AD
Chu-Han-Dynastie	221 – 263 n. Chr.	Chu Han Dynasty	221 – 263 AD
Wu-Dynastie	222 – 280 n. Chr.	Wu Dynasty	222 – 280 AD
Westliche Jin-Dynastie	265 – 316 n. Chr.	Western Jin Dynasty	265 – 316 AD
Östliche Jin-Dynastie	317 – 420 n. Chr.	Eastern Jin Dynasty	317 – 420 AD
Die Süd-Dynastien	420 – 589 n. Chr.	The Southern Dynasties	420 – 589 AD
Song-Dynastie	420 – 479 n. Chr.	Song Dynasty	420 – 479 AD
Qi-Dynastie	479 – 502 n. Chr.	Qi Dynasty	479 – 502 AD
Liang-Dynastie	502 – 557 n. Chr.	Liang Dynasty	502 – 557 AD
Chen-Dynastie	557 – 589 n. Chr.	Chen Dynasty	557 – 589 AD
Die Nord-Dynastien	386 – 439 n. Chr.	The Northern Dynasties	386 – 439 AD
Nördliche Wei-Dynastie	386 – 534 n. Chr.	Northern Wei Dynasty	386 – 534 AD
Östliche Wei-Dynastie	534 – 550 n. Chr.	Eastern Wei Dynasty	534 – 550 AD
Nördliche Qi-Dynastie	550 – 577 n. Chr.	Northern Qi Dynasty	550 – 577 AD
Westliche Wei-Dynastie	535 – 556 n. Chr.	Western Wei Dynasty	535 – 556 AD
Nördliche Zhou-Dynastie	557 – 581 n. Chr.	Northern Zhou Dynasty	557 – 581 AD
Sui-Dynastie	581 – 618 n. Chr.	Sui Dynasty	581 – 618 AD
Tang-Dynastie	618 – 907 n. Chr.	Tang Dynasty	618 – 907 AD
Fünf Dynastien	907 – 960 n. Chr.	Fife Dynasties	907 – 960 AD
Die spätere Liang-Dynastie	907 – 923 n. Chr.	The later Liang Dynasty	907 – 923 AD
Die spätere Tang-Dynastie	923 – 936 n. Chr.	The later Tang Dynasty	923 – 936 AD
Die spätere Jin-Dynastie	936 – 946 n. Chr.	The later Jin Dynasty	936 – 946 AD
Die spätere Han-Dynastie	947 – 950 n. Chr.	The later Han Dynasty	947 – 950 AD
Die spätere Zhou-Dynastie	951 – 960 n. Chr.	The later Zhou Dynasty	951 – 960 AD
Liao-Dynastie	916 – 1125 n. Chr.	Liao Dynasty	916 – 1125 AD
Song-Dynastie	960 – 1279 n. Chr.	Song Dynasty	960 – 1279 AD
Nördliche Song-Dynastie	960 – 1127 n. Chr.	Northern Song Dynasty	960 – 1127 AD
Südliche Song-Dynastie	1127 – 1279 n. Chr.	Southern Song Dynasty	1127 – 1279 AD
Jin-Dynastie	1115 – 1234 n. Chr.	Jin Dynasty	1115 – 1234 AD
Yuan-Dynastie	1271 – 1368 n. Chr.	Yuan Dynasty	1271 – 1368 AD
Ming-Dynastie	1368 – 1644 n. Chr.	Ming Dynasty	1368 – 1644 AD
Qing-Dynastie	1644 – 1911 n. Chr.	Qing Dynasty	1644 – 1911 AD
Republik (Minguo)	1912 – 1949 n. Chr.	Republic (Minguo)	1912 – 1949 AD
Volksrepublik	seit 1949 n. Chr.	People's Republic	since 1949 AD

Introduction

This publication is based on a documentation project, called Lao Fangzi, published by the Jiangsu Fine Arts Publishing House in Nanjing. Since the early 1990s, photographers have been travelling around the provinces of China to take pictures of traditional houses and courtyards. Historians, architects and art experts have contributed to the project and made their research available.

The Chinese Empire covers 27 provinces with a total area of 9.6 million square kilometres and extends over climatically and geographically different areas. Cold and dry zones in the north, dry deserts and rather moderate areas in Central China and subtropics with extreme rainfall in the south, mountainous highlands, plateaus, lowlands and plains along the large rivers determine the scenery. The population consists of more than fifty ethnic minorities, living in different, mostly autonomous regions. On trade routes and as a result of migrations caused by military conflicts their cultures continuously influenced each other; in architecture a variety of characteristics were transferred and new styles developed.

The two philosophies of Confucianism and Taoism represented the two poles of Chinese life and culture, and influenced architecture as well. Living in harmony with nature was the basic principle of the Taoist philosophy. By using the art of Chinese geomancy, called *fengshui* by the layman, they succeeded in realizing this principle in architecture by choosing the best location for any kind of human settlement according to natural conditions and aesthetic aspects. From the Han Dynasty (206 BC – 220 AD) onwards, Central China had a defining influence on the cultural development of all other provinces, stressing the southern and south eastern regions. Thus the conception of the traditional courtyards which are arranged following the Confucian order of succession, and defined as being in harmony with the laws of nature, were transferred and modified according to the respective landscapes.

The buildings presented here are built in the Ming (1368 to 1644 AD) and Qing Dynasty (1644–1949 AD) with a few that are important in their traditional design dating from the Minguo Period (1912–1949 AD). Only a few municipal and sacred buildings or fragments of residential buildings or courtyards have survived from earlier periods.

This is an attempt to convey insights into architectural traditional styles without making any claims to completeness. Presented here are the highly developed cave buildings of the yellow earth (loess) areas in Central China, stilt houses with their successors, the overhanging houses

wickelten Höhlenbauten aus den Gebieten gelber Erde (Lößboden) Zentralchinas, Pfahlbauten und ihre Abkömmlinge, zu denen die überhängenden Häuser gehören, die in Gebirgsregionen im Süden Chinas ein bevorzugter Baustil sind, sowie die sogenannten reitenden Stockwerke, die an den Flüssen in Jiangsu und Zhejiang zu finden sind. Ferner werden Höfe aus den als Schatzkammer der Baukunst geltenden Provinzen Shanxi und Anhui gezeigt sowie Freilichthöfe der Altstadt Beijings und ein Hof der Roten Backsteinbaukunst Fujians, die im Kontrast zu der Grauen Backsteinbaukunst Zentralchinas steht. In Fujian beeindrucken die aus Erde gestampften Festungsgebäude *(tulou)* und Erdschlösser *(tubao)*, die im Stil der traditionellen Höfe angelegt sind; als Ergänzung werden die Wachtürme und Bunkergebäude des Zang-Volkes in West-Sichuan vorgestellt, die ihren Ursprung in Tibet (Xizang) haben.

Die ausgewählten Aufnahmen reflektieren die Ästhetikprinzipien der chinesischen Kultur auf zweifache Weise, sie lassen den Betrachter die Bilder als Kunstwerke der Fotografie empfinden, und sie zeigen die Baustrukturen der Häuser mit Betonung lokaler Besonderheiten, technischer Einzelheiten und ästhetischer Finessen und können so als eine Schule für die Architektur betrachtet werden. Die Kunst des *fengshui* lebt in den substantiellen *yinyang*-Kräften der Natur, und somit ist die Schwarzweißfotografie, die mit den Kunstgriffen der Kontraste Hell und Dunkel, Licht und Schatten arbeitet, ein besonders geeignetes Medium, um Verständnis für die chinesische Baukunst zu vermitteln. Farbfotos wurden hier gewählt, um die Schönheit der natürlichen Materialien oder die zarte Stimmung einer Stadtlandschaft für das verwöhnte Auge zu betonen sowie Besonderheiten farbiger Dekorationen zu zeigen.

and the so-called riding storeys, which are preferred in areas with a warm, humid climate, in mountainous areas and in the plains along the rivers in Jiangsu and Zhejiang; there are also courtyards from the old cities of Beijing, Shanxi and Anhui, provinces considered as treasury of traditional architecture, and a famous courtyard in Red-Brick-Architecture in Fujian which contrasts with the Grey-Brick-Architecture of Central China. In Fujian the famous rammed earth buildings *(tulou)* and the earth castles *(tubao)*, which are arranged in the traditional courtyard style impress the visitor; in addition the Zang fortresses in West Sichuan, derived from the fortresses in the pill-box style in Tibet (Xizang), are also presented here.

The pictures chosen reflect the aesthetic principles of Chinese culture in two different ways: they allow viewers to enjoy the images as works of art, and they show how the buildings are constructed. Particular attention has been paid to special local features, technical details and aesthetic subtleties, so that overall the pictures can act as a school of architecture. The art of *fengshui* draws its power from the substantial *yinyang* forces of nature. This means that black-and-white photography, which exploits the contrasts between bright and dark, light and shade, is a particularly suitable medium for conveying an understanding of Chinese architecture. Color photographs have been chosen here to enhance the beauty of the natural materials and the delicate atmosphere of a townscape for the discerning eye, and to show the special qualities of colored decorations

Danksagung

Mein Dank gilt vornehmlich Herrn Li Yuxiang, dem Cheffotografen des Projektes, und Herrn Zhu Chengliang, dem Herausgeber der Publikation des Dokumentationsprojektes „Lao Fangzi", die ihr Bildmaterial zur Verfügung gestellt haben und mit Rat und Tat zu Seite standen.

Ich danke Herrn Wang Qijun für Erklärungen zu seinen Texten und für Hinweise auf weiterführende Literatur seines Fachgebietes. Mein Dank gilt ferner Herrn Yu Hongli, dem Kunstexperten, der in Huizhou beheimatet ist und seine Kenntnisse der Baukunst dieser Region vermittelt hat.

Wertvolle Hinweise zur chinesischen Baukunst verdanke ich Herrn Chen Zhihua, Herrn Zheng Guangfu und Herrn Hong Wenxiong.

Zu Dank verpflichtet bin ich Herrn Manfred Boetzkes, dem Direktor des Roemer- und Pelizaeus Museums in Hildesheim, dessen Aufgeschlossenheit und Interesse am kulturellen Austausch die Ausstellung „Lao Fangzi – Traditionelle chinesische Baukunst in China" – im Frühjahr 1999 ermöglicht hat.

Sehr herzlich danke ich allen Freunden, die Teile meines Manuskripts gelesen und mir mit Anregungen zur Seite gestanden haben.

Herrn Michael Robinson verdanke ich die Endfassung der englischen Übersetzung.

Schließlich danke ich Herrn Thomas Rosenstock, dessen technisches Sachverständnis und Geschick unverzichtbar für die Qualität der Reproduktion waren.

Almut E. I. Bettels

Acknowledgement

My thanks go first and foremost to Li Yuxiang the principal photographer and Zhu Chengliang, the editor-in-chief of the Lao Fangzi project publications who provided me with the opportunity to write this book and arrange the exhibition Lao Fangzi – Old houses – Traditional Architecture in China.

I am grateful to Wang Qijun for his explanatory comments and for introducing me to secondary literature about his subject and to Yu Hongli, the art expert, who lives in Huizhou and has generously shared his profound knowledge of the architecture in that region.

I thank Chen Zhihua, Hong Wenxiong and Zheng Guangfu for helpfully drawing my attention to special features of Chinese architecture.

I am indebted to Manfred Boetzkes, whose open mind and interest in cultural exchange made the exhibition in the Roemer and Pelizaeus Museum in Hildesheim possible in spring 1999.

My warm thanks go to all my friends, who listened to parts of the manuscript and made helpful suggestions.

Special thanks go to Michael Robinson for the final English version.

Last but not least I want to thank Thomas Rosenstock, whose technical skill and expertise were invaluable for the type setting and repro quality.

Almut E. I. Bettels

Elefant und Affe auf der Brüstung vor einer Ahnenhalle. Ming-Dynastie
Monkey and elephant on the parapet in front of an ancestor hall. Ming Dynasty
Shanxi, Yangcheng, Runchengzhen

Die Höfe im Stil der Höhlen in Shanxi 山西

Die Baukunst Chinas hat ihren Ursprung in den Höhlen- und Pfahlbauten, die in geographisch verschiedenen Landschaften entstanden sind. Beide Formen führten zu den Hofanlagen im *siheyuan*-Stil, die später in allen Provinzen des Festlandes verbreitet waren. Die Höhlenbauten sind in den Gebieten der Gelben Erde im Norden Chinas entstanden, und bis heute werden in den Provinzen Henan, Shanxi, Shaanxi und Gansu Höhlenbauten bewohnt. Sie werden zwei Stilarten zugeordnet, dem Stil der an das Ufer angelehnten Höhlen und dem Stil der versenkten Höhlen. Letztere wurden mit rechteckigem Innenhof angelegt und können als Vorstufe der traditionellen *siheyuan* betrachtet werden. In die Gruppe der Höhlenbauten werden ferner die freistehenden Höhlen eingeordnet, deren Räume nach dem Vorbild der versenkten Höhlen angelegt sind.

Der Stil der versenkten Höhlen
(xiachenshi yaodong) 下沉式窰洞

進村不見村，
樹冠露三分，
麥垛星羅布，
戶戶窰洞沉。

Du betrittst das Dorf, doch Du siehst es nicht,
Baumkronen kommen zum Vorschein,
Weizenschober sind verstreut wie Sterne,
Familien leben in versenkten Höhlen.

Diese Volksweise beschreibt anschaulich die Dörfer mit Höfen im Stil der versenkten Höhlen. Der Bezirk Pinglu im Süden Shanxis ist berühmt für Höfe in diesem Stil, und die gut erhaltenen darunter werden bis heute bewohnt.

Vor der Tang-Dynastie (618–907 n.Chr.) hieß die Stadt mit ihrem Bezirk Taiyin oder Dayin. Diese Namen bedeuten größte oder große Finsternis und weisen darauf hin, daß die Menschen hier in Höhlen lebten. Im Jahre 742 n.Chr. wurde die Stadt Pinglu (ebenes Land) genannt. Der Name läßt vermuten, die Stadt läge auf flacher Ebene, doch breitet sich der Bezirk über gebirgiges Land aus, das im Norden eine

The cave style courtyards in Shanxi

Chinese architecture originates from the cave buildings and stilt houses, two sources from areas with different geographical conditions and climate. Both forms led to the classical courtyards in the *siheyuan* style which became common in all of the mainland provinces. The cave buildings developed in the regions of Yellow Earth in the north and in the provinces Henan, Shaanxi, Shanxi and Gansu. Many of them are still inhabited today. They were constructed in two different styles, the draw alongside cave and the sunken cave. The last-named are laid out with a rectangular inner yard and can be seen as forerunners of the *siheyuan* courtyards. Courtyards built on the surface with their rooms arranged and installed in the same style as the sunken caves are also classified in this group and called cave buildings in the standalone style.

The sunken cave style
(xiachenshi yaodong)

*jin cun bu jian cun
shu guan lu san fen
mai duo xing luo bu
hu hu yao dong chen.*

No village is seen, while entering it
Only treetops make it visible,
Covered with stacks of wheat, like stars,
The families live in sunken caves.

This folksong describes the villages with courtyards in the sunken cave style. Pinglu county in the south of Shanxi is famous for courtyards in the sunken cave style and for the courtyards in the draw alongside side caves.

Before the Tang Dynasty (618 – 907 AD) the town and its district were called Taiyin or Dayin. These names mean utmost or great darkness and refer to the fact that people used to live in caves. In 742 AD the town was renamed Pinglu (flat land). From this name alone, one might think Pinglu is a district on the plains, but actually it spreads over the mountains, sloping down from 1600 meters above sea level in the north

Eingang in einen versenkten Höhlenbau mit Blick auf eine Schutzmauer
Entrance of a courtyard built in the sunken cave style with a screen wall
Shanxi, Pinglu, Nancun

Hof im Stil der versenkten Höhlen in Pinglu
Courtyard in the sunken cave style in Pinglu

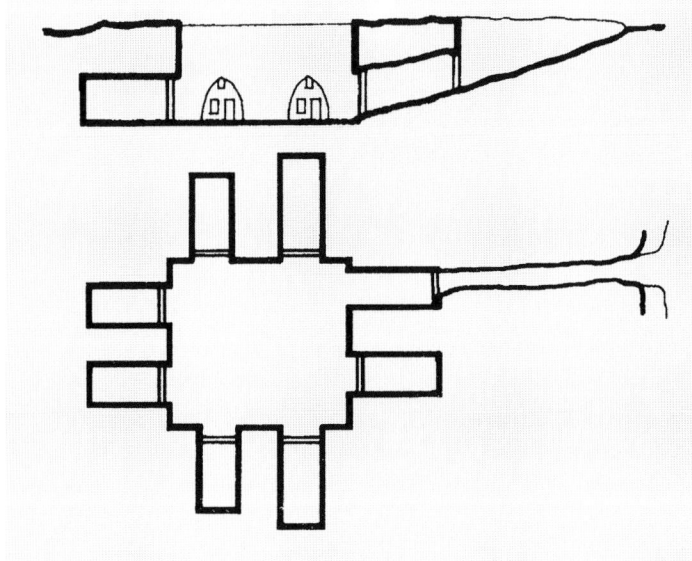

Skizze eines Hofes im Stil der versenkten Höhlen
Sketch of a courtyard in the sunken cave style

Höhe von 1600 m erreicht und im Süden entlang des Gelben Flusses auf 330 m ü. d. M. abfällt. Eben erscheint die Stadt durch die Höfe im Stil der versenkten Höhlen. Ihre Innenhöfe werden mit einer Tiefe von zehn bis elf Metern, einer Länge von etwa zehn Metern und einer Breite von drei bis vier Metern in die Erde gegraben. Ihr oberer Rand wird von einer kleinen Schwelle umsäumt, auf der manchmal dekorative Brüstungen gemauert sind, die vor Regen schützen. Die Längsachse der Innenhöfe verläuft entsprechend dem *fengshui* in Zentralchina von Nord nach Süd. Dadurch ist die Sonneneinstrahlung so günstig, daß die Höhlen auch im Winter mit genügend Licht versorgt werden. In die Seiten der Höfe sind die Höhlen eingegraben. Ihre Decken sind drei bis fünf Meter dick, um eine Durchfeuchtung des Bodens zu vermeiden und Stabilität zu garantieren, und sie sind gewölbt, um die Last des Bodens seitlich abzutragen. Im Norden liegt die Ahnen- und Empfangshalle mit Seitenräumen für die ältere Generation. An der West- und Ostseite sind Wohn-, Schlafräume und Küchen eingerichtet. In den Räumen sorgen Ofenbetten für eine ausgeglichene Temperatur. Vorhänge vor den Eingängen begünstigen die Luftzirkulation. Die Grundfläche der Räume liegt etwas höher als die Grundfläche der Innenhöfe. Zusätzlich schützen an der Südwestseite der Räume angelegte Sickerbrunnen vor Überschwemmung. Sie sind in einer Tiefe von etwa zehn Metern mit Ziegeln ausgekleidet und mit einer Mahlscheibe bedeckt, die bei Regen entfernt werden kann.

to 330 meters in the south along the Yellow River. But the surface of the town appears even, since the inhabitants live in courtyards in the style of the sunken caves. Box-like cavities, ten to eleven meters in depth, ten meters in length, and three to four meters in width were dug out to form sunken yards. The upper edges of the yards are a little above ground level and sometimes parapets, laid with patterns of tiles, are added. According to *fengshui* in Central China the longitudinal axes run from north to south, and the narrow axes from east to west. Consequently the sun can light and warm up the yards sufficiently even in winter. A gate leads into the yards, usually at the south-east corner, and caves are excavated in the sides. Their ceilings are vaulted to distribute the load on both sides to the ground, and they are three to five meters thick to guarantee stability and offer protection from rain. In the north the central hall is set up, subdivided into ancestor hall, guest hall and side rooms for the older generation. Bedrooms and kitchens are installed in the side caves. Curtains in front of the entrances help to keep the air circulating. In front of the windows beside the entrance, oven beds keep the rooms warm in the winter. The surfaces of the sunken yards are slightly lower than the floor levels of the living rooms, and raised thresholds prevent flooding. There is only little rainfall, but wells are installed at the southwestern corner of the rooms with their shafts tiled at least ten meters below ground level. Millstone slabs, removed when it rains, cover the wells.

Nach alter bäuerlicher Tradition wird in Shanxi bei Jahreswechsel über dem Tor der Höfe das Bild eines goldenen Ochsen angeheftet, das den Frühling symbolisiert und Wohlstand verspricht. Ein langes Leben und Harmonie für das neue Jahr besiegelt folgender Spruch.

Following the tradition of the old peasant culture a picture of a golden ox is fixed above the entrances to the courtyards around New Year, symbolizing spring and promising wealth. Long life and harmony in all the seasons of the new year are guaranteed by the following proverb.

新春正月二十三，太上老君去煉丹，
家家門上貼金牛，一年四季永平安。

Xin chun zheng yue ershisan, Taishang Laojun qu lian dan, jiajia menshang tie jin niu, yi nian si ji yong pingan.

Am 23. Tag des neuen Jahres raffiniert Taishang Laojun Pillen (Arznei für ein Langes Leben). An die Türen ist das Bild eines Goldenen Ochsen zu heften, und die vier Jahreszeiten werden friedvoll und harmonisch sein.

On the 23rd day of the new year, Taishang Laojun refines pills (for long life). Above all the doors a golden ox has to be fixed, and the four seasons will be peaceful and harmonious.

Hinter dem Eingang der Höfe steht nach altem Brauch eine Schutzmauer mit eingelassenem Schrein für den Erdherrscher. In Pinglu werden bis heute Höfe bewohnt, deren Baujahr aus der Qing-Dynastie datiert. Einer der ältesten Höfe zählt mehr als hundert Jahre. Die Haupthalle des Hofes ist viereinhalb Meter hoch, fünf Meter breit und achtzehn Meter tief. Nach Angaben des Hausherrn war die Anlage nach dem *fengshui* bestimmt worden, doch waren die Höhlen zu Anfang recht klein. Erst nach mehreren Jahren, als die Bewohner sich der Qualität des Bodens sicher waren, hatten sie die Räume vergrößert, um sich eines angenehmen Lebens darin zu erfreuen.

Bei schlechter Erdbeschaffenheit wird die Oberfläche der Höhlen rissig, das Regenwasser beginnt durchzusickern, und die Höhlen stürzen daraufhin ein. Obwohl solche Fälle selten sind, geben die Bewohner sorgsam acht; sofern Risse entstünden, würden diese mit Ziegeln bedeckt und der Hof müßte umgehend verlassen werden.

Heute werden kaum noch Höfe im Stil der versenkten Höhlen gebaut. Der wesentliche Grund dafür liegt in den Bestimmungen der Baubehörden. Sie schreiben für die Baugrundstücke der Bauernfamilien eine Größe von 0,2 bis 0,3 *mu* vor (1 *mu* = 1/15 Hektar). Ein Hof im Stil der versenkten Höhlen beansprucht jedoch eine Grundfläche von ein bis zwei *mu*. In der direkten Umgebung darf kein Ackerbau betrieben werden, und die Oberfläche der Höhlen wird nur als Trockenplatz für Getreide benutzt. So sind die Höfe im Stil der versenkten Höhlen dem Niedergang geweiht.

Der Stil der an das Ufer gelehnten Höhlen, der in gebirgigen Gebieten der gelben Erde bevorzugt wird, ist hier mit einigen Bildern und Skizzen präsentiert (s. S. 18,19).

According to custom a shrine for the Earth Ruler is inset on the screen wall behind the yard gate. Many courtyards in the sunken cave style in Pinglu, which are inhabited today, were built in the Qing Dynasty. One of them is more than a hundred years old. The cave in this courtyard's main hall is four and a half meters high, five meters wide and eighteen meters deep. According to the owner, the courtyard was constructed following the laws of *fengshui*, but at first with very small caves excavated. The rooms were not enlarged until several years later, when the inhabitants found it was a success, as they had enough space to enjoy a comfortable life.

If the location is wrongly determined and it turns out that the soil is not firm, cracks will appear on the surface, rain water will penetrate into the caves and within a short time the surface will collapse. Such cases rarely happen, but if cracks appeared, the inhabitants would cover them with tiles and immediately leave their courtyard.

Today they do not build sunken caves in Pinglu any more. The main reason is that the planning department and the building control offices only allocate 0,2–0,3 *mu* (1 *mu* = 1/15 hectare) for a farming estate, while a courtyard in the sunken cave style measures one or two *mu* on average. The land in the immediate vicinity cannot be farmed, and the surface of the caves only provides a drying area for the harvest. Consequently the courtyards in the sunken cave style have declined.

The style of the draw alongside cave which was preferred in mountainous areas of the yellow earth is presented with some pictures and sketches below (cf. pp. 18,19).

Blick in einen versenkten Höhlenbau
Courtyard in the sunken cave style
Shanxi, Pinglu, Nancun

Eingang in einen versenkten Höhlenbau
Way into a building in the style of the sunken cave
Shanxi, Pinglu, Nancun

An das Ufer angelehnte Höhlen *(kaoanshi yaodong)* 靠岸式 窑洞
Draw alongside caves *(kaoanshi yaodong)*

An das Ufer angelehnte und freistehende Höhlenbauten
Caves in the draw alongside and standalone style
Shanxi, Lingshi, Jingshengzhen

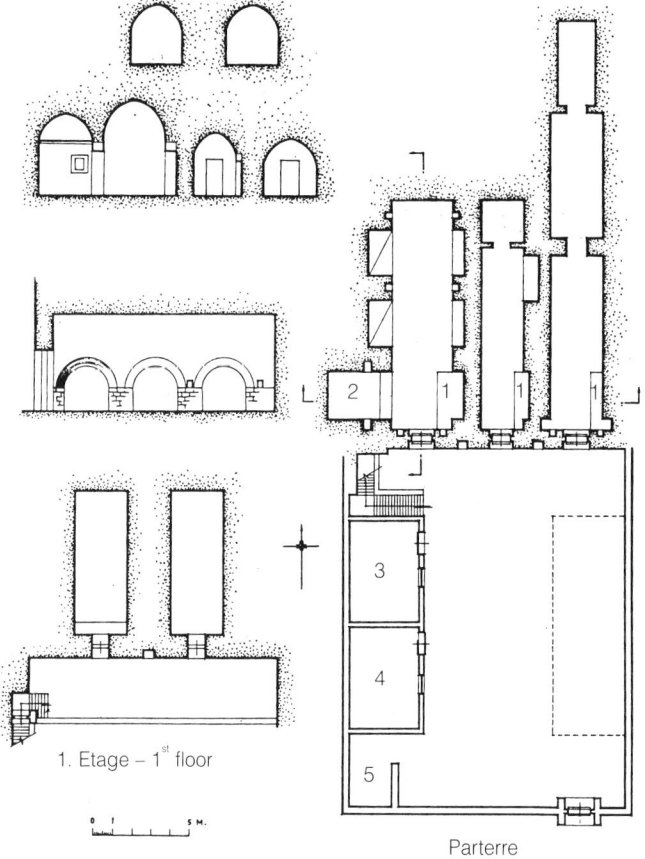

1. Etage – 1st floor

Parterre

An das Ufer angelehnte Höhle
Draw alongside cave
Henan
1 Küche – kitchen
2 Vorratsraum – store room
3 Gästezimmer – drawing room
4 Wohnraum – living room
5 Toilette – toilet

An das Ufer angelehnte Höhlenbauten in Baode, Qiaotouxian, Shaanxi
Caves in the draw alongside style in Baode, Qiaotouxian, Shaanxi

Schulklasse an der Brüstung eines Gebäudes im Stil der an das Ufer angelehnten Höhlen
Schoolboys with their teacher behind a parapet of a building in the draw alongside cave style

Courtyards in the style of standalone caves (dulishi yaodong)

Skizze eines Hofes im Stil der freistehenden Höhlen
Outline of a courtyard in the style of the standalone caves

1 Schutzmauer des Zentralgebäudes – Screenwall of the central building
2 Schornsteine der Ofenbetten – Chimneys of the oven beds *(kang)*
3 Galerie des Zentralgebäudes – Gallery of the central building
4 Treppenaufgang – Staircase
5 Innenhof – Inner yard
6 Seitengebäude – Wing of the courtyard
7 Tor der hängenden Blumen – Hanging flower gate
8 Zentraltor – Central gate
9 Götterschrein – Shrine for idols
10 Treppe im Innenhof – Stairs in the inner yard
11 An die Gebäudewand lehnende Schutzmauer – Screen wall set in the gable wall of a wing
12 Haupteingang – Main entrance

Historically Pingyao is one of the most important towns in China. It is famous for its colossal city walls and the courtyards in the style of standalone caves, which are surrounded by high and massive walls stress its fortress character.

Since Pingyao lies in the center of Shanxi, not far away from Pinglu, the same *fengshui* applies to both districts. Consequently the longitudinal axis of the yards runs from north to south. The ground level of the yards ascends wing by wing, step by step up to the main hall. The main entrance is placed at the south-east corner of the front wall. It faces a screen wall, which is set in the gable wall of the wing opposite. Passing the second gate, designed in the hanging flower style, the path leads to the central yard. Both the main building and the wings are usually subdivided into three bays *(kaijian)* with the entrance leading into the middle bay, their style is called 'one light two dark *(yiming liangan)*'. The single layered roofs of the wings are concave in form. They slope from the ridge towards the inner yard, while the main building has a flat roof edged by parapets. Since the flat roof is lower than the roofs of the

Hof im Stil der freistehenden Höhlenbauten
Courtyard in the standalone cave style
Shanxi, Lingshi, Jingshengzhen

während das Hauptgebäude ein Flachdach hat, das mit einer Brüstung eingefaßt ist. Darauf stehen an der Rückseite Schutzmauern, die vor Wind schützen, den Einblick aus den Nachbarhöfen versperren und das Zentralgebäude betonen. Ein Hof in dem beschriebenen Stil wird hier mit Bildern und einer Skizze gezeigt (s. S. 31–33).

Seit in der Ming-Dynastie der Außenhandel in Pingyao florierte, wurden die Höfe prachtvoller ausgestattet und dekoriert. Oft wurden an den Seiten der Hofeingänge gemeißelte Steinsockel zum Besteigen und Manneshöhe überragende Steinpfosten zum Festbinden der Pferde aufgestellt, um die Wirkung der imposanten Tore zu betonen. Auf den Pfosten sitzen Löwen oder Affen, denen zugesprochen wird, Pferde vor Krankheit schützen zu können.

Eine skurrile Geschichte erzählt der Hof mit dem Namen Qijian, Qilin Baoxiating, dessen Haupt- und Seitengebäude jeweils sieben Buchten *(jian)* in der Breite und sieben Dachpfetten in der Tiefe messen und im *siheyuan*-Stil den zentralen Innenhof umfassen. Der Hof datiert aus der Qing-Dynastie, einer Zeit, in der nur die kaiserlichen Palasthallen neun Buchten und neun Dachpfetten maßen und es hohen Beamten vorbehalten war, in Haupthallen zu residieren, die sieben Buchten und sieben Dachpfetten maßen.

Unter Tong Zhi (1865–1877 n.Chr.) war in Pingyao eine Bank mit dem Namen Rishengchang (Die Sonne, die Tag für Tag Wohlstand hervorbringt) gegründet worden. Dieses Geldinstitut gelangte zu so hohem Ruhm, daß die Bewohner in Pingyao zu sagen pflegten: „Rishengchang ist das erste Bankhaus unter dem Himmel". Als im August 1900 die vereinte Armee der acht Mächte (20000 Soldaten, aufgestellt von England, Rußland, Japan, USA, Deutschland, Frankreich, Italien und Österreich) in Beijing einzog, um den Boxeraufstand niederzuschlagen, flohen die Prinzessin Cixi und der König Guang Xu über Shanxi nach Shaanxi. In Pingyao nahm die Prinzessin eine Geldanleihe auf und wählte dafür das Kreditinstitut Rishengchang. Dies verleitete den Bankeigentümer Hou Dianyuan anzunehmen, seinen Einfluß noch stärker geltend machen zu können, und um seine Position zu betonen, ließ er den prachtvollen Hof Qijian Qilin Baoxiating bauen. Da er keine offizielle Position bekleidete, lief er damit Gefahr, zum Tode verurteilt zu werden. Zwar gelang es ihm, die Beamten zu bestechen und sein Leben zu retten, doch mußte er seinen Hof verkaufen, dessen prachtvolle Gebäude daraufhin dem Verfall überlassen waren.

wings, screen walls were set up on the parapets of the back wall, to protect against the wind, and they accentuate the site of the ancestor hall, where the owner used to reside. A very beautiful courtyard in the style of the standalone caves is presented here with some pictures and a little sketch (cf. pp. 31–33).

Foreign trade flourished from the Ming Dynasty onwards and consequently the residences were furnished more splendidly. Stone pedestals to mount horses and posts to tether them, higher than a man, were set up on both sides of the main gate to emphasize the splendor of the main gate. Lions or monkeys, believed to protect horses from illness and to tame them, decorate the posts.

The courtyard in the standalone style with the name Qijian, Qilin Baoxiating tells a peculiar story. The main hall as well as the wings of this courtyard measure seven bays *(jian)* in width and seven purlins in depth and surround the central yard in the *siheyuan* style. The courtyard was built in the Qing Dynasty, when only the main halls of the Emperors' Palaces measured nine bays and nine purlins. The right to reside in main halls of seven bays and seven purlins was reserved for officials of the highest rank.

Under Tong Zhi (1865–1877 AD) a financial institution was founded in Pingyao called by the name Rishengchang (The sun, day by day producing prosperity). This bank became so influential that in Pingyao people used to say: "Rishengchang is the first bank in the world". When in August 1900 the United Army of eight countries (20000 soldiers organized by the U.K., Japan, USA, Russia, Germany, France, Italy and Austria) marched into Beijing to quell the Boxer Rebellion, the Dowager Cixi accompanied by the King Guang Xu left their residence and went to Shaanxi. The escape route led them through Shanxi, and in Pingyao Rishengchang was the bank chosen by the Dowager for a loan. Thereafter Hou Dianyuan further emphasized his influence, and to stress his position he built the magnificent courtyard called Qijian Qilin Baoxiating. Since Hou Dianyuan was not a high ranking official, he ran the risk of being sentenced to death. He succeeded in avoiding capital punishment only by bribing the authorities, but he had to sell his courtyard, and its magnificent buildings were allowed to fall into disrepair.

Frontansicht und Innenhof des Qijian, Qilin Baoxiating (Sieben Buchten, Sieben Dachpfetten Hofes)
Front view and inner yard of the Qijian, Qilin Baoxiating (Seven Bays, Seven Purlins Courtyard)
Shanxi, Pingyao, Chengguanzhen

Oben: Haupttor eines Hofes im Stil der freistehenden Höhlen mit Blick auf eine in die gegenüberliegende Giebelwand eingelassene Schutzmauer; an den Seiten Steinsockel und -pfosten zum Besteigen und Festbinden der Pferde. Shanxi, Pingyao, Chengguanzhen
Links: Steinpfosten zum Festbinden der Pferde, dekoriert mit einem Affen, dem Tier mit der Gabe, Pferde zu zähmen und sie vor Krankheit zu schützen. Shanxi, Xiangfen, Dingcun

Above: Main entrance of a courtyard in the standalone style, with a screen wall let in the gable wall behind, and stone pedestals to mount horses and pillars to tether them on both sides.
Shanxi, Pingyao, Chengguanzhen
Left: Stone pillar to tether horses, decorated with a monkey, the animal supposed to tame and to protect horses from illness. Shanxi, Xiangfen, Dingcun

Oben: Ortsteil mit Ruinen freistehender Höhlenbauten
Links: Blick über die Dächer eines freistehenden Höhlenbaus auf die Berge vor dem Ort
Shanxi, Lingshi, Jingshengzhen

Above: Dilapidated courtyards in the standalone cave style
Left: View overlooking the wing of a courtyard in the standalone style and the mountains
Shanxi, Lingshi, Jingshengzhen

Oben: Blick vom Innenhof auf das zweite Tor eines Hofes im Stil der freistehenden Höhlen mit Schutzmauer und Schrein zu beiden Seiten. Shanxi, Pingyao, Chengguangzhen
Rechts: Zwei Schreine, eingelassen in die Schutzmauern eines Hofes, gestaltet als Miniatur eines zweiten Durchgangstores mit Schutzmauer zu beiden Seiten. Shanxi, Lingshi, Jingshengzhen

Above: Second gate in a courtyard in the standalone style with a shrine let in the screen wall on both sides of the entrance. Shanxi, Pingyao, Chengguangzhen
Right: Two shrines let in a screen wall, imitating the design of second gates with screen walls on both sides. Shanxi, Lingshi, Jingshengzhen

Zweites Tor in einem Hof im Stil der freistehenden Höhlen
Second gate in a courtyard in the standalone style
Shanxi, Pingyao, Chengguanzhen

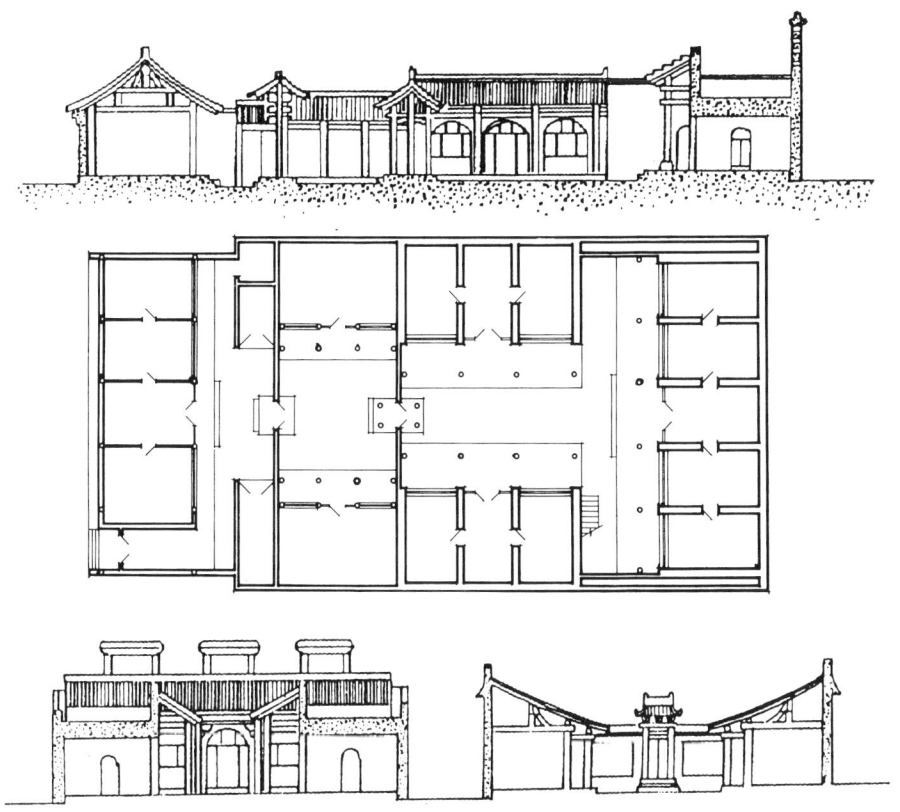

Skizze des freistehenden Höhlenbaus in der Renyi-Gasse Nr. 4 in Pingyao
Sketch of the courtyard in the standalone cave style in no. 4 Renyi alley in Pingyao

Schutzmauern auf der Brüstung des Hauptgebäudes (oben) und Innenhof
(S. 32/33) des Hofes im Stil der freistehenden Höhlen in der Renyi-Gasse Nr. 4 in Pingyao

Screen walls set up on the parapets of the main building (above) and inner yard
(cf. pp. 32/33) of the courtyard in the standalone style in no. 4 Renyi alley in Pingyao

Die Pfahlbauten *(ganlan)* 幹欄 und ihre Abkömmlinge

Die Pfahlbauten in Yunnan 雲南

In den Provinzen Guizhou und Yunnan im Südwesten Chinas sind bis heute Pfahlbauten zu finden, die als geschlossene Dörfer angelegt sind und sich harmonisch in die Landschaft einfügen. Sie werden von Minoritäten bewohnt, die in autonomen Gebieten leben. Die Häuser, genannt *ganlan,* haben ihren Ursprung im Südwesten Chinas, und wie durch Ausgrabungen belegt wurde, waren sie bereits in der Shang-Dynastie der übliche Baustil. In den Ruinenstätten in Haimenkou im Bezirk Jianchuang wurden neben Bronzen und Stein Urformen der Pfahlbauten aus dem Jahre 1150 v.Chr. entdeckt. Aus dem Jahre 400 v.Chr. wurden in dem Dorf Dapona in Xiangyuan kleine Bronzepfahlbauten gefunden, die den heute von der Jingpo-Minorität bewohnten Häusern gleichen.

Der Begriff *ganlan* wurde zuerst in der Literatur der Tang-Dynastie in folgendem Lehrtext über die Völker des Südens (Jiu Tangshu – Nanmanfu) beschrieben: „In den Bergen gibt es giftige Pflanzen und Grubenottern, dort leben die Menschen zusammen in Stockwerken, in die sie über Treppen hinaufgelangen. Genannt werden sie *ganlan.*" Zu den bedeutenden Völkern des Südens gehören die Dai-Sippen. Mit einer Bevölkerung von 1,138 Millionen Menschen besiedeln sie das autonome Gebiet Xishuangbanna. Sie leben in Kleinfamilien zusammen in ihren sogenannten Bambushäusern. In früheren Zeiten wurden die Häuser auf Bambuspfählen errichtet, mit Wänden aus Bambusgeflecht eingeschalt und mit Stroh überdacht. Die Böden wurden in Bambusmatten gemessen und mit Bambusmatten ausgelegt. Bambus war das Lebenselixier, beschrieben mit dem Spruch „Bambus zum Essen, Wohnen und Feuer machen (*Chi zhu, zhu zhu, chao zhu*)!" Später ging man dazu über, mit Nutzholz und Ziegeln zu bauen. Der Boden der Häuser ist auf Holzpfeiler gestützt und von einem Holzrahmen eingefaßt. An die Hausfront ist eine Veranda angeschlossen, auf der sich das alltägliche Geschehen abspielt und Gäste empfangen werden. Auf einem seitlichen Balkon wird Regenwasser aufgefangen. Im Erdgeschoß sind die Vorratsräume und die Ställe für das Vieh eingerichtet. Das Privatleben der Familien findet in den sogenannten Familienhallen *(jiating)* statt, mit dem Feuerplatz als ihrem Zentrum. Dieser Raum war nach Tradition ein geheiligter Ort, der nicht übertreten werden durfte. Die Dächer sind als Walmdächer (ruhender Berg) mit Frontgiebel, Rückgiebel und kurzem First konstruiert und mit flachen Ziegeln

The stilt houses *(ganlan)* and their offspring

The stilt houses in Yunnan

Stilt houses laid out as complete villages that fit in with the scenery beautifully are found in the provinces Guizhou and Yunnan in the south-west of China. They are inhabited by different minorities who live in autonomous regions. Excavation has verified that the houses called *ganlan* originate in the south-west of China and were the common architectural style even in the Shang Dynasty. Along with bronze and stone finds architectural prototypes of stilt houses, dating from 1150 BC, were discovered in Haimenkou in the district of Jianchuan. In the village of Dapona in Xiangyuan little bronze stilt houses, dating from 400 BC, were found which are shaped like the dwellings that are still inhabited by the Jingpo minority in Yunnan.

The name *ganlan* was first described in the literature of the Tang Dynasty in the following text on the tribes of the south (Jiu Tangshu – Nanmanfu): "In the mountains where there are poisonous plants and vipers, people live together in upper storeys into which they walk up the stairs. They are called *ganlan.*" The Dai, 1.138 million people, living in the autonomous region of Xishuangbanna are among the most important old-established tribes of the south. Nuclear families live in dwellings also called "bamboo houses". In former times the houses were built only using bamboo. They were supported on bamboo stilts, surrounded by walls of bamboo wickerwork and roofed with thatched straw. The ground floors were covered with and measured in bamboo mats. Bamboo was the elixir of life, described with the proverb: "Bamboo for eating, dwelling, and making fire! *(Chi zhu, zhu zhu, chao zhu!)*" Later they changed to houses built using timber and tiles. The almost square base of the houses is edged by a timbered frame, and supported on timbered stilts. A veranda is built on in front and here guests are received and daily life takes place. Rainwater is collected on a balcony behind. The ground floor is used for storing food and keeping animals. The private life of the families takes place in the so-called family hall *(jiating)* with the fireplace at its center. According to tradition, this place is holy and should not be stepped over. The houses are covered with combined gable and hip roofs (resting mountain), supported by timbered beams and tiled with flat tiles. On all four sides the steep slopes of the roof extend as projecting eaves which protect the buildings from violent rain and intense sunlight. Roofed gates in the *ganlan* style mark the boundaries of the villages. The Dai people

Ein Dai-Mann im Hauptwohnraum *(jiating)* eines Bambushauses aufrecht auf einer Matte sitzend
A Dai man sitting upright on a straight mat in the main room *(jiating)* of a bamboo house
Yunnan, Ruili, Nongdao

Dorftor im *ganlan*-Stil
Village gate in the *ganlan* style
Yunnan, Ruili, Nongdao

Zwei elliptische Häuser des Wa-Volkes
Two elliptical houses of the Wa people
Yunnan, Cangyuan, Mengjiao

Unterbau eines „Auf tausend Beinen stehenden Hauses" des Lisu-Volkes
Foundation of a "House Built on Thousand Legs" of the Lisu people
Yunnan, Fugong

gedeckt. Steile Dachhänge mit weit ausladenden Dachvorsprüngen schützen gegen Regen, Wind und starke Sonneneinstrahlung. Überdachte Eingangstore im *ganlan*-Stil begrenzen die Orte. Die Dai-Sippen verehren ihre Vorfahren, und sie sind teilweise Anhänger des Buddhismus. So schmücken Ahnentempel und buddhistische Tempel das Bild der Dorflandschaften.

Das Jingpo-Volk lebt mit 1,26 Millionen Menschen in Gebirgsregionen (Yinjiang, Longchuan, Ruili, Luxi etc.), die ein- bis zweitausend Meter über dem Meeresspiegel liegen. Ihre Häuser genannt „Langer First, kurzer Dachvorsprung (Haus)" blicken auf eine Geschichte von mehr als zweitausend Jahren zurück und werden bis heute in ihrer ursprünglichen Form gebaut. Der Name beschreibt klar ihren Stil. Die Häuser sind rechteckig und mit hängenden Strohdächern gedeckt, die im Winkel von 45 Grad geneigt sind und über dem Eingang einen Meter überstehen. Die Grundfläche liegt, je nach Topographie der Landschaft, entweder einen oder ca. zwei Meter über dem Erdboden. Vorratsräume und Ställe befinden sich im Erdgeschoß; das Leben der Familien spielt sich im oberen Stockwerk ab, in dessen Zentrum der Feuerplatz liegt.

Als ein Gedicht des Bambus werden die ellipsenförmigen Häuser des Wa-Volkes betrachtet, dessen Vorfahren zu den Pu-Sippen, den ältesten Einwohnern Yunnans, gehörten. Mit einer Bevölkerung von 380000 siedelt das Wa-Volk in der Gebirgsregion Awashan. Aus Stroh gearbeitete Walmdächer bedecken wie ein Teppich ihre Häuser und überdachen die Eingänge im Halbkreis. Aus Holz oder Bambusrohr geformte Front- und Rückgiebel kreuzen am First und erscheinen wie Schwalbenschwänze. Zu den Seiten neigen sich die Dächer im Winkel von 60 Grad zum Boden, ohne von Außenwänden gestützt zu werden. In den Dörfern sind die Häuser Reihe an Reihe mit einem zentralen Gartenhäuschen angeordnet.

Der Name „Auf tausend Beinen stehendes Haus" bezeichnet anschaulich die Wohnhäuser des Lisu-Volkes, das mit 614000 Einwohnern in der Schlucht des Nu-Flusses im Nordwesten Yunnans lebt. Einfache Dächer aus Stroh bedecken die rechteckigen Häuser; die Wände sind aus Bambus geflochten. In ihrem Zentrum befinden sich ein oder zwei Feuerstellen. Die Häuser ruhen auf Holzpfählen unterschiedlicher Stärke, die in ihrer Länge den Unebenheiten des Bodens und dem Neigungswinkel der Berghänge angepaßt sind. Sie wirken wie Tausendfüßler und können als einfache Vorstufe der überhängenden Häuser betrachtet werden.

worship their ancestors, and most of them are followers of Buddhism. Thus ancestor temples and Buddhist temples adorn the villages.

The Jingpo minority live with 1.25 million people in mountainous regions (Yinjiang, Longchuan, Ruili, Luxi, etc.) which rise from one thousand up to two thousand meters above sea level. Their dwellings, called Long Ridge, Short Eaves House, look back on a history of more than two thousand years, and they are constructed in their original shape to this very day. The name describes their simple style precisely. The houses are rectangular and covered with thatched roofs which slope down at an angle of 45 degrees and project one meter above the front. Depending on the topography of the landscape, the ground floors are about one or two meters above the ground. Store room and shed are located in the storey below, in the upper storey family life takes place with the fireplace at its center.

The elliptical houses of the Wa people, whose ancestors belong to the Pu tribes, the oldest inhabitants of Yunnan, are considered as a poem in bamboo. With a population of 380000 in number the Wa minority live in the mountainous area of Awashan. Hipped roofs, made of thatched grass, soft as a carpet, cover the houses. Front and rear gables, made of bamboo canes or wood, cross at the ridge and look like swallow tails. The roofs slope down towards the ground at an angle of 60 degrees, without being supported by exterior walls. The front veranda has a semi-circular roof. In the villages the houses are arranged row upon row with a pavilion in the center.

The name House Built on Thousand Legs illustrates the dwellings of the Lisu people, who, 614000 in number, live in the gorge of the Nu River in the north-west of Yunnan. Simple gable roofs, thatched with straw, cover rectangular houses, the walls are woven from bamboo. One or two fireplaces are located in the center. The storey rests on wooden posts, which are different in length and thickness, according to the unevenness of the ground and the gradient of the mountain slopes. They look like millepedes and can be seen as an early form of the overhanging houses.

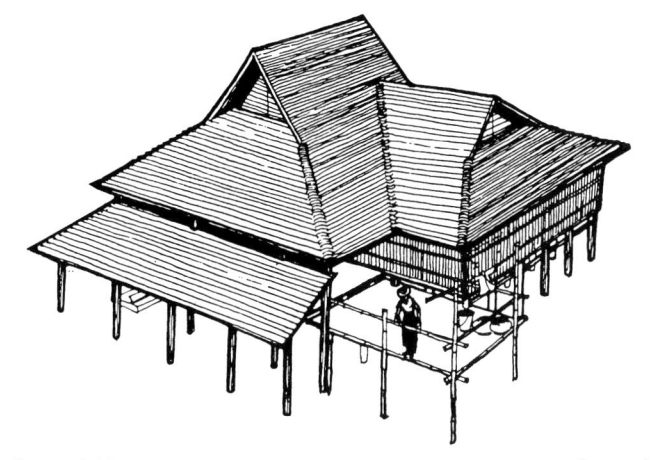

Außenansicht   Outer view

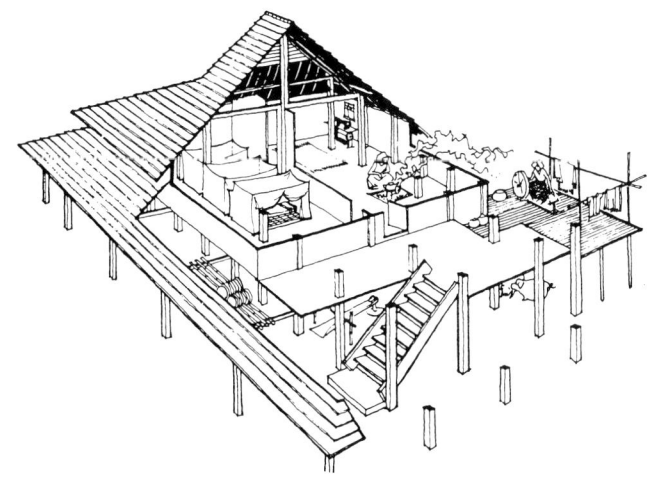

Innenansicht   Inner view

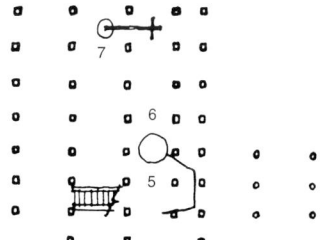

Parterre

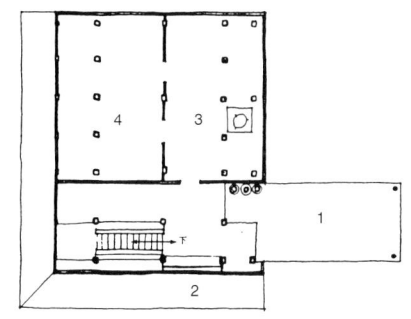

1. Etage – 1st floor

Skizze eines Pfahlbaus *(ganlan)* des Dai-Volkes

1 – Trockenterrasse, 2 – Frontveranda, 3 – Hauptraum,
4 – Schlafraum, 5 – Futterplatz, 6 – Speicher, 7 – Reismühle

Sketch of a stilt house *(ganlan)* of the Dai people

1 – drying terrace, 2 – front veranda, 3 – main hall,
4 – bedroom, 5 – feeding place, 6 – granary, 7 – rice mill

Frontansicht eines Bambushauses des Dai-Volkes
Front view of a Dai bamboo house
Yunnan, Ruili, Nongdao

Rückansicht eines Bambushauses des Dai-Volkes
Rear view of a Dai bamboo house
Yunnan, Ruili, Nongdao

Dachlandschaft des Ortes Mengla des Dai-Volkes im Bezirk Menglun, Yunnan
Roof scenery in the Dai village of Mengla in the Menglun district, Yunnan

Doppelhaus des Dai-Volkes im *ganlan*-Stil
Dai twin house in the *ganlan* style
Yunnan, Jinghong, Menghanzhen

Die überhängenden Häuser (diaojiaolou) 吊腳樓 der Tujia 土家

Die überhängenden Häuser sind Abkömmlinge der Pfahlbauten, die als Balustraden, Pavillon Balustraden und Hanf Balustraden *(ganlan, gelan, malan)* bezeichnet werden. Auf Schildkrötenknochen sind unter anderen die Zeichen 帛（京）*(jing* – Hauptstadt), 亳（亳）*(po* – nördlicher Bezirk in Anhui), 畗（享）*(xiang* – erfreuen) *(xiangtang* – Ahnenhalle) und 高（高）*(gao* – hoch) zu lesen, deren Struktur die überhängenden Häuser beinhaltet. Daraus läßt sich entnehmen, daß dieser Stil in frühen Zeiten in Zentralchina verbreitet war. Nachdem die Baiyue-Völker über die Grenzen Zentralchinas hinaus verstreut siedelten, breitete sich der *ganlan*-Stil in Ost- und Südasien, Korea und Japan aus.

Die Balustraden *(ganlan)* haben ihren Ursprung im Südwesten Chinas. Ihr Weg führte über das Yungui-Plateau durch die Wuling-Gebirge, das historische Ursprungsland der Ba-Völker, nach Zentralchina. Nachdem die Ba-Völker mit den Chu-Völkern, den ältesten Völkern Zentralchinas, in Kontakt getreten waren, hielt ihr Bau- und Wohnstil in Zentralchina Einzug. Später, als die Chu- mit den Han-Völkern als führende Klasse vereint waren, wurde ihre Baukunst Vorbild, und der Stil, auf Matten zu leben, behielt daraufhin Vorrang in Zentralchina in den zweitausend Jahren der Xia-, Shang-, Zhou- und Qin-Dynastie. Nach der Han-Dynastie (220 v.Chr.–207 n.Chr.) wurden die auf Balustraden konstruierten überhängenden Häuser zu lebenden Fossilien der Chu-Baukunst erklärt. In der Östlichen Jin-Dynastie (317–420 n.Chr.), als die Qiang- und Di-Völker im Gefolge der Rebellion der fünf nicht Han-Völker *(wu hu luan hua)* nach Süden zogen, wurde dieser Bau- und Wohnstil wiederum über die Grenzen Chinas transferiert. Als nach der Sui- (581–618 n.Chr.) und Tang-Dynastie (618–917 n.Chr.) der Südosten erschlossen war, kehrte er an seinen Ursprungsort, den großen Südwesten Chinas, zurück.

Die Tujia sind Nachfahren der Ba-Völker. Mit einer Bevölkerungszahl von 5,7 Millionen zählen sie zu den bedeutenden ethnischen Nationalitäten Chinas. Sie haben ihr eigenes Symbol, den Tigerlotus, ihr eigenes Musikinstrument, hergestellt aus Bronze mit einem Tigergriff. Ihre Sprache gehört zu der Familie der tibetisch-burmesischen Sprachen und somit zu dem sino-tibetischen Sprachsystem. In der Baukunst sind die überhängenden Häuser ihre Charakteristika.

Die Wuling-Gebirgszüge erstrecken sich im Grenzgebiet der Provinzen Hubei, Hunan, Guizhou und Sichuan. Sie werden von Seitenarmen des Yangtse-Flusses durchzogen, deren schmale fruchtbare Ebenen zugunsten der Landwirtschaft nicht besiedelt werden. Die Tujia bauen ihre Häuser an den Berghängen entlang der Flüsse. Dabei kommen die

The overhanging houses (diaojiaolou) of the Tujia

The overhanging houses *(diaojiaolou)* are offspring of the stilt houses, named as *ganlan, gelan, malan* (balustrades, pavilion balustrades, hemp balustrades). Old characters, engraved on turtle bones, as for instance 帛（京）*(jing* – capital), 畗（享）*(po* – northern part of Anhui), 高（高）*(gao* – high), and 亳（亳）*(xiang* – enjoy) *(xiangtang* – ancestor hall), which carry the meaning of overhanging storeys built on balustrades, show that this style was prevalent in Central China in primeval times. After the Baiyue people living in Central China migrated to different countries in Asia, the *ganlan* style was transferred to the South and East of Asia, Korea and Japan.

The balustrades *(ganlan)* originated in the south-west of China, crossed the Yungui Plateau and continued their way along the Wuling Mountains, where the Ba people are historically rooted. Contact with the Chu people, the oldest race of Central China, meant transfer of the matting system and the *ganlan* style. After the uniting of the Chu and Han people this architectural style and way of living became common and remained in favor throughout the two thousand years of the Xia, Shang, Zhou and Qin Dynasty. After the Han Dynasty (207 BC–221 AD), the matting system and the *ganlan* style were given up in Central China and the overhanging houses were declared living fossils of Chu architecture. In the East Jin Dynasty (317–420 AD) at the time of the Five No Han Upheaval in China *(wu hu luan hua)*, when the Di and Qiang people migrated to the south, this architectural style and way of living were transferred abroad, and after opening up the south-east in the Sui (581–618 AD) and Tang Dynasty (618–907 AD), they went back to their place of origin, the Great South-west of China.

Overhanging houses came to be characteristic of Tujia architecture, descendants of the Ba people, living in the Wuling Mountains. With 5.7 million people they are one of the most important independent minorities in China. They have their own symbol, a tiger totem, and their own musical instrument, made of bronze with a tiger handle. They speak their own language, which is one of the Burma-Tibetan, and consequently the Sino-Tibetan, family of languages. Thus they have developed their independent culture.

The Wuling Mountains extend through the border area of the four provinces Hubei, Hunan, Guizhou and Sichuan. The Qing, Apeng, Youshui, and Loushui, tributaries of the Yangtze River, meander through the mountains, but their fertile plains are so narrow that the Tujia try to keep them clear of settlement. Since overhanging houses need little

Blick auf überhängende Häuser
View of overhanging houses
Sichuan, Longtan, Xiyang

Vorzüge der überhängenden Häuser zur Geltung, denn sie lassen sich beliebig an Höhenunterschiede anpassen. Als Baumaterial wird Kiefernholz verwendet. Die Gerüste werden mit großer handwerklicher Geschicklichkeit gezimmert, so daß einfache Häuser innerhalb eines Tages fertiggestellt werden können, und selbst komplexere Konstruktionen nie länger als einen halben Monat beanspruchen.

Da sich die Wuling-Gebirgszüge wie eine Halbinsel vom Yungui-Plateau nach Zentralchina ziehen, haben sich beide Kulturen kontinuierlich beeinflußt. So hielten in der Baukunst die Brunnenhöfe in die Gebirgsregion Einzug. Die Höfe der Tujia konnten jedoch nicht exakt symmetrisch wie ihre traditionellen Vorbilder angelegt werden, denn sie mußten den geographischen Bedingungen der Berge gehorchend gebaut werden. Sorgloses Fällen von Bäumen sowie Ausgraben kostbaren Bodens wurden vermieden, und Prinzipien der Ästhetik hatten Vorrang. Raum hat seine eigene Ästhetik, und die Berge bieten eine Schule des *fengshui*, als deren Meisterwerke die Höfe der Tujia zu sehen sind.

Bei der Anlage der Höfe und der Gestaltung der Dekorationen folgten die Tujia den im Buch der Riten *(Liji)* aufgezeichneten Lehrsätzen der Kunst und Baukunst. So wie ein Gelehrter den ethischen Prinzipien entsprechend wirkte und dabei Entspannung in der Meisterschaft der literarischen Kunst fand *(shi yi yu de, you yu yi)*, suchte der Handwerker, den Vorschriften der Anordnungen und Maße folgend, Freude in ihrer Variation *(gong yi yu fa, you yu yue)*.

Die Grundrisse der Höfe folgen dem Prinzip „zum Wachsen bringen" *(shengzhang)*. Die elementare Form mit drei linear angeordneten Räumen wird nach dem Charakter für die Zahl eins — Eins-Häuschen *(yiziwu)* genannt. Umschliessen die Gebäude einen Brunnenhof, wird das Hauptgebäude als Sattelgebäude bezeichnet. Die Zentralgebäude wurden grundsätzlich nicht überhängend konstruiert. Ausnahmen bilden Häuser in Wufeng, die mit dem Ziel besserer Anpassung an die Gebirgsformationen an einer Seite eine freitragende Dachtraufe haben. Dem Eins-Häuschen folgt der Grundriß genannt Schlüssel *(yaoshi)*. Ein Seitengebäude wird im rechten Winkel an das Hauptgebäude angeschlossen. Die nächst größere Anlage mit einem Hauptgebäude und zwei im rechten Winkel angeschlossenen Seitengebäuden wird Wasser von drei Seiten *(sanheshui)* oder Kehrrichtschaufel *(cuojikou)* genannt. Wird ein Frontgebäude angefügt, so ist der Brunnenhof vervollständigt. Diese Anlage wird Wasser von vier Seiten *(siheshui)* genannt. Weitere Gebäude und seitliche Brunnenhöfe werden nach Bedarf angefügt.

ground space and can withstand all extremities of the warm and humid climate as well, they are still the most suitable constructions. Pine wood is the only material used, and since the craftsmanship of the Tujia people is highly developed, they often start their construction at sunrise, and by sunset the house is finished. Buildings more varied in structure need up to ten days, but never more than a fortnight.

Since the Wuling Mountains extend like a peninsula from Yunnan to Central China, both their cultures contin-uously influenced each other. Consequently the Tujia built their houses as well yards. But their layout does not follow the traditional rules of the courtyards they were modelled on precisely, since the houses had to be built to conform with the geographical conditions of the mountains. No careless excavations or tree felling were allowed and aesthetic principles were given priority. Space has its own aesthetic and the mountains offer a school of *fengshui* topography; and the works of the Tujia can be seen as a masterly demonstration of this.

When laying out their courtyards and shaping decorations the Tujia followed the principles of art and craft written in the Book of Rites *(Liji)*. Just as scholars followed ethical principles and thus striving for relaxation in the mastery of literary art *(shi yi yu de, you yu yi)*, craftsmen following the principles of arrangement and sizes sought their joy in variation *(gong yi yu fa, you yu yue)*.

The ground plans in their layout follow the rule give birth to growth *(shengzhang)*. The simplest form, which has three rooms, is called *yiziwu* (house shaped in the figure one —). If the rooms surround a well yard, the main or central building is named saddle building. Most of the central buildings are not overhanging. Houses in Wufeng built with raft eaves, overhanging on one side, to adjust to the topography of the mountains, are an exception to the rule. The construction following the house shaped like the figure one is called key *(yaoshi)*. One wing is added to the main building at an angle of 90 degrees. Houses in this design are the most common. The layout of the next larger one, which has one main building and two wings added at rectangular angles, is called water from three sides *(sanheshui)* or dustpan-mouth *(cuojikou)*. The first courtyard unit is completed by adding a gate building. This construction is named water from four sides *(siheshui)*. Further buildings enclosing well yards can be added when required.

Holztür neben einem *tianjing*, verziert mit dem Doppelzeichen *xi* 囍 (Glückssymbol der Eheschließung)
Wooden door carved with the double character *xi* (symbol of luck in marriage) facing a *tianjing*
Buermen, Yongshun, Hunan

Galerie genannt *meirenkao*, gestützt von hängenden, mit Kürbissen verzierten Säulen vor den Wohnräumen *kanzi* genannt. Lichuan
Gallery named *meirenkao* along the so-called *kanzi*, supported by hanging pillars carved with pumpkins instead of flowers. Lichuan

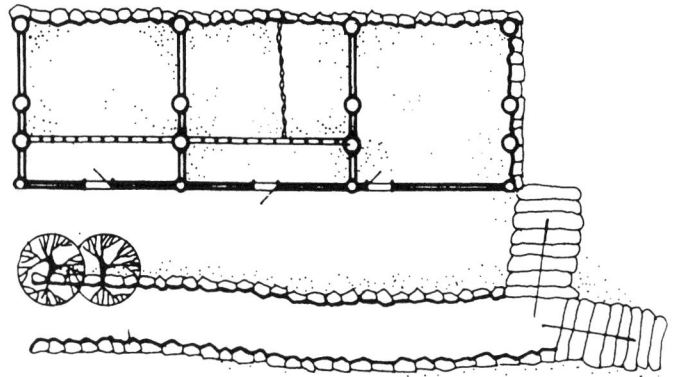

Grundriß eines Eins-Häuschens *(yiziwu)*
Floor plan of a house shaped like the figure one *(yiziwu)*

Kanzi werden die Räume mit freitragenden Veranden genannt, in denen die Kinder des Hauses wohnen. Der Begriff *kanzi*, von den Tujia *qianzi* ausgesprochen, bezeichnet ursprünglich Nischen für Idole. Die Veranden werden von Dachvorsprüngen mit Schutzgiebel *(siyan)* geschützt und von hängenden Säulen getragen. Dieses Arrangement wird mit den in Zentralchina üblichen Veranden, genannt *meirenkao* (Anlehnen der schönen Menschen), verglichen.

Die Schutzdächer *(siyan)* der freitragenden Veranden sind als Dachvorsprünge an die Dächer der Häuser, genannt hängender Berg *(xuanshan)*, angefügt und ähneln dadurch den ruhender Berg *(xieshan)* genannten, seitlich gegiebelten Walmdächern der traditionellen chinesischen Baukunst (s. S. 130). Das Wort Schutz *(si)* ist in den Bezeichnungen Windschutzdach *(siding)* und gedeckter Wachturm *(fusi)* wiederzufinden, die beide den gegiebelten Walmdächern gleichen (s. S. 51). So ist anzunehmen, daß der Begriff *xieshan* historisch aus dem Begriff *siyan* entstanden ist, denn *xie* soll eine Kurzform der beiden Zeichen *si* und *yan* sein. Die Schutzdächer schmücken anmutig die Häuser und gelten als Besonderheit der Tujia-Baukunst.

Die Kommandeurssäule *(jiangjunzhu)* steht im Schnittpunkt der Mittelachsen von Haupt- und Seitengebäude und trägt die Last beider Gebäude. Sie wird auch Schirmgriffsäule oder gen Himmel gerichtetes Geschütz genannt. Parallel angeordnete Balken, die auf Holzpfeiler gestützt sind, vollenden die Konstruktion. Der Fuzhongtao-Tempel beeindruckt durch ein perfektes Arrangement dieser Art, genannt eine Säule, zwölf Balken *(yi zhu shier liang)*.

Zu den häufigsten freitragenden Gebäudeteilen *(xuantiao)*, als Besonderheit der Tujia Höfe, gehört die überhängende Dachtraufe. Sie steht gewöhnlich mindestens eine (Balken) Maßeinheit (2,5 – 3,0 *shichi*) über (1 *shichi* = 1/3 m). Die freitragenden Veranden der *kanzi* werden von hängenden Säulen gestützt, die an der Dachtraufe verkürzt sind und zwei Maßeinheiten überstehende Holzplanken tragen. Auf den daraufliegenden Brettern werden Ernteprodukte gestapelt. Dadurch entsteht eine Schwalbenwohnung *(yanzilou)* unter der Dachtraufe.

Holzschnitzereien dekorieren Veranden, Säulen, Fenstergitter, Türen und Dachtraufen. Mit Ausnahme des als Pferdekopf *(fantiaofang)* geschnitzten tragenden Balkens der Dachtraufen in Hefeng (s. S. 46) gibt es jedoch nur wenige lokale Charakteristika. Die Dächer haben flache Firste, gerade Dachtraufen und -sparren. Dächer vom Typ *taishan* (steigender Berg) haben flügelartige Giebel, die je weiter Richtung Süden zu finden umso stärker geschwungen sind.

Kanzi, pronounced *qianzi* by the Tujia, is the name for overhanging rooms on the second floor, where the children of the family usually live (the original meaning of this term is niche of idols). In front of the rooms is a veranda supported by hanging columns. This arrangement is compared with the *meirenkao* (beautiful persons leaning), a borrowing from the Han culture. The hanging columns are decorated with pumpkins, a special Tujia feature.

Siyan (screen eave) is the name for the roof protecting the *kanzi*. The screen eaves are added to the roofs, shaped like the common roofs called hanging mountains (*xuanshan*). They look like the hipped and gabled roofs of the royal palace architecture in Central China (cf. p. 130), called *xieshan*. The vaulting called *siding* and the decorative screen roof or connecting watchtower (*lianque*) called *fusi* are comparable constructions (cf. p. 51). The *si* in these terms means protect. That is why it has been suggested from the etymological point of view that the syllable *xie* in *xieshan* is just the short form of the two characters *si* and *yan*. The *siyan* give shelter, embellish the houses, and they are seen as special features of Tujia architecture.

The commander's column (*jiangjunzhu*) supporting the main building and the wing, is placed on the intersection point of their central axis. This column was also called umbrella-handle column or rifle towards the sky. Crossbeams, arranged next to each other, are added for support. The framework of the Fuzhongtao (Buddhist) Temple, called one column twelve crossbeams (*yi zhu shier liang*), offers a splendid example of this kind of construction.

Overhanging eaves are the most common of all the overhanging constructions (*xuantiao*). They protrude by at least one beam-unit (2.5–3.0 *shichi*), (1 *shichi* = 1/3 m), and south of Laifeng even more than two units. The verandas of the *kanzi* (described above) are supported by hanging columns and wooden beams. The columns taper towards the top and form a hanging bench at the opening of the eave, jutting out two steps. Boards for drying harvest products are put on the bench, thus creating a home for swallows.

Wooden carvings decorate the verandas, the pumpkin-columns, the hanging beams, the joining eaves, the partition doors and windows. Since the culture of Central China was adopted and intermingled with the local culture, the Tujia designs and decorations can only be distinguished in a few features. In Hefeng, the turned overhanging beam (*fantiaofang*), carved as a horse's head, is considered a local feature (cf. p. 46). The roofs are made up of flat ridges, straight eaves, straight rafters; but so-called raising moun-

Kommandeurssäule *(jiangjunzhu)* 將軍柱 in einem Haus der Tujia
Commander's column *(jiangjunzhu)* in a house of the Tujia
Hunan, Liangjia, Maoba, Lichuan

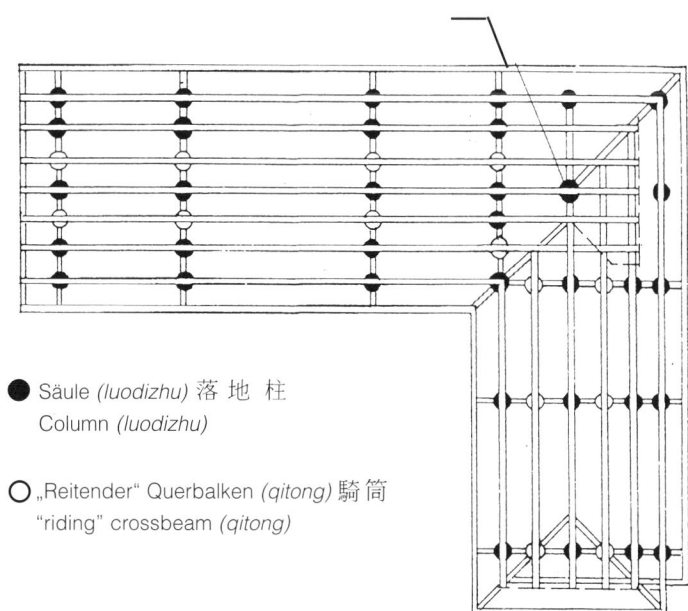

● Säule *(luodizhu)* 落地柱
Column *(luodizhu)*

○ „Reitender" Querbalken *(qitong)* 騎筒
"riding" crossbeam *(qitong)*

In den Städten wurden die Gebäude mit Steinmeißeln und -schnitzereien dekoriert, wobei bestimmte Gesetze der Ästhetik befolgt wurden. Die Steinsockel der Säulen wurden nach dem Prinzip *gong yi yu fa, you yu yue* des Handwerks modelliert. Die Sockel wurden in vertikaler Richtung dreigeteilt; ihr Querschnitt mußte rund, quadratisch, sechs- oder achteckig sein, während Größe, Proportionen und Muster nach Belieben variiert werden konnten. In dem Sanyuan-Tempel in Lichuan (s. S. 52/53), der nach dem Vorbild des Liulong-Tempels der südlichen Han-Dynastie konstruiert ist, finden sich kunstvoll gearbeitete Steinsockel, die in ihrer Vielfalt eine Schule dieses Prinzips sind.

Die Feuerplatz-Schlafstätten *(huopu)* im Zentrum der Häuser sind aus Holz konstruiert, werden jedoch mit den gemauerten Ofenbetten *(kang)* verglichen. Sie sind um eine Maßeinheit höher als der Fußboden. In ihrer Mitte ist eine Feuerstelle angelegt. Dort brennt stets das Feuer, um die Luftzirkulation in Gang zu halten, die Temperatur auszugleichen, Bambus und Holzkonstruktionen vor Fäulnis und oberhalb der Feuerstelle eingelagertes Getreide vor Schimmelbildung zu schützen. Der *huopu* ist eine tradierte Einrichtung der Chu aus den Zeiten, in denen die Familien auf Matten in einem Wohnraum, genannt *huopu*-Halle, zusammenlebten. Nach Ablösung einheimischer Würdenträger durch Beamte der Zentralmacht unter Yong Zheng (1723–1736 n. Chr.) der Qing-Dynastie wurden die *huopu* als Schlafstätten verboten, und die Eltern mußten getrennt von Sohn und Schwiegertochter nächtigen. Seitdem werden die *huopu* außer bei Anlässen, an denen Gäste geladen sind, nicht mehr von der Familie als Schlafstätte benutzt. Doch sind die Feuerplätze bis heute Zentrum des Familienlebens in den Häusern der Tujia geblieben.

tain roofs *(taishan)* can also be found, which have eaves formed like raised wings; the further south they are, the more they curve upwards.

Stone carvings decorate the buildings of the courtyards in the cities, with high fireproof walls in the horse head style, pedestals and drum stones. Their design follows the principle *gong yi yu fa, you yu yue* of craftsmen. The stone pedestals, for instance, are divided vertically into three parts. Their cross section can be round, square or octagonal according to the *yi*, while the *you* does allow three parts to be combined in size and proportion at random. A school following this rule is the Sanyuan Temple in Lichuan (cf. pp. 52/53), where all the stone pedestals are different in size, proportion and carvings. They are similar to those in the famous Liuliang Temple of the Southern Han Dynasty.

The fire-sleeping-places *(huopu)* are timbered, but are comparable to the brick-oven beds *(kang)*. The area is one step higher than the ground floor and the hearth is set in the center. The fire is kept burning day and night and all the year round to circulate the air and to protect wooden scaffolding from rot. Harvest products are stapled above to dry, and salted foods are hung up to smoke. The *huopu* can be traced back to the Chu people. They were set up in the centers of the houses in the room called fire-sleeping-place-hall *(huoputang)*, and the whole family used to sleep in this room. Under Yong Zheng (1723–1736 AD), when the local authorities were replaced by officials of Central China, it became forbidden for parents to use the same sleeping area as their sons and daughters-in-law. Since this time the *huopu* is only used as sleeping place for the whole family when feasts are held and guests are accomodated. But daily life still revolves around the fireplace.

Überhängende Häuser gebaut im Fachwerk *(chuandou)* mit geraden, überstehenden Schutzgiebeln entlang des Weges in das Dorf Longtan, Xiyang, Sichuan

Overhanging houses built in the framework *(chuandou)* style with straight projecting eaves, along the way into the village of Longtan, Xiyang, Sichuan

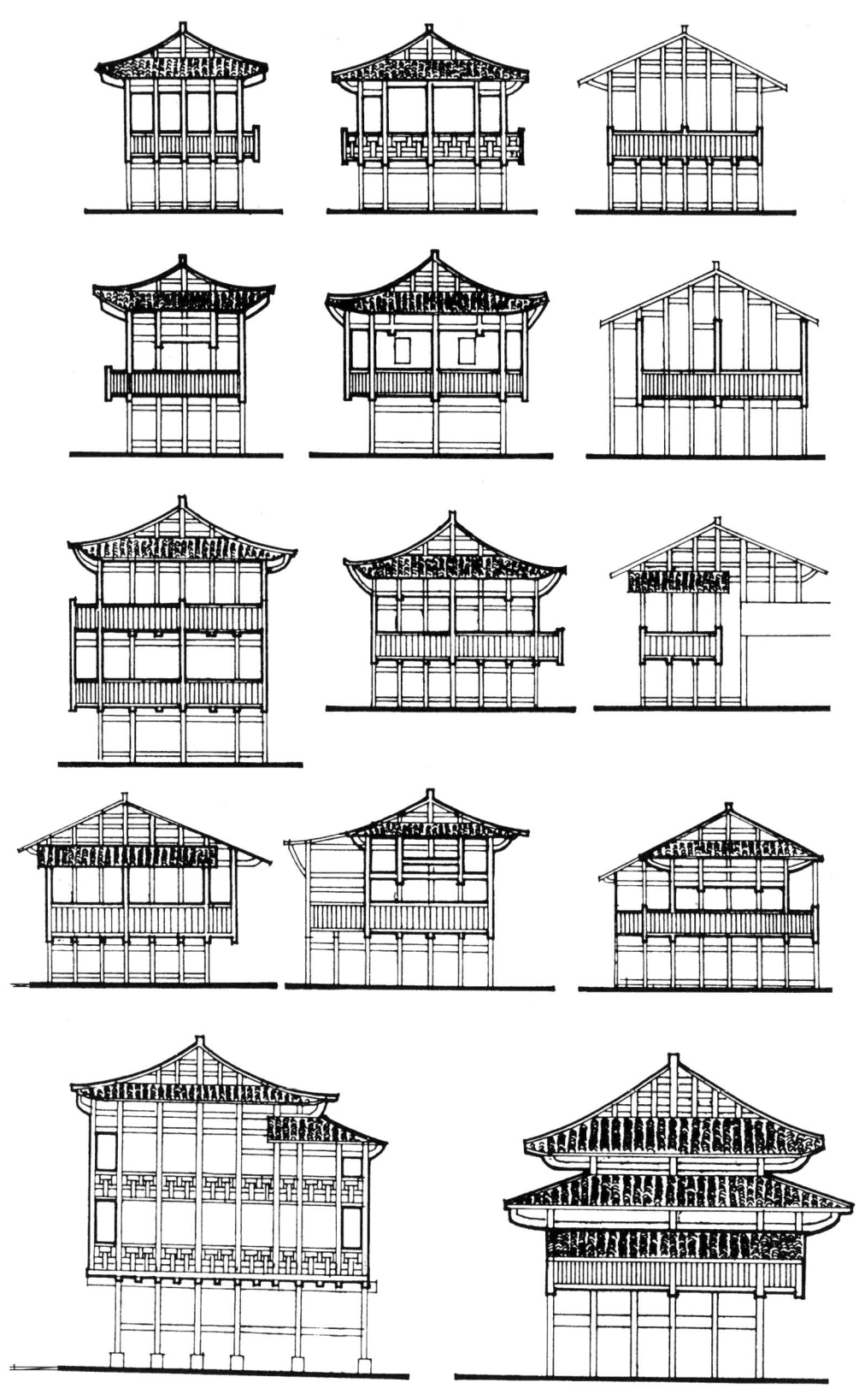

Skizzen von Variationen überhängender Stockwerke genannt *kanzi*
Sketches of different kinds of overhanging storeys called *kanzi*

Überhängende Häuser mit Schwalbenwohnungen und Schutzgiebeln über den Stockwerken, genannt *kanzi* in Hunan, Zejia, Yongshun (oben) und in Hunan, Baoping, Yongshun (unten)

Overhanging houses with swallow dwellings and screen eaves protecting the rooms called *kanzi* in Hunan, Zejia, Yongshun (above) and in Hunan, Baoping, Yongshun (below)

Haus im Stil der überhängenden Häuser
House in the style of the overhanging houses
Hunan, Zejia, Yongshun

Dächer und Wachturm *(fusi)* des Hofes der Familie Zhang
Roofs and watchtower *(fusi)* of the courtyard belonging to the Zhang family
Hubei, Fumenba, Yangdong, Xianfeng

Säulensockel im Sanyuan (Buddhist)-Tempel
Stone pedestals in the Sanyuan (Buddhist) Temple
Hunan, Zhonglu, Lichuan

Innenhof mit *tianjing* des Sanyuan-Tempels
Inner yard with *tianjing* of the Sanyuan Temple

Oben und rechts: Überhängende Häuser mit Wänden aus Fachwerk und überstehenden Schutzgiebeln, ein Charakteristikum der überhängenden Häuser in Sichuan
Sichuan, Longtan, Xiyang

Above and right: Overhanging houses with timber frame walls and projecting eaves, a characteristic of the overhanging houses in Sichuan
Sichuan, Longtan, Xiyang

Die Baukunst des Dong-侗 Volkes

Vor langer Zeit gab es an einem fernen Ort ein Gebirge mit dem Namen Gawa-Berge. Eines Tages kamen ein La-Bursche und ein La-Mädchen die Berge herab. Sie wollten am Fuß der Berge ein Haus bauen. Der La-Bursche war recht träge, und er sagte zu dem La-Mädchen: „Wir kriechen auf dem Berg in eine Steinhöhle und werden darin wohnen." Das La-Mädchen hörte auf die Worte des La-Burschen, und so krochen die beiden auf dem Berg in eine Steinhöhle.

Als es Abend geworden war, kam eine alte Schlange aus ihrer Höhle heraus und sprach zu ihnen: „Die Steinhöhlen hat der Satianba-Geist uns zugedacht, darin zu wohnen. Wenn ihr nicht hinausgeht, werde ich die Ratten rufen, euch totzubeißen." Darauf blieb dem La-Burschen und dem La-Mädchen nichts anderes, als aus der Höhle herauszukriechen. Das La-Mädchen sagte zu dem La-Burschen: „Laß uns ein Haus bauen!" Doch der La-Bursche war recht träge und sagte zu dem La Mädchen: „Wir kriechen am Fuß des Berges in eine Erdhöhle und werden darin wohnen." Das La-Mädchen hörte auf die Worte des La-Burschen, und so gingen die beiden den Berg hinab und krochen in eine Erdhöhle.

Als es Abend geworden war, kam ein Ohrenschuppentier in die Höhle und sprach zu ihnen: „Die Erdhöhlen hat der Satianba-Geist uns zugedacht, darin zu wohnen. Wenn ihr nicht hinausgeht, werde ich die Ameisen rufen, euch in Bewegung zu setzen." Darauf blieb dem La-Burschen und dem La-Mädchen nichts anderes, als aus der Höhle herauszukriechen, und das La-Mädchen sagte zu dem La-Burschen: „Laß uns ein Haus bauen!" Doch der La-Bursche wehrte träge mit der Hand ab und sagte zu dem La-Mädchen: „Wir werden auf dem Gipfel des Berges in eine große Baumhöhle kriechen und darin wohnen." Das La-Mädchen hörte auf die Worte des La-Burschen, und so krochen die beiden auf dem Gipfel des Berges in eine große Baumhöhle.

Als es Abend geworden war, kam eine große Fledermaus in die Baumhöhle geflogen und sprach zu ihnen: „Die Baumhöhlen hat der Satianba-Geist uns zugedacht, darin zu wohnen. Wenn ihr nicht hinausgeht, werde ich die Moskitos rufen, euch totzustechen." Darauf blieb dem La-Burschen und dem La-Mädchen nichts anderes, als aus der Baumhöhle herauszukriechen. Das La-Mädchen sagte zu dem La-Burschen: „Diesmal werden wir uns selbst ein Haus bauen." So blieb dem La-Burschen nichts anderes, als seine Hände zu rühren und ein Haus zu bauen. Er sammelte ein paar Bambusstämme, stellte ein Gerüst auf, verknüpfte Bambusbast zu einer Strohmatte, legte sie darauf, baute so auf dem Berg ein Strohmattenhäuschen, und die beiden krochen hinein, darin zu wohnen.

The Dong people's architecture

Once upon a time, far away, there was a mountain range called Gawa-mountain. One day a La-boy and a La-girl came down from the mountains, they wanted to build a house down the hill to live in. The La-boy did not feel like doing anything, and he said to the La-girl: "Let us crawl into a stone cave on a mountain and live in it." The La-girl obeyed the La-boy, and both of them crawled into a stone cave on the mountain.

In the evening an old snake came out of a stone cave and spoke to them: "The Satianba Spirit has conferred the right upon us to live in the stone caves, if you do not leave, I shall call on the rats to chew you to death." There was nothing left for the La-girl and the La-boy but to crawl out of the stone cave. The La-girl said to the La-boy: "Wouldn't it be better to build a house." The La-boy still did not feel like doing anything, and he said to the La-girl: "Let us crawl into an earth cave down the hill and live in it." The La-girl obeyed the La-boy, and both went to crawl into an earth cave down the hill.

In the evening a scaly anteater came into the cave and spoke to them: "The Satianba Spirit has conferred the right upon us to live in the earth caves, if you do not leave, I shall call on the ants to make you move." There was nothing left for the La-boy and the La-girl but to crawl out of the earth cave. Again the La-girl said to the La-boy: "Wouldn't it be better to build a house." The La-boy still did not feel like lifting a finger, and he said to the La-girl "Let us crawl into a cave of a huge hollow tree on top of a hill and live in it." The La-girl obeyed the La-boy, and both went to crawl into a cave of a hollow tree on top of a hill.

In the evening a huge bat came flying along into the cave of the hollow tree and spoke to them: "The Satianba Spirit has conferred the right upon us to live in the caves of the hollow trees, if you do not leave, I shall call on the mosquitoes to bite you to death." There was nothing left for the La-girl and the La-boy but to crawl out of the cave. The La-girl said to the La-boy: "This time we have to build our own house." There was nothing left for the La-boy but to lift his fingers and to build a house. He collected some bamboo

Dorftor mit Trommelturm, an der Treppe ein kleiner Erdherrscher-(Tudi) Schrein
Village gate combined with a drum tower, beside the stairs a little shrine for the Earth Ruler (Tudi)
Hunan, Yanglan, Tongdao

Feuerplatz in einem Haus des Dong-Volkes
Fireplace in a Dong house
Guangxi, Longsheng

Eines Tages kam der Berggeist, das Gebirge zu inspizieren. Als er das Strohmattenhäuschen erblickte, das der La-Bursche gebaut hatte, gebar er Zorn und dachte: „Ohne meine Erlaubnis eingeholt zu haben, wer kann es da wagen, auf dem Berg ein Haus zu bauen." Er blies, sein Atem verwandelte sich in einen starken Gebirgswind und fegte das Mattenhäuschen fort, ohne eine Spur zu hinterlassen. So blieb dem La-Burschen und dem La-Mädchen nichts anderes, als sich dicht aneinander zu schmiegen, und das La-Mädchen sagte zu dem La-Burschen: „Laß uns ein Haus bauen, aber eines, das der Wind nicht fortblasen kann." So blieb dem La-Burschen nichts anderes, als viele große Steine zu sammeln und am Fuße des Berges ein Haus zu bauen. Obenauf legte er eine große Steinplatte, und die beiden krochen hinein, darin zu wohnen.

Eines Tages kam der Wassergeist, den Fluß zu inspizieren. Als er das Steinhaus erblickte, das der La-Bursche gebaut hatte, gebar er Zorn und dachte: „Ohne meine Erlaubnis eingeholt zu haben, wer kann es da wagen, am Fuß der Berge ein Haus zu bauen!" Er blies, sein Atem verwandelte sich in eine große Flut, überschwemmte das Steinhaus und stürzte es um. So blieb dem La-Burschen und dem La-Mädchen nichts anderes, als auf den Berg zu eilen; und sie seufzten. Da kam eine gutherzige Elster herbeigeflogen und rief: „Holzgitter, mit Baumrinde bedeckt, keine Angst vor dem Wind, keine Angst vor dem Regen." Das La-Mädchen hatte verstanden, und es sagte zu dem La-Burschen: „Sieh wie geschickt das Nest der Elster gebaut ist. Wir werden von ihr lernen, ein Haus zu bauen." So geschah es. Der La-Bursche und das La-Mädchen legten gemeinsam Hand an, suchten große Spießtannen, richteten ein Holzgerüst auf, legten in der Mitte eine Holzplatte hinein, bedeckten es mit Baumrinde und stellten so ein sehr, sehr hübsches Holzhäuschen fertig. Der La-Bursche und das La-Mädchen wohnten nun in diesem Holzhäuschen.

Der Berggeist gebar Zorn, indem er Wind blies, und der Wind zog durch das Gerüst, doch das Haus bewegte sich nicht. Der Wassergeist gebar Zorn, indem er die Flut schickte, und das Wasser floß zwischen den Pflöcken hindurch, doch das Haus bewegte sich nicht. Die alte Schlange und der Rotwolf gelangten nicht hinauf, und die giftigen Insekten und Mücken gelangten nicht hinein. Der La-Bursche und das La-Mädchen lebten nun friedlich und sorglos in ihrem Holzhaus. Als der Satianba-Geist dies sah, dachte er das Holzhaus sogleich den Menschen zu, darin zu wohnen, und so blieb es bis heute.

canes, put up a frame, on top of it he spread bamboo splints double layered with grass, and a thatched hut was completed on the mountain. Both of them crawled into the thatched hut to live in it.

One day the Mountain Spirit went on tour of inspection along the mountains; having caught sight of the thatched hut built by the La-boy, he flew into a rage and thought: "Without my permission, who dares to build a house on a mountain." He blew, and gave rise to a strong mountain wind, and the wind blew away the thatched hut without a trace, without a shadow left. Nothing was left for the La-girl and the La-boy but to snuggle up closely. The La-girl said to the La-boy: "Let us build a house which cannot be blown away by the mountain wind." The La-boy had to collect big stones, and on the foot of a mountain he piled up the stones, on top of them he put a stone slab, and both crawled into the stone house to live in it.

One day the Water Spirit went on tour of inspection along the river; having caught sight of the stone house, built by the La-boy, he flew into a rage and thought: "Without my permission, who dares to build a house at the foot of a mountain." He blew, and whipped up a great flood, and the water flowed over the stone house from east to west and swept it away. The La-girl and the La-boy had to run up the mountain slope, and they sighed. A goodhearted magpie came flying along, and cried: "A wooden frame, covered with tree bark, no fear of wind, no fear of rain!" The La-girl understood, and she said to the La-boy: "Look how skillfully the magpie has built her nest! We shall learn from her and build a house like hers." Together the La-boy and the La-girl went to it, they collected fir trees, raised a scaffold, fixed the center with wooden boards, on top of the scaffold they spread tree bark, and a very, very nice wooden house was completed. The La-girl and the La-boy moved in to live in it.

The Mountain Spirit vented his rage by whipping up the wind, and the wind blew right through the center of the framework, but the wooden house stood. The Water Spirit vented his rage by sending the flood, and the water raced through the pillars, but the wooden house stood. The old snake and the jackal could not get up into it, and the mosquitoes and wasps could not fly into it. The La-girl and the La-boy enjoyed a peaceful life in the wooden house. The Satianba Spirit caught sight of it, and conferred the right upon men to live in wooden houses, as they still do to this day.

This is a didactic *fengshui* story which is still told at the fireplace in the center of the Dong peoples' houses. The

Diese lehrhafte Geschichte des *fengshui*, die sehr anschaulich Entstehung und Vorzüge der Pfahlbauten schildert, wird von den Dong am Feuerplatz im Zentrum ihrer Häuser erzählt.

Die Dong-Sippen leben im Grenzgebiet der vier Provinzen Guizhou, Guangxi, Hunan und Hubei; sie siedeln in autonomen Bezirken, verstreut vom Südwesten Hunans bis in den Nordwesten von Guangxi, vom Yunnan-Guizhou-Plateau bis zu den Flußebenen in Guangxi, in Hunan von den Ebenen hinauf zu den höheren Gebieten im Nordwesten und in dem hügeligen Land im Südosten. Im Norden erstrecken sich die Wuyi-, im Süden die Yuecheng-Gebirgsketten, im Westen liegen die Miao- und im Osten die Xuefeng-Gebirge. Von Nordwesten nach Südosten erstrecken sich die Leifeng-Berge, in denen die Flüsse Yuan, Qingshui, Wuyang, Qushui, Zhujiang, Liu und Xun, Seitenarme des Yangtse-Flusses, ihre Quellen haben.

In diesen Gebieten leben verschiedene ethnische Gruppen, die von den Ba-Völkern abstammen. Darunter gehören die Dong neben den Tujia zu den bedeutendsten. Kiefern sind der Reichtum der Landschaft. Deswegen bauen sie ihre Häuser mit dem wertvollen Holz der Kiefern und legen sie nach *fengshui*-Gesetzen an. Den topographischen Bedingungen angepaßt, werden die Häuser in verschiedenen Stilen gebaut. Die Dörfer liegen meist an Berghängen entlang der Flüsse. Dort werden die überhängenden Häuser

story describes the origin of the stilt houses and the advantages they offer for withstanding all the inclemency of the mountainous areas where the Dong people live.

The border area of the Guizhou, Guangxi, Hunan, and Hubei provinces is their native country. They settled mainly in their autonomous districts, spread from the south-west of Hunan to the north-west of Guangxi, with Sanjiang, one of their main districts, from the Yunnan-Guizhou-Plateau to the river plains in Guangxi, in Hunan from the plains up to the higher areas in the north-west, and in the hilly land in the south-east. In the north are the Wuyi Mountains, in the south the Yuecheng Ridges, in the west the Miao Ranges and in the east the Xuefeng Mountains. The Leifeng Mountains run through the country, from north-west to south-east, and here the Yuan, Qingshui, Wuyang, Qushui, Zhujiang, Liu and Xun rivers, tributaries of the Yangtze River, have their sources.

Different ethnic groups, offspring of the Ba people, are settled in these regions. The Dong are next in importance to the Tujia. Since pines make up the wealth of their country, the houses are exclusively timbered with pines and laid out following *fengshui* rules, avoiding any careless excavations and felling of trees. The houses are built in different styles according to the topography of the countryside. Most of the villages slope uphill from the plains of the river. There overhanging houses, with their floors terraced upwards, are

Holzhäuser mit terrassenförmig angelegten Stockwerken
Timber houses with terraced floors

Das Dorf Zhaoxing in Liping, Guizhou
The village of Zhaoxing in Liping, Guizhou

mit terrassenförmig angelegten Stockwerken bevorzugt. Die unteren Stockwerke dienen als Schuppen, die oberen als Lagerräume für Getreide, in den mittleren sind die Wohnräume eingerichtet. In Dörfern auf feuchten Ebenen werden die Häuser im Pfahlbaustil konstruiert, während die Häuser auf trockenen Flächen mit 0,3 bis 0,4 Meter über dem Erdboden liegenden Holzböden zu ebener Erde gebaut werden. Häuser dieser Art werden in den Städten mit Schutzmauern eingefaßt und Siegel *(yinzi)* genannt.

„Bevor das Eingangstor des Ortes gebaut wird, ist ein Platz für den Erdherrscher, bevor die Häuser gebaut werden, ist der Gerichtshof für den Satianba-Geist einzurichten." Von den Dong befolgt, war dieses alte Gesetz zur Tradition geworden. Vor den Eingangstoren und neben den Häusern stehen Schreine für den Erdherrscher (Tudi). Die Halle für den Satianba-Geist, den Schutzgeist aller Ba-Völker, ist in größeren Dörfern im Zentrum eingerichtet; daneben steht ein Trommelgebäude, das ebenfalls zu den traditionellen Gebäuden der Dong gehört. Sie werden mit den Phönixgebäuden der königlichen Paläste verglichen, in denen bei offiziellen Ankündigungen eine Glocke geläutet wird. Im Trommelgebäude wird bei offiziellen Anlässen getrommelt, und bei drohender Gefahr können die Bewohner der Nachbardörfer alarmiert werden. In kleineren Orten sind Trommelgebäude, Halle des Satianba-Geistes und Eingangstor in einem Gebäude integriert. Zu den Baustilen gehören der Pavillon-, Turm-, Pfahlbau- und der Hallenstil. Ihre Dächer sind in ungerader Zahl überlappend angeordnet. Walmdächer dekorieren die rechteckigen, im Hallenstil gebauten Trommelgebäude. Der höchste Trommelturm ist 20 Meter hoch, hat 17 Stockwerke und wird König der Trommeltürme genannt.

Die Wind-Regen-Brücken ähneln im Stil den Trommeltürmen. Zu den berühmtesten gehört die Chengyang-Brücke (s. S. 72/73). Sie ruht auf fünf Steinblöcken, deren drei mittlere im Flußbett aufgerichtet und als Kanu geformt sind. Fünf Pavillons rahmen und unterteilen ihre Korridore. Überlappende Dächer, die an den Seiten der Brücke in fünf und in der Längsachse in drei Stufen vom Dach der Korridore ansteigen, schützen die Pavillons. Der zentrale, als Flaschenkürbis geformte Pavillon schließt mit sechseckigem Spitzdach ab, die Dächer der beiden folgenden sind viereckig, während die äußeren Pavillons als Walmdächer abschließen. Im Kontrast zu dem rotbraunen Holz sind die Dächer mit ihren geschwungenen Traufen gelb und jadegrün bemalt. Dadurch erscheint die Brücke wie ein schillernd gepanzerter Drachen, der den Fluß überquert.

preferred. The lower floors are used as sheds, the ones in the middle as living rooms, and harvest products are stored in the upper floors. Stilt houses supported by wooden pillars are mainly built on wet plains. The ground-level style is suitable for settlements in flat and dry areas, since the wooden planks of their ground floors are only 0.3 to 0.4 meters above the ground. In the cities fireproof walls are added on both their sides, which make them look like a seal *(yinzi)*.

When laying out their villages the Dong people have followed an old proverb which says: "Do not build the village gate, but first fix the place for the Earth Ruler (Tudi); do not build the houses, but first set up the Satianba Spirit court well." In front of the village gate a little temple for the Earth Ruler is set up. The hall for the Satianba Spirit, the tutelary genius of all Ba people, is installed in the center of the villages. Next to his hall a drum tower is set up, which is used for official ceremonies and feasts. The villagers like to compare the drum towers with the phoenix building in the royal palaces. There a bell rings for official announcements, while in the *gulou* a drum is used for convening people and to contact neighbouring villages. In smaller villages gate buildings serve these different purposes. The drum towers are designed in the pavilion, watch-tower, stilt, close-eaves and hall styles. Their cross sections are square, hexagonal or octagonal. The roofs are layered in the style of resting mountains or sloping mountains and overlap up to the top of the tower. The highest drum building, which is called King of the Drum Towers, has 17 storeys and is 20 meters high.

The wind-rain-bridges are designed in the pavilion, gallery or tower style. One of the most famous is the Chengyang-Bridge (cf. pp. 72/73). Its timbered body rests on five huge stone blocks piled with bricks. The three middle ones are set up in the riverbed in shape of a canoe and can withstand any storm or flood. Five pavilions frame and subdivide the corridors of the bridge. The three in the middle are formed like gourds, tied up under the top roof. The roofs of the pavilions rise in five steps from the two lowest roofs, which protect the corridor and the side galleries from rain and wind. The top roof of the central pavilion is hexagonal and converges at the top, the top roofs of the two side pavilions are square. The corners of the eaves turn upwards, as is traditional in Chinese architecture. In contrast with the red brown timber the roof eaves are painted yellow and jade green, and make the bridge look like a dragon crossing the river dressed in an iridescent coat of mail.

Blick auf das Dorf Dudong
View of the village of Dudong
Sanjiang, Guangxi

Oben: Dorftore im *ganlan*-Stil, links in Guangxi, Sanjiang, Ruxie, rechts in Sanjiang, Yanzhu
Rechts: Dorfgasse, zwei Wachhunde auf der Treppe eines terrassenförmigen Hauses
Guangxi, Pingdeng, Longsheng

Above: Village gates in the *ganlan* style in Guangxi, Sanjiang, Ruxie (left), in Sanjiang, Yanzhu (right)
Right: Village alley, two watchdogs on the stairs of a terraced house. Guangxi, Pingdeng, Longsheng

Gerüst eines terrassenförmigen überhängenden Hauses mit Schrein für den Erdherrscher (Tudi)
Frame of a terraced overhanging house with a shrine for the Earth Ruler in front (Tudi)
Guangxi, Linxi, Sanjiang

Haus im *ganlan*-Stil
Stilt house in the *ganlan* style
Hunan, Hengliang, Tongdao

Oben: Kleine Wind-Regen-Brücke im *ganlan*-Stil mit Pavillon. Guangxi, Heli, Sanjiang
Rechts: Wind-Regen-Brücke vor dem Dorf Hualian des Dong Volkes, angelegt mit Trommelturm und Theater (Halle) im Zentrum. Guangxi, Sanjiang

Above: Wind-rain-bridge in the *ganlan* style with a pavillon. Guangxi, Heli, Sanjiang
Right: Wind-rain-bridge in front of the Dong village of Hualian with drum tower and performance hall in the center. Guangxi, Sanjiang

Trommelgebäude *(gulou)* im Hallenstil
Drum building *(gulou)* in the hall style
Mapang, Sanjiang, Guangxi

Wind-Regen-Brücke und Trommelturm im Pfahlbau *(ganlan)*-Stil im Zentrum des Dorfes Zhaoyue in Liping, Guizhou
Wind-rain bridge and drum tower in the stilt-house *(ganlan)* style in the center of Zhaoyue village in Liping, Guizhou

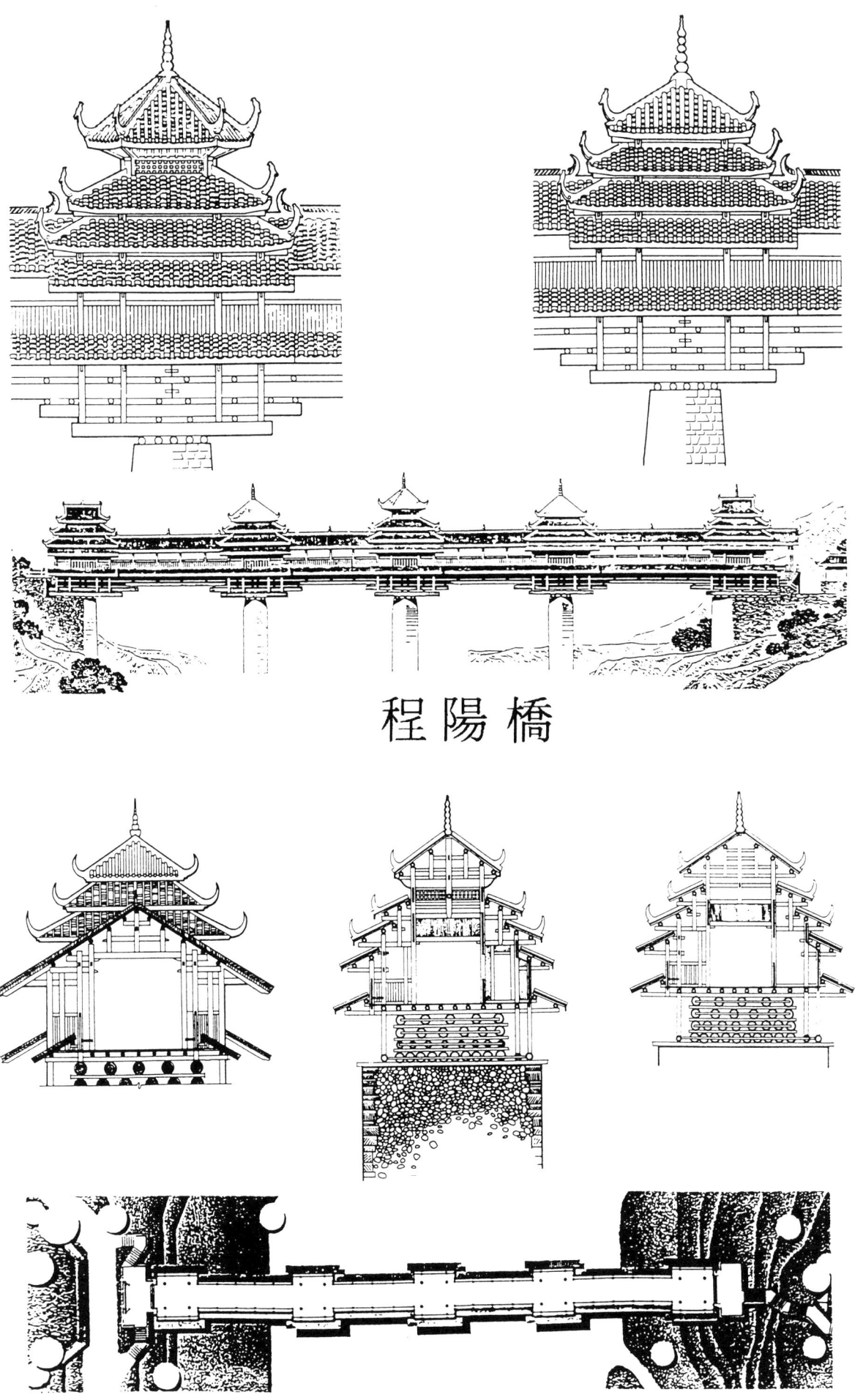

程陽橋

Die Chengyang-Brücke
The Chengyang-Bridge
Linxi, Sanjiang, Guangxi

Die reitenden Stockwerke (qilou) 騎樓 in Jiangnan 江南

Die traditionelle Baukunst in Jiangsu und Zhejiang beeindruckt durch ihre Eleganz und Kunstfertigkeit. Die Landschaft in der Tiefebene des Yangtse ist von Flüssen durchzogen, die als Lebensadern des Landes bezeichnet wurden; denn Binnenschiffahrt und Handel brachten die Provinzen zu kultureller Blüte. Boote zogen durch Städte und Dörfer, und die Familien hatten ihre eigenen Anlegeplätze. Bambus und Blauregen schützten vor der Sonne. Dunstschleier liegen in den Morgenstunden über Flüssen und Seen, die gegen Mittag von heißen Sonnenstrahlen durchbrochen werden. In diesem Klima waren Häuser mit sogenannten reitenden Stockwerken (qilou) eine bevorzugte Bauform. Sie sind als Varianten der überhängenden Stockwerke Abkömmlinge der Pfahlbauten, die zu den ältesten Baustilen Chinas gehören und auf eine Geschichte von 7000 Jahren zurückblicken. Die reitenden Stockwerke bilden Kolonnaden entlang der Wasserstraßen, indem sie die Wege überqueren und auf Holzsäulen am Ufer gestützt sind. Im Schutz der überdachenden Stockwerke konnte sich ein reges Alltagsleben abspielen. Zur Rast und für ein besinnliches Geplauder begrenzen hier und da als Bänke gezimmerte Geländer die Ufer. Hohe, kalkweiß getünchte Feuerschutzmauern grenzen die Nachbarhäuser voneinander ab, überqueren bogenförmig die Uferwege und unterteilen die Kolonnaden.

In der Ming-Dynastie wurden die Giebel der Schutzmauern häufig im 人 (ren – Mensch)-Stil konstruiert. In der Qing-Dynastie waren Pferdekopfmauern und bogenförmige Mauern, genannt guanyindou (Blick und Klang einhüllen), beliebt. Beide Namen sind etymologischen Ursprungs. Die Pferdekopfmauern sind treppenförmig oder geschwungen wie die Anlegeplätze an den Flüssen. Beide Namen entsprechen einander im Klang matou bei unterschiedlichen Zeichen. Der Name der bogenförmig geschwungenen Mauer guanyindou leitet sich aus dem Wort doumao ab. Ihr Profil erinnert an einen Kopf, den eine Mütze bedeckt.

Über die Flüsse führen Brücken verschiedener Stilrichtungen und pointieren reizvoll das Bild der Städte. Die Höfe in Jiangnan wurden nach traditionellen Prinzipien als Brunnenhöfe im siheyuan-Stil angelegt. In ihrer kunstfertigen Gestaltung und Dekoration waren sie Vorbild für die Baukunst der benachbarten Provinzen.

The riding storeys (qilou) in Jiangnan

Jiangsu and Zhejiang are provinces where traditional architecture flourished most splendidly being both elegant and beautiful. Rivers criss-cross the plains of the Yangtze Delta. They are the country's commercial and social life blood and made the culture prosper and flourish. Boats floated along the waterways and every family had its private pier. Bamboo and wisteria offer shade above the entrances, leading from the piers into the houses. In the morning, mist covers the lakes and rivers, but the sun plays on the water as noon approaches. In this humid and warm climate houses with riding storeys (qilou) were the favored constructions. They are variants of the overhanging houses, and these again are offspring of the stilt houses, which are among the oldest architectural styles in China and look back on 7000 years of history. The riding storeys form colonnades, projecting over the paths and supported on wooden columns along the bank of the waterways. An active daily life was lived out under the shelter of the roofing storeys. Wooden railings, constructed as benches, intended for taking a rest und having a little chat, framed the waterways at intervals. High whitewashed fireproof walls divide off the neighbouring houses from each other, cross the paths as arcades and intersect the colonnades.

In the Ming Dynasty the gables of the fireproof walls were shaped in the 人 (ren – human being) style. In the Qing Dynasty, horse-head (matou) and sight-sound-wrapping (guanyindou) walls were common. Both names are etymological in origin. Matou also means pier and they both have the same pronunciation for different characters. The horse-head walls, shaped like a staircase or curved on both sides, look like the private piers of their houses. The word dou is part of the saying doumao (mao – cap), and the profile of this kind of wall is reminiscent of a person's head covered with a cap.

Bridges in different style and size cross the rivers and emphasize the picturesque character of the cities. The courtyards in the traditional siheyuan style were constructed so superbly that the layout and decoration of courtyards and gardens in many other provinces were modelled on those in Jiangnan.

Rechts: Zwei Frauen vor den Trenntüren eines Hauseinganges
Right: Two women in front of an entrance with partition doors
Zhaoxing, Zhejiang

Oben: Kolonnade unter reitenden Stockwerken mit Bogendurchgängen der unterteilenden Feuerschutzmauern. Zhejiang, Nanxun, Huzhou
Rechts: Blick von einem Wandelgang unter einem reitenden Stockwerk auf die von einer Feuerschutzmauer im *ren*-Stil getrennten Häuser am gegenüberliegenden Ufer
Zhejiang, Deqing

Above: Colonnade under riding storeys with the arched gateways of the subdividing fire-proof walls. Zhejiang, Nanxun, Huzhou
Right: Way under a riding storey, facing houses across the channel, protected by a *ren* style fire-proof wall. Zhejiang, Deqing

Alltagsleben in der Mitte des 20. Jahrhunderts auf den Uferwegen unter sogenannten reitenden Stockwerken in Zhejiang, Zhaoyu, Keqiaozhen (oben) und in Hejing, Yinxian, Qiuaizhen (links)

Everyday life in the middle of the 20th century on the bank alleys below so-called riding storeys in Zhejiang, Zhaoyu, Keqiaozhen (above) and in Hejing, Yinxian, Qiuaizhen (left)

Bogenbrücke, gebaut in der Song-Dynastie
Arched stone bridge built in the Song Dynasty
Zhejiang, Shaoxing

Oben: Seitenkanal mit im Wasser reflektierender Bogenbrücke. Jiangsu, Kunshan
S. 84/85: Fluß mit privaten Anlegeplätzen und Bogenbrücke in Suzhou, Luxu, Wujiang

Above: Bridge shaped like a crescent moon reflected in the channel. Jiangsu, Kunshan
pp. 84/85: River with private piers and a vaulted bridge in Suzhou, Luxu, Wujiang

81

Anmerkungen zu den Grundlagen der traditionellen Baukunst

Bei der Betrachtung der traditionellen Baukunst stellen sich Fragen zu den Materialien, Dekorationen, Strukturen und Anordnungen und ihrer historischen Entwicklung, die hier nur kurz gestreift werden können.

Die Städte und Höfe wurden im Einklang mit den Prinzipien der chinesischen Philosophie und Gesellschaftsordnung angelegt. Eine faszinierende Stimmung liegt in den alten Städten mit ihren gewachsenen Strukturen. Ahnentempel, Theater, Gerichtshöfe, Tempel und Schulen bestimmten die Zentren der Orte. Tore begrenzten und Mauern umschlossen die Städte. Die Anlagen der Städte lassen sich historisch bis in die Zhou-Dynastie zurückverfolgen. In jener Zeit wurde die Baukunst der Shang-Dynastie verfeinert und weiterentwickelt. Im Zhou Li (Gesetzbuch der Zhou-Dynastie) ist zu lesen: „Handwerker(meister) bestimmen das Land; quadratisch, neun li an den Seiten mit je drei Toren, durch das Zentrum des Landes verlaufen neun Längen und neun Breiten, die Längen entsprechen neun Wagenspuren, links befindet sich die Ahnenhalle, rechts der Tempel des Erdgottes, vorn liegt der Kaiserhof, hinten liegt der Markt". Nach diesem Gliederungsprinzip wurden während der folgenden Dynastien die Hauptstädte und Städte der kleineren Fürstentümer angelegt. Die Palastanlagen der Herrscher wurden mit fünf Toren begrenzt und unterteilt und mit einem Wachturm geschützt. Der Kaiserhof für offizielle Staatsangelegenheiten war in den äußeren, inneren und in den Haupthof unterteilt. Der hier als Beispiel traditioneller Stadtanlagen gezeigte Plan datiert aus der Song-Dynastie. Er zeigt Pingjiang, die heutige Stadt Suzhou, die seit der Frühlings- und Herbstperiode (770–476 v. Chr.) Hauptstadt des Landes Wu, eines der Drei Reiche (220–280 n. Chr.), war. Die Stadt ist rechteckig, mit der Längsachse von Norden nach Süden verlaufend, angelegt. In gleicher Richtung verlaufen die Wasserwege. Hohe mit Zinnen versehene Mauern umgeben die Stadt. Die Grabanlagen liegen im

Notes on the principles of traditional architecture

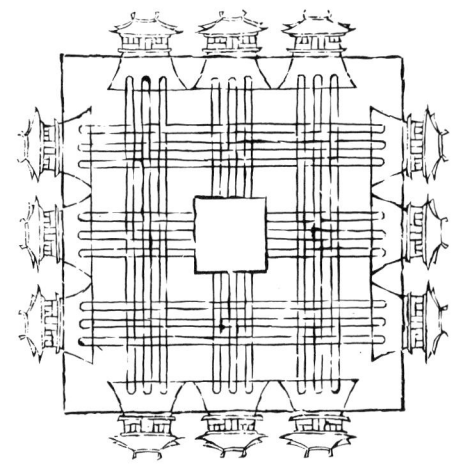

When looking at traditional Chinese architecture, many questions arise about building material, structure, design, rules of order and arrangement and their historical development. They can only briefly be touched on here.

Towns and courtyards were laid out according to the Chinese philosophy and the social order of their hierarchical feudal system. The old cities are still strangely attractive as an organic whole. Ancestor halls, courts, temples, schools and markets defined their center. The individual buildings were obviously related to each other and drew attention to each other. High walls with gates surrounded the cities. The layout of the cities can be traced back to the Zhou Dynasty, a period in which the architecture of the Shang Dynasty was developed and refined. In the Zhou Li (Law of the Zhou Dynasty) it says: "Craftsmen explore the land, a square with nine li on each side with three gates, nine verticals and nine horizontals cross the land, the long sides measure nine wheel ruts each, on the left side there is the ancestor hall, on the right side the shrine for the earth spirit, in front (of the center) there is the imperial court, behind there is the market". Under subsequent dynasties the capitals and also many smaller cities of the little principalities were basically arranged according to this principle. A watch tower was set up in front of the Imperial palace, which was bounded and subdivided by five gates. The imperial court, where state affairs were handled, was subdivided into the outer, inner and main court. The city map shown here as an example of traditional cities dates from the Song Dynasty (960–1276 AD). It shows the city of Pingjiang, later renamed Suzhou, which in the Spring and Autumn Period became the capital of the Wu Kingdom, one of the Three Kingdoms (220–280 AD). The city is laid out as a rectangle with its longitudinal axis running from north to south. High crenellated walls with five gates surround the city. The waterways run from north to south, the graves are located on the

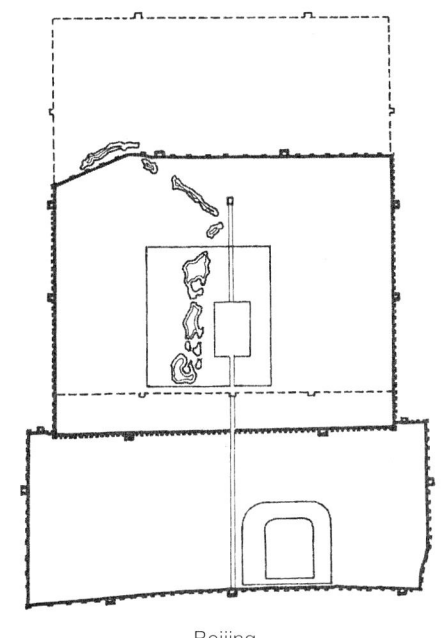

Beijing

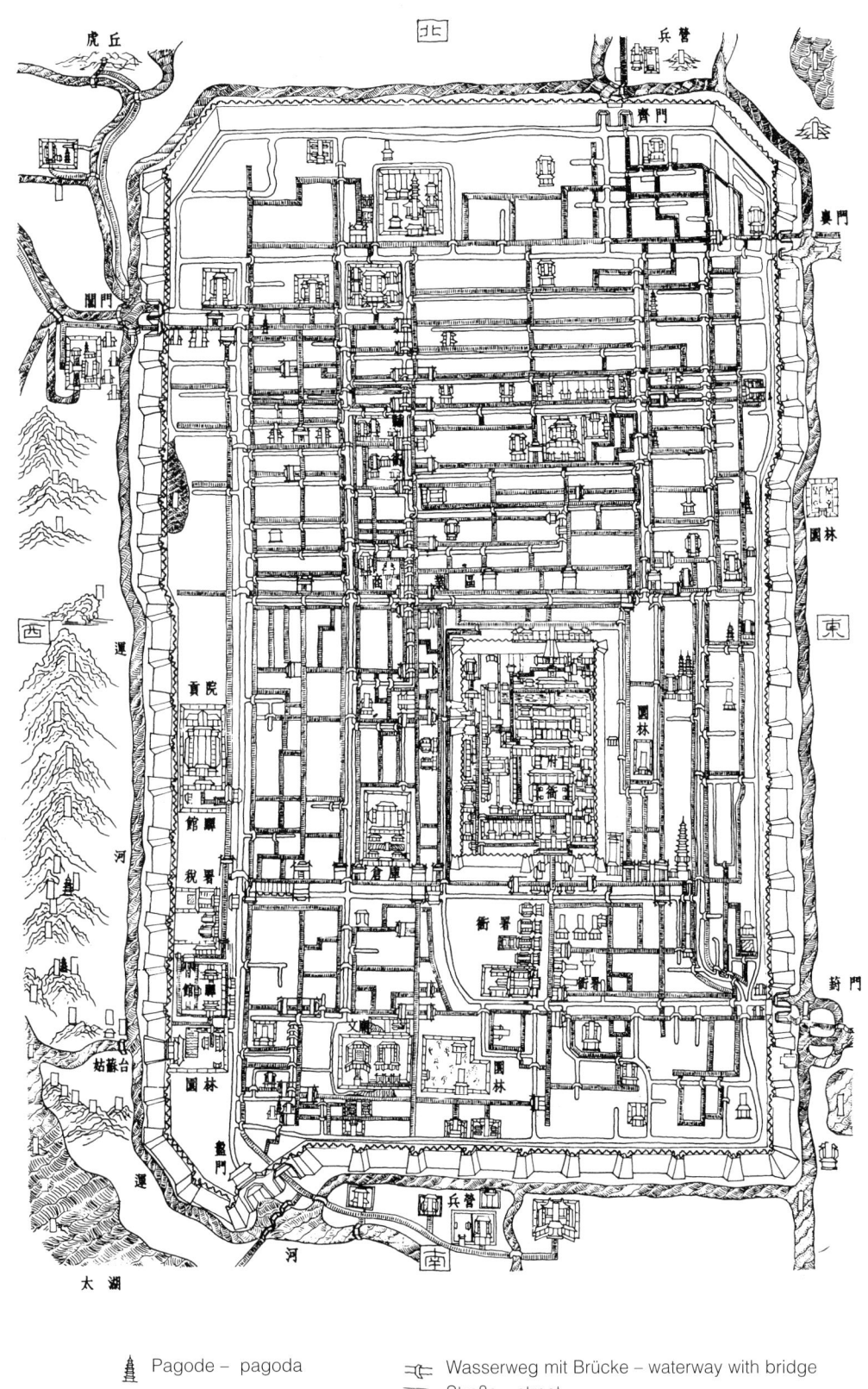

- Pagode – pagoda
- Tempel – temple etc.
- Wasserweg mit Brücke – waterway with bridge
- Straße – street
- Gedenkbogen – memorial arch

Skizze der Stadt Pingjiang (heutiges Suzhou), mit der Kaiserstadt *(zicheng)* im Zentrum
Outline of the Pingjiang town (today Suzhou), with the emperor's city *(zicheng)* in the center

Fliegende Apsaras in einem Buddhist-Tempel. Quanzhou, Fujian
Flying Apsaras in a Buddhist temple. Quanzhou, Fujian

Hausfront im westlichen Stil. Hebianzhen, Dingxiang, Shanxi
House front in the occidental style. Hebianzhen, Dingxiang, Shanxi

Westen außerhalb der Stadt. Die zentrale Königsstadt *(zicheng)* ist in den offiziellen Hof *(tingtang)* im Süden und den daran anschließenden Palast unterteilt, der im *siheyuan*-Stil mit drei Quergebäuden, das Zeichen 王 *(wang – Kaiser)* bildend, angelegt ist. Die Stadt Beijing, die in der Yuan-Dynastie angelegt und in der Ming-Dynastie rekonstruiert worden war, ist nach vergleichbaren Prinzipien geordnet. Der Einfluß westlicher Kulturen trat in der Baukunst vorrangig an Sakralbauten in Erscheinung. Philosophisch in einigen Punkten mit dem Taoismus verwandt, gewann der Buddhismus den größten Einfluß aller fremden Religionen, und nachdem er zu Beginn des 6. Jahrhunderts offiziell anerkannt worden war, erlebte er während der Tang-Dynastie seine Blütezeit. Obwohl er mit dem Taoismus um den Vorrang rivalisierte und zeitweise durch den Einfluß des Konfuzianismus offiziellen Restriktionen unterlag, stellte er eine so starke Ergänzung des philosophischen und spirituellen Gedankengutes dar, daß er in den folgenden Dynastien offiziell anerkannt blieb. Buddhistische Tempel wurden mit künstlerischem Geschick vielfältig ausgestattet, sie folgten dabei den Grundprinzipien des traditionellen chinesischen Baustils (s. S. 52/53). Als Missionare des Christentums verstanden die Jesuiten ihre Aufgabe, Glauben und Kultur in Bildern zu übertragen, zwar dergestalt, daß sie Gebäude als Kontrapunkt zur chinesischen Baukunst konstruierten, wie zum Beispiel die katholische Universität in Peking zeigt, jedoch blieben die Kirchengebäude meist Fremdkörper. Besonders zur Geltung kam der jesuitische Einfluß durch den Maler Guiseppe Castiglione (1688 – 1766 n. Chr.), der nach China entsandt worden war, um kulturell Einfluß zu

west side *(yin* side) of the town. The central emperor's city *(zicheng)* is subdivided into the official court in the south with the palace lying behind. The palace is laid out in the *siheyuan* style with three transverse buildings, forming the character 王 *(wang –* emperor). The city of Beijing, which was laid out in the Yuan Dynasty and reconstructed in the Ming Dynasty, followed comparable rules.

In China the influence of foreign cultures in architecture mainly showed in sacred buildings. Based on philosophy in some points related to Taoism, Buddhism was the most influential foreign religion and became officially accepted in the early 6th century, enjoying its heyday in the Tang Dynasty. Even though competing with Taoism for supremacy, and at times being officially suppressed by the government following Confucian principles, Buddhism provided such an important complement to philosophical and spiritual life in China that it remained officially accepted throughout all dynasties. Buddhist temples were skillfully decorated especially in the south of China but mostly designed in the traditional Chinese style (cf.pp. 52/53). As representatives of Christianity the Jesuits knew very well how to pass on their beliefs and culture in pictures by laying out buildings in a way that was contrapuntal to the Chinese style, as in the Catholic university in Beijing, but most of the church buildings appeared as alien elements. The Jesuitical influence was expressed in a very special way by the artist Guiseppe Castiglione (1688 – 1766 AD), who was sent to China to establish some form of cultural influence. He tried his hand at paintings in the Chinese style, and though his pictures were not considered as masterpieces by the court

Oben: Blick von der zentralen Ahnenhalle des Ortes auf ein Theater. Im Hintergrund der Bühne ein Bild mit den drei Sterngenii Shouxing, Wenchang und Dongfangshuo, langes Leben, Literatur und glückliches Geschick bezeichnend. Hunan, Tuojiangzhen, Fenghuang
Rechts: Theater gebaut auf einem die Erde symbolisierenden Mauerwerk und gedeckt mit einem den Himmel symbolisierenden Dach mit geschwungenen Giebeln. Zhejiang, Wuzhen, Tongxiang

Left: View from the village's ancestor hall of a theatre. On the wall behind the stage a picture of the three star sages Shouxing, Wenchang, and Dongfangshuo, signifying long life, literature, and good fortune. Hunan, Tuojiangzhen, Fenghuang
Above: Theatre, constructed on brickwork, symbolizing the earth, and covered with a roof, decorated with upturned eaves, symbolizing heaven. Zhejiang, Wuzhen, Tongxiang

gewinnen. Er versuchte sich an Malereien im chinesischen Stil, die zwar von den Hofästhetikern nicht als Meisterwerke bezeichnet wurden, aber der Herrscher Qian Long begünstigte ihn, und so brachte er in der Baukunst die Kaiserliche Parkanlage Yuanmingyuan im italienischen Barockstil hervor. Die Gebäude blieben bereits Ende des 18. Jahrhunderts dem Verfall überlassen. Doch es wurde Mode, Fassaden europäischer Häuser und Kirchen zu imitieren, und in der Minguo-Zeit propagierte unter anderen der in Anhui lebende Kunstexperte Hu Kaiwen diesen Stil. Die Innenstrukturen der Höfe behielten dabei ihren ur-sprünglichen Charakter. Erst nach der industriellen Revolution wurden die traditionellen Strukturen aufgebrochen.

In der Ming-Dynastie waren die Normen und Maximen des Konfuzianismus noch einmal besonders hervorgehoben worden, und demzufolge galten in der Baukunst streng traditionelle Richtlinien. Die Gebäude wurden symmetrisch und schlicht gestaltet und haben dadurch eine suggestive Wirkung (s. S. 212/213). Seit Mitte der Qing-Dynastie veränderten sich durch den Einfluß des Großbürgertums die Gebäude in ihrer Ausstattung. Unverändert blieben die traditionellen Gesetzgebungen und Baubestimmungen in Kraft. Sie waren auch in dieser Zeit nicht zu umgehen, wie das Beispiel des Hofes Qijian, Qilin Baoxiating (s. S. 23) zeigt.

aesthetician, he found favor with by the Emperor Qian Long. In architecture he supervised the construction of the Emperor's Yuanmingyuan designed in the Italian Baroque style; these buildings were allowed to fall in disrepair as early as the end of the 18th century. But the western style was favored by some people, and in the Minguo Period for instance, the artist Hu Kaiwen, living in Anhui, modelled his own property on western facades and thus paved the way for this style. The inner structure of the courtyards was still arranged according to traditional rules. Only after the industrial revolution did the traditional structures crumble.

In the time of Neo-Confucianism in the Ming Dynasty, they once more laid stress on moral principles and ethics and so architecture followed strict traditional guidelines. Due to their symmetrical layout and to their unpretentiousness (cf. pp. 212/213), the inner and outer decor of the buildings are visually captivating. From the Qing Dynasty onwards the building styles and decorations changed, caused by the influence of the upper middle class. But it was still almost impossible to evade the traditional laws and building regulations, which remained in force, as the example of the courtyard Qijian, Qilin Baoxiating (cf. p. 23) shows.

Notes on fengshui

The historical continuity of China is demonstrated in architecture in the laws and rules of geomancy (fengshui). Even in early dynasties it was the custom that the ruler, as the son of heaven, invested in land and had the land assigned to be built on explored by his officials. Kanyu 堪輿 is the original term for the empirical science used for exploring nature and establishing settlements. As usual in classical Chinese, the character of a term changed while keeping the same pronunciation and thus showing the change of meaning in pictures. The early kan 勘 means 'officially investigate (explore)', the later character kan 堪 means 'cover the soil' which is above the subsoil and vegetation. Yu means territory. In this way the original term 'officially investigate a territory' had changed to the term 'heaven and earth', signifying the placing of territories according to astrology and natural conditions. Palaces, temples and courtyards were up on the basis of the magic square (Luoshu). This was divided into nine squares, allocated to the nine stars of the Plough. The stars move, which suggests that the divisions made for various uses of the rooms would have had to move as well, provided that enough space was available. As a basic scheme for the division of the rooms, the sequence of numbers was arranged with the number five wu in the center. The courtyards were additionally arranged according to the eight trigrams (ba gua), whose original sequence correspond with the cosmic yinyang. Their sequence as fixed later (circa 1160 BC), reflected the points of the fengshui compass. These were read in comparison with the original sequence, in order to bring the cosmic and local yinyang into harmony. Qualities, natural phenomena, animals, parts of the body, family relationships and social positions were allocated to the eight trigrams. The theory of the Five Elements (wu xing), emerged by 330 BC, was seen in accord with this scheme as well. The elements wood, fire, earth, metal,

Above: The four points of the compass and their symbols

North	– the black warrior (tortoise) – the lesser yin
East	– the (qing) lightgreen dragon – the greater yang
South	– the red phoenix – the lesser yang
West	– the white tiger – the greater yang
Center	– yellow earth/heaven – equivalence

Lehre der Fünf Elemente *(wu xing)* gesehen. Den Elementen wiederum waren Objekte und Phänomene aus den drei Kategorien Himmel, Erde und Mensch zugeordnet, und sie oblagen den legendären Herrschern. (Zur Berechnung der Zentralachse der Höfe nach dem Geburtsdatum des Eigentümers wurden ferner die vierundzwanzig Mondzyklen, die zehn Himmelsstämme und die zwölf Erdzweige etc. einbezogen.)

Im konfuzianischen System wurden Vorschriften für die Ausstattung der Residenzen nach dem Rangsystem erlassen (s. S. 125). So durften nur höchste Beamte die Tore ihrer Residenzen rot kolorieren, mit der Farbe des Feuers, des Sommers, des Phönix und des Südens, der Farbe des kleineren *yang*. Das lichte *(qing)* Grün des Bambusholzes, des Frühlings, des Drachens und des Ostens etc., die Farbe des höheren *yang*, war die Farbe der Ming-Dynastie und nur die Ziegel der Dächer von Palästen der Prinzen durften in diesem Ton glasiert werden. Gelb, die Farbe des Zentrums, der Entsprechung von Himmel und Erde, war in der Ming- und Qing-Dynastie zur Kolorierung den Dächern der Kaiserpaläste vorbehalten.

Die Gestaltung des *fengshui* lebte in metaphorischer Zuordnung. Dies ebnete der Vorstellung den Weg, diese Kunst sei Gegenstand des Aberglaubens. (Die Jesuiten haben allerdings, laut Needham, den Aberglauben nicht in der Eigenschaft einseitiger Verstandesmenschen bekämpft: Nicht, daß sie nicht an die Kunst der Geomantik geglaubt hätten, sie haben sie als diabolisch betrachtet). Einer der Punkte, die diese Meinung bestärkten, kann darin gesehen werden, daß aus der Raumaufteilung in den Höfen nach Familienbeziehungen, die den acht Trigrammen zugeordnet sind, Hypothesen entwickelt wurden, die vom einfachen

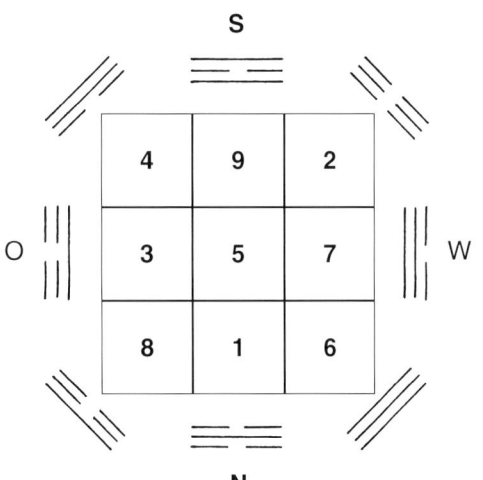

water were ruled by the legendary emperors and objects relating to the three categories heaven, earth, human beings were assigned to them. (To determine the axis of the courtyards according to the birth date of the owner, the twenty four half moons, the ten heaven trunks and twelve earth branches etc. were included.)

As described in the article about status systems, building regulations were made under the Confucian system. This prescribed the furnishings of the residences according to their official rank (cf. p.125). Thus only high officials were allowed to paint their main gates red, the color related to fire, the south, the summer, the phoenix etc., as a color of the lesser *yang*. Only princes were allowed to glaze the roof tiles in light green *(qing)*, the color related to (bamboo) wood, the east, the spring, the dragon etc., as a color of the greater *yang*. The color of the Yellow Emperor (Huang Di) and the yellow earth, reflected in the light of the sun and the moon, as the color of the balanced *yin* and *yang*, was in the Ming and Qing Period reserved for the roofs of the emperors' palaces.

The fact that the *fengshui* arrangements were made on the basis of metaphor prepared the way for the idea that *fengshui* arose from superstition. (Though according to Needham, the Jesuits did not combat superstition in the capacity of rationalists: it was not that they did not believe in the art of geomantics, they considered it diabolical). One of the points that reinforced this opinion can be seen in the fact that conclusions like these were drawn from the way in which the space in the yards was allocated on the basis of family relationships assigned to the eight trigrams. Simple people could not understand this, as the appropriate division of the rooms could not be carried out in every case

Oben: Beziehungen und Zuordnungen der Trigramme für die spätere Himmelsreihenfolge (circa 1160 v. Chr.)

kan	N	das Abgründige	mittlerer Sohn	Mond	Ohr	Wasser
yin	NO	das Stillehalten	jüngster Sohn	Berg	Hand	(Holz)
zhen	O	das Erregende	ältester Sohn	Donner	Fuß	(Holz)
xun	SO	das Sanfte	älteste Tochter	Wind	Schenkel	Holz
li	S	das Haftende	mittlere Tochter	Sonne	Auge	Feuer
kun	SW	das Rezeptive	Mutter	Erde	Bauch	Erde
dui	W	das Heitere	jüngste Tochter	See	Mund	Wasser/Metall
qian	NW	das Kreative	Vater	Himmel	Kopf	Metall

Above: The trigram associations and correlations for the later heaven sequence (circa 1160 BC)

kan	N	danger	middle son	moon	ear	water
yin	NE	stillness	youngest son	mountain	hand	(wood)
zhen	E	exciting	oldest son	thunder	foot	(wood)
xun	SE	gentleness	oldest daughter	wind	thighs	wood
li	S	adherence	middle daughter	sun	eye	fire
kun	SW	receptive	mother	earth	belly	earth
dui	W	joy, serenity	youngest daughter	lake	mouth	water/metal
qian	NW	creative,	father	heaven	head	metal

Volk nicht nachvollzogen werden konnten, da die entsprechende Aufteilung der Räume aus Platzmangel nicht unbedingt zur Anwendung kam. Zu den Folgerungen gehört z. B. die Meinung, daß bei Schäden des Bodens im Osten eines Hofes der älteste Sohn des Hauses krank wird und bei Schäden des Bodens im Westen die jüngste Tochter.

Unumstößlich für die Baukunst sind die Regeln, die sich aus den klimatischen und geomorphologischen Bedingungen ergaben. Der im Volksmund für *kanyu* verwendete Begriff *fengshui* ist die Kurzform des Satzes *Zang feng de shui* (den Wind bergen und das Wasser bekommen), ein Prinzip, nach dem die Höfe angelegt und gestaltet wurden. Dachneigungen, Giebel, verstellbare Türen und Schutzmauern bergen den Wind und lenken die Energie. Im Zentrum der Höfe, in die das Sonnen- und Mondlicht einfloß, wurde das Wasser in den Brunnen der *tianjing* aufgefangen; das Wasser war fruchtbringend, so waren die Zentralhallen in Urzeiten heilig und wurden Tradition. *Zang feng ju qi* (den Wind bergen und die Energie sammeln) hieß ein weiterer Leitsatz. Diese Naturprinzipien waren mit den Kunstprinzipien einer Hochkultur im Einklang. Die Höfe wurden aus freistehenden Holzgerüsten konstruiert und von Mauern eingefaßt. „*Fang dao, wu bu ta*. Stürzt auch das Gebäude ein, so bricht doch das Haus nicht zusammen," charakterisierte die Eigenschaft der Konstruktionen. Die Mauern hatten primär Schutzfunktion. Der individuelle Gestaltungswille der chinesischen Menschen fand Raum in der Kalligraphie. Sie ist Basis der anderen Kunstkategorien. Dies gilt sowohl für die bildliche Darstellung als auch für die Art ihrer Ausführung. Eleganz der Linienführung ist bedingt durch den meisterhaft gelenkten *Qi*-Fluß des Gestalters. In der Baukunst ist deshalb Holz das bevorzugte Material. Es läßt sich schnitzen, es ist biegsam und schmiegsam, es federt, atmet und gibt Energie weiter. Es läßt sich verknüpfen, und bei der Gestaltung werden mit Winkeln und Biegungen Bilder gezeichnet. Somit konnten Außen- und Innendekorationen modelliert werden, die nie Kunst am, sondern im Bau und des Baues waren.

because there was not enough space available. Thus, for example, the commonly held opinion that if there was subsidence in the east of the courtyard the eldest son of the household would fall ill and if the ground on the west subsided the youngest daughter would fall ill is possibly one of the phenomena that could lead to the opinion that *fengshui* is mere superstition.

Principles derived from the natural climatic and geographical conditions must on no account be ignored in architecture. The term *fengshui*, popularly used for *kanyu,* is the abbreviation for: *Zang feng de shui* (hide the wind and get the water). This is the proposition followed when the outer and inner design of the traditional courtyards is decided. Roofs, eaves, screen walls and partition doors were set up to hide the wind, and to keep the energy circulating. The water was collected in the *tianjing* of the center, where the sun- and moonlight stream in. Water brought life. Thus in primeval times the center was holy and central halls became traditional. *Zang feng ju qi* (hide the wind but keep the energy) is the next rule. These natural principles harmonized with the aesthetic of their highly sophisticated culture. Chinese houses were constructed with wooden frames. "The building may fall down, but the house will not collapse *(fang dao, wu bu ta),*" was the principle behind these constructions. The surrounding walls were built mainly for protection against the dangers of the outside world. The individual creative will of the Chinese found its expression in calligraphy, their principal art form, from which the other arts derived. This goes for both for pictorial presentation and for the way in which things were carried out. The elegance of drawn lines depends on masterly control of the *Qi*-current of the creator. Therefore in architecture wood is the favored material. It can be carved, it is pliable, soft and springy, it breathes and transfers energy. It can be joined and shaped, and by drawing angles and curves, pictures are painted as in calligraphy. Thus exterior and interior decorations were modeled that do not appear as ornament, but as part of a whole.

Oben: Das *yinyang*-Symbol umgeben von den acht Trigrammen, angeordnet nach der alten Regel mit dem absoluten *yin* im Norden, gerahmt von fünf Fledermäusen als Glückssymbole

Above: The *yinyang* symbol encircled by the eight trigrams, set up according to the old rule with the absolut *yin* in the north, framed by five bats symbolizing luck

Löwenkopfkapitell einer die Galerie der oberen Etage tragenden Säule in einem Hof im Stil der freistehenden Höhlen
Capital of a pillar supporting the gallery of the upper floor in a courtyard in the standalone style, carved as a lion's head
Shanxi, Pingyao, Chengguanzhen

Blick durch die Trenntür der Ahnenhalle mit dem Namen Caiyitang auf das Haupttor im Hof des Weng Tonghe
Partition door of the ancestor hall named Caiyitang in the courtyard of Weng Tonghe, and view of the main gate
Jiangsu, Changshu

Wohnraum unterteilt durch eine geschnitzte Trennwand mit Mondhöhlentor *(yuedongmen)*
Living room subdivided by a carved partition wall with a moon cave gate *(yuedongmen)*
Jiangsu, Suzhou

Holzschnitzerei der freudigen Begegnung der zwei Unsterblichen Hanshan und Shide auf einer Trenntür *(Hehe er xian)*
Zhishan, Yixian, Huizhou

Wooden carving of the cheerful encounter of the two immortals Hanshan and Shide on a partition door *(Hehe er xian)*
Zhishan, Yixian, Huizhou

Dem Primat der Natur in der taoistischen Philosophie entsprechend, waren die unerschöpfliche Pflanzenwelt und das Tierreich vorrangige Quellen für die Motive der bildenden Kunst. In ihrer Gestalt und im Zusammenspiel versinnbildlichten Blumen und Kreaturen ethische Werte, glückliche Fügung der Geschehnisse, langes Leben und Wohlstand. So symbolisierten Bambus, Pflaumenblüte und Kiefer, die drei Freunde des Winters, Bescheidenheit, Unschuld und ein langes Leben. Häufig anzutreffen ist die Elster als Symbol der Freude, denn baute sie ihr Nest in der Nähe eines Hauses, so meinte man, verspräche dies Glück für alle Nachbarn und Gäste der Familie. Fledermaus und Hirsch, gleichklingend im Laut mit Glück und Wohlstand, sind in allen Häusern als Glücksbringer unter den Dekorationen zu finden. Beliebt waren auch narrative Malereien und Schnitzereien legendärer und dokumentierter historischer Anekdoten, ferner Darstellungen der taoistischen Gottheiten des Wohlstandes, des langen Lebens, des Glücks etc. sowie der vergötterten Unsterblichen mit der besonderen Gruppe der acht Unsterblichen des Taoismus, die als entfernt vom irdischen Treiben in den Kunlun-Bergen wohnend vorgestellt wurden. Sie wirkten als mit Zauberkräften und Verwandlungskünsten begabte Genii, die menschliche Daseinsformen und Verhaltensweisen reflektierten und persiflierten und dabei als die Härten der gesellschaftlichen Normen ihrer Zeit zu glätten und Glück zu bringen imstande betrachtet wurden. Oft wurden nur ihre acht Embleme Fächer, Schwert, Kürbisflasche, Kastagnetten, Blumenkorb, Bambusstock, Flöte und Lotus zur Dekoration verwendet. Zu den buddhistischen Motiven der Dekorationen gehörten zum Beispiel der Elefant mit der geweihten Almosenschale auf dem Rücken sowie die acht Symbole Krug, Tritonshorn, Schirm, Baldachin, Lotus, Rad des Rechts, Fische und mystischer Knoten. Da entsprechend den acht Trigrammen *(ba gua)* die yin-Zahl acht das Leben eines Mannes bestimmt, zählen auch die gern als Dekoration verwendeten Symbole des Gelehrten (Perle, Musikinstrument, Münze, Rhombus, Bücher, Bilder, Horn des Rhinozeros, Blatt der Artemisia) acht an der Zahl.

In der Qing-Zeit waren die Dekorationen sehr mannigfaltig. Aussparungen der bildlichen Motive und narrativen Darstellungen wurden mit verschiedenen Mustern wie Acht- und Viereck, Fischrogen, Netzarbeit und Waben unterlegt, mit Ornamenten wie Zepter *(ruyi* – Glückssymbol), und Schriftzeichen wie *shou* (langes Leben) und der Unendlichkeit symbolisierenden Zahl 10000 *wan* ausgeschmückt. Arabesken wie Mäander, Ranken in T-Form und Schlüssel-

In accordance with the primacy of nature in Taoist philosophy, the inexhaustible plant world and the animal kingdom were the preferred sources for the motifs used in fine art. Flowers and creatures symbolized ethical values, a happy outcome for events, long life and prosperity, in their form and interplay. Bamboo, plum blossom and pine, for example, were the friends of the winter, symbolizing modesty, innocence and long life. The magpie often crops up as a symbol of joy: it was said that if it built its nest close to a house this promised happiness for all the family's neighbours and guests. Bat and stag, homophones for happiness and prosperity, can be found among the decorations in every house as bringers of happiness. Narrative paintings and carvings of legendary and documented historical anecdotes, and also depictions of the Taoist gods of prosperity, of long life etc. and of the deified immortals with the special group of eight principal immortals holding their emblems were favored. The immortals were presented as living in the Kunlun Mountains, far away from human activities, and worked as genii endowed with magic powers and arts of transformation. They reflected and satirized human forms of existence and behaviour, and were thus considered capable of smoothing out the hardships that were the social norm in their day, and bringing happiness. Often only their eight emblems were used as decoration: fan, sword, bottle gourd, castanets, flower basket, bamboo cane, flute and lotus. The Buddhist motifs for decoration included the elephant with a consecrated alms-bowl on its back, and the eight symbols jug, triton's horn, umbrella, baldacchino, lotus, wheel of justice, fish and mystical knot. Since according to the eight trigrams *(ba gua)* the *yin* number eight rules the life of a man, the symbols of the scholar (pearl, musical stone, coin, rhombus, books, paintings, rhinoceros horn, artemisia leaf) which were often used for decoration also count eight in number. The pictorial motifs and narrative accounts were often lined with patterns like octagon and square, fish roe, network and honeycomb, embellished with ornaments like sceptre *(ruyi* – symbol of luck) swastika and calligraphy characters as for instance *shou* (long life) or *wan* (10000) symbolizing infinity, and framed with motifs including meanders and arabesques in key, T or *hui* (return) form. Often panels with a variety of antiques were added to complete the decorations.

From the Song Dynasty (960–1279 AD) onwards, it was the custom in many provinces to decorate the facades with brick carvings. The clay was molded, washed and baked up to the point when a light greenish grey color, indicating

Obere Galerie eines *tianjing* mit stützenden Querbalken und Säulen, verziert mit Holzschnitzereien. Unter dem Zeichen Harmonie ein Hirsch, ein Kraut der Unsterblichkeit *(zhi)* kauend, und sein Kitz. Zwei der acht Unsterblichen als Stützen der Querbalken: Lü Dongbing und sein Lieblingsschüler Han Xiangzi, eine Flöte spielend.
Zhejiang, Changyue, Lanxi

Beams and columns supporting the upper gallery in a *tianjing*, decorated with wooden carvings. Under the character harmony a deer, chewing a herb of immortality *(zhi)* and protecting a fawn. Two of the eight immortals supporting the cross beams: Lü Dongbing and his favorite disciple Han Xiangzi, playing a flute.
Zhejiang, Changyue, Lanxi

Holzfenster dekoriert mit der Darstellung einer Fledermaus als Glückssymbol
Wooden window carving of a bat symbolizing luck
Huangxi, Qianjiang, Sichuan

Holzschnitzereien mit der Darstellung eines Hirsches mit zwei Ricken unter einer Kiefer gerahmt mit Ranken im *hui* (Rückkehr) Muster und verziert mit *ruyi* (Glückssymbol) Ornamenten und Kakiblüten auf einem Fensterquerbrett. Fensterflügel verziert mit Schnitzereien von eine Münze haltenden Fledermäusen. Zhejiang

Wooden carvings of a stag with two roe deers under a pine tree framed with arabesques in the *hui* (return) style and carvings in the *ruyi* (symbol of luck) pattern embellished with persimmon flowers on a window cross board. Window wings decorated with carvings of bats holding a coin. Zhejiang

Dachreiter auf dem Giebel des Kaiserpalastes in der Verbotenen Stadt *(Zijincheng)* in Beijing

Roof turrets on the eave of the emperor's palace in the Forbidden City *(Zijincheng)* in Beijing

Runde Ziegel einer Dachtraufe dekoriert mit dem *Yinyang*-Symbol, Phönix und Kranich der Bai-Völker in Yunnan, Dali, Xizhou

Round eaves tiles decorated with the *yinyang*-symbol, phoenix, and crane of the Bai people in Yunnan, Dali, Xizhou

muster rahmen, und Tafeln, verziert mit einer Vielzahl von antiken Utensilien. ergänzen die Dekorationen.

Seit der Song-Dynastie wurden die Fassaden der Häuser mit Backsteinschnitzereien geschmückt. Hierzu wurde Lehm modelliert und gebacken, bis ein grün schimmernder Grauton die zur Bearbeitung notwendige Festigkeit anzeigte. Danach wurden die Motive ausgeschnitten, geschnitzt und poliert. Die Hofeingänge wurden nach altem Brauch mit Trommelsteinen eingerahmt. In Tempeln und in Höfen hoher Beamter war ein Löwenpaar als Hüter zu den Seiten der Tore aufgestellt. Der an der Westseite plazierte weibliche Löwe hält ein Junges unter der Tatze, der männliche Löwe an der Ostseite eine Zauberkugel, in der ein imaginäres Junges verborgen ist.

Bräuche zum Schutz vor Unbilden der Natur fanden in den Dekorationen der Häuser Gestalt. Giebel und Dächer wurden mit Glückssymbolen und mythologischen Kreaturen geschmückt. Der Drache war die mächtigste, beschützende und deshalb die bevorzugte, doch ihn als Figur zu dekorieren, war den Königspalästen und den Residenzen der Prinzen vorbehalten. Auf ihren Dachgiebeln wurden die Dachreiter Drache, Phönix, Löwe, Meeres- und Himmels-(Luft)pferd aufgereiht, angeführt von auf einem mythologischen Vogel reitenden Genius *(xianren)* und gefolgt von einer schützenden Bestie. In den Königspalästen folgten der 'Kerberos' des Huang Di Olymp *yayu*, das schnell wie ein Löwe laufende Wildpferd *suanni*, die Hybride aus Einhorn und kriechendem Reptil *xiazhi* und der Ochse des Zödiakus *douniu;* vervollständigt wurde die Reihe durch einen geflügelten Krieger einer zehn Mann starken Heeresbatterie *xingshi*. In den Residenzen der einfachen Bevölkerung wurden die nicht glasierten Ziegel der Dachtraufen mit Blüten, Schriftzeichen oder Motiven des Tierreichs verziert. Um den Erdherrscher zu ehren und gnädig für das Wohl der Familien zu stimmen, wurden nach Tradition Schreine in die Schutzmauern der Höfe eingelassen. Der sogenannte Taishan-Stein mit Tigerkopf als Wächter, versehen mit der Aufschrift „der Stein des Taiberg führt Aufsicht", gehörte zu den unverzichtbaren Schutzfiguren des *fengshui*.

Die besondere Art, Wesen der Natur in Metamorphosen darzustellen, hat ihren Ursprung in der Philosophie des Taoismus und war Tradition in der bildenden Kunst. Sie diente als Kunstmittel in philosophischen und politisch satirischen Abhandlungen und Anekdoten bis hin zu volkstümlichen, scheinbar naiven Darstellungen, wie hier mit dem Motiv eines Drachenkopfes mit Menschengesicht auf einem roten Backsteingiebel gezeigt wird (s. S. 101).

the required degree of hardness for processing was obtained. Then the bricks were cut, carved and polished. The main gates of the courtyards were framed with drum stones with carved ornaments. In temples and in courtyards of high officials a pair of lions was set up as guardians on both sides of the main entrance. The female, placed at the west side, keeps a cub under her right paw, while the male at the east side keeps an ornamental ball under his left paw, suggesting a hidden cub.

Customs used as protection against inclement nature and disadvantages affected the decoration of the houses. Roofs and eaves were decorated with symbols of good fortune and mythological creatures. The dragon was the most powerful and protecting creature, and thus the most favored, but to present him as a figure was allowed only for princes' palaces. Dragon, phoenix, lion, sea- and heaven-(air)horse were lined up as ridge turrets on the eaves of their palaces. On the eaves of the emperor's palace these five mythological creatures were followed by the 'cerberus' of the Huang Di Olympus *(yayu)*, a hybrid of a wild horse and a lion *(suanni)*, able to run 500 miles a day, a hybrid of a unicorn and a reptile *(xiazhi)* which can identify good and evil men and a zodiacal ox *(douniu)*. A winged warrior *(xingshi)* completed the set of ten creatures, similar to a basic military file in China. An immortal *(xianren)* riding a mythological bird is the leader of the creatures, followed by a hanging beast *(chuishou)*. In the residences of common people, Chinese characters, motifs of the animal kingdom and plant world were favored as decorations. The gutter-head tiles of the eaves for instance were patterned with flowers, characters symbolizing long life, or a cat's head, while dragon patterns were only allowed for the emperors' palaces. To worship the Earth Ruler and dispose him for protecting the family, shrines were let in the screen walls of the courtyards. The so-called Taishan stone with a tiger's head as guard provided with the inscription "the Tai Mountain stone is supervising and ready to act boldly" is an indispensable tutelary spirit of *fengshui*.

The very peculiar way of depicting natural creatures of nature in metamorphosed forms is based on the philosophy of Taoism and was common in all categories of fine art. It was used as an artificial device in philosophical essays and superficially naive satires going as far as popular apparently naive depictions such as the motif of a dragon's face looking like a very human face decorating the red-brick eaves shown here (cf. p. 101)

Platte zur Abwehr des Windes *(bofeng bantou)* mit Drachenkopf und Fischpaar. Shanxi, Chengguanzhen, Baode
Fight the wind board *(bofeng bantou),* with a dragon head and a pair of fish. Shanxi, Chengguanzhen, Baode

Mythischer Drache als Späher *(tantou)* am Haupttor eines Hofes
Mythical dragon as spy head *(tantou)* at the main gate of a courtyard
Shanxi, Chengguanzhen, Baode

Taishan Steinwächter mit Tigerkopf
Taishan Stone Guard with a tiger's head
Sichuan, Taoping, Lixian

Giebel eines Hauses im Roten Backsteinstil. Drache mit Menschengesicht über Wolken, Guanyin mit Hirsch in einem runden Juwel haltend. Fujian, Huixian

Gable of a house in the Red-Brick-style. Dragon with the face of a human being above clouds, keeping Guanyin with a deer in a round jewel. Fujian, Huixian

Versetzter, aus Backstein geschnitzter Drache unter dem Giebel eines Hoftores
Displaced brick carved dragon under the gable of a courtyard gate
Shanxi, Lingshi, Jingshengzhen

Schutzmauer mit Schrein hinter dem Haupttor eines Hofes
Screen wall with a shrine behind the main gate of a courtyard
Shanxi, Jingshenzhen, Lingshi

Oben links: Trommelstein dekoriert mit Ornamenten, Blumenschnitzereien und Löwen neben dem Haupttor eines Hofes in Shanxi, Lingshi, Jingshengzhen
Oben rechts: Spielende Steinlöwen auf einer mit Ornamenten verzierten, auf einem Steinsockel ruhenden Zauberkugel neben dem Haupttor eines Hofes in Shanxi, Lingshi, Jingshengzhen
Rechts: Trommelstein verziert mit Schnitzerei einer auf einem Einhorn reitenden Fledermaus unter einer Kiefer im Mäanderring. Sockel verziert mit Lotusblume.
Residenz des Beamten Wen Yu in Beijing

Left above: Drum stone decorated with carved flowers, ornaments and lions beside a main gate of a courtyard in Shanxi, Lingshi, Jingshengzhen
Right above: Stone lions playing on an ornamental ball, resting on a stone pedestal beside a main gate of a courtyard in Shanxi, Lingshi, Jingshengzhen
Right: Drum stone with carvings of a bat riding a unicorn below a pine tree encircled by meander ring. Socle decorated with lotus flower.
Residence of the official Wen Yu in Beijing

Oben: Zwei Fenster mit Steinschnitzereien von Pflaumenblüten, Bambus und Kiefer, bezeichnet als die drei Freunde des Winters *(sui han san you)*. Huizhou, Xidi, Yixian
Rechts: Backsteinschnitzerei an der Seite eines Haupttores mit glückverheißenden Elstern auf einem Pflaumenblütenzweig, gerahmt von der Kontour eines Blattes. Fujian, Xiamei, Wuyishan

Above: Two windows with stone carvings of plum blossoms, bamboo and pine, the so-called three friends of the winter *(sui han san you)*. Huizhou, Xidi, Yixian
Right: Brick carving on the side of a main gate, magpies on a twig of plum blossoms, a symbol of luck and fortune, framed by the outline of a leaf. Fujian, Xiamei, Wuyishan

Rechts: Haupttor eines Hofes im Bezirk der Grauen Backsteinbaukunst. Fujian, Xiamei, Wuyishan
Oben: Dekorierende Backsteinschnitzereien mit der historischen Darstellung des Mu Wang (5. Kaiser der Zhou Dynastie) und seines Gefährten Zao Fu mit acht Pferden auf der Inspektionsreise durch das Reich. Die Quertafeln verziert mit Schnitzereien buddhistischer Geräte.

Right: Main gate of a courtyard in the district of Grey-Brick-Architecture. Fujian, Xiamei, Wuyishan
Above: Stone carvings decorating the main entrance, presenting the historic narration of Mu Wang (5th emperor of the Zhou Dynasty) with his companion Zao Fu and eight horses on tour of inspection through his country. The cross boards decorated with carvings of Buddhist tools.

In China wurde gern im Schutz der Berge gesiedelt. Vom westlichen Kunlun-Gebirge verlaufen drei Gebirgsketten durch das Land zum Pazifik. Sie wurden als drei durch das Land ziehende Drachen gesehen. Die trennenden Ströme des Yangtze und des Gelben Flusses mit ihren Nebenflüssen wurden als Blutgefäße der Drachen bezeichnet. Den Drachen, sprich die Gegend zu erforschen und das Fundament mit Sorgfalt im angemessenen Zeitraum zu bestimmen *(san nian xun long, shi nian dian xie),* war Voraussetzung für die Anlage der Ortschaften und Höfe. Ein Hof der She-Minorität in Fujian zeigt anschaulich die Kunst, wie in gebirgiger Landschaft gesiedelt wurde. Der Hof liegt im Schutz des Haus- oder Sitzberges *(zuoshan/zhushan)* mit einem Wäldchen, das im Bogen den Hang säumt. Vor dem Hof liegt ein Teich, zur rechten Seite steht ein Baum, der ein glückliches Geschick verspricht. Die Eingangstore rahmen nach dem Prinzip gegenüber der Szenerie *(duijing)* ein anmutiges Landschaftsbild ein.

Die Küstenregionen im Süden Chinas sind oft von Taifunen bedroht, und es herrscht starke Sonnenstrahlung. Deshalb wurden die Höfe hier meist im Gegensatz zu den Höfen in Zentralchina mit der Front nach Westen gerichtet im Schutz der Berge gebaut, die an der linken Seite jedoch nie höher sein durften als an der rechten (die zugeordneten Symboltiere wanderten im Kreis mit).

In den Tiefebenen der Flüsse herrschten wiederum andere *fengshui*-Bedingungen als in den gebirgigen Landschaften. Die Wendigkeit dieser Kunst reflektiert sich in dem Spruch „Lehnst du am Berg, so ernähre dich von den Bergen; lehnst du am Wasser so ernähre dich durch das Wasser *(Kaoshan chishan; kaoshui chishui).*" In Jiangnan war es

In China people preferred to settle in the shelter of the mountains. From the western Kunlun Range, three chains of mountains run south-eastwards to the Pacific Ocean. These chains were seen as three dragons roaming through the country *(san long ru guo).* The Yellow River and the Yangtze River, which flow between them, were called the dragons' blood vessels. The rule for setting up the courtyards was established by exploring the 'dragon' and carefully placing the foundations in the appropriate period of time *(san nian xun long, shi nian dian xie).* A beautiful example of the art of settling in mountainous areas is provided by a farmyard of the She minority in Fujian. The yard is built in the shelter of the so-called house or seat mountain *(zuoshan/zhushan)* with a little forest curling round the slope. In front of the yard there is a little pool. On the right side in front of the yard a tree signifies good fortune. The gates frame and set off beautiful scenery according to the aesthetic principle *duijing* (opposite the scenery).

People living in the coastal areas of southern China need protection against typhoons and strong summer sunshine. This is why they used to built their courtyards facing west, different from Central China, protected by the mountains behind and on both sides, but never higher on the left than on the right. (The related symbolic animals also turned round.)

In the river plains, on the other hand, different *fengshui* rules have to be followed. The adaptability of this art is reflected in the proverb: "Leaning on the mountain one depends on the mountain for food, leaning on the water one depends on the water for food. *(Kaoshan chishan, kaoshui chishui.)*" The dragon is seen as the ruler of the streams.

Oben: Frontansicht eines Hofes des She-Volkes
Links: Blick von innen und außen durch das linke Tor eines Hofes des She-Volkes
Fujian, Xingshuicun, Yonganxian

Above: Front view of a farmyard of the She people
Left: View of the left gate of a farmyard of the She people
Fujian, Xingshuicun, Yonganxian

deshalb üblich, die Häuser am Ufer lehnend (ungern mit dem Rücken dem Fluß zugewandt) zu bauen, und mit ihrer Front auf den (Ufer-) Weg blicken zu lassen (s. S. 78–83).

In Flußgebieten folgten die Anlagen der *fengshui*-Regel: Abhängig von der Form ist die Kraft, preise die Länge, meide die Kürze! *(Yixing jiushi; yangchang yiduan!)*. Deshalb wurden Dörfer und Höfe in der Nähe des konkaven und nicht in der Nähe des konvexen Flußufers angelegt, um Überschwemmungen und Verschmutzungen zu vermeiden. Die Dörfer in der mittleren Region des Nanxi-Flusses bieten dafür anschauliche Beispiele. Die Orte grenzen an im Bogen verlaufende Flüsse, die sorgfältig mit Steinen gelegte Wasserreservoire speisen. Die Dörfer müssen hier vor starken Regenfällen, Sturm und Feuer geschützt werden, deshalb sind die Häuser auf hohen Sockeln gebaut und entlang der Gassen mit Mauern eingefaßt. Mauern und Gassen sind mit vom Flußwasser geschliffenen Steinen gelegt. Der Hof mit dem Namen 'Kiefernwind-Wassermond (Songfeng-Shuiyue)' in dem Dorf Daitou im Bezirk Yongjia ist ein Hof der Ming-Zeit, der hier als Beispiel eines nach *fengshui*-Regeln angelegter Höfe dieser Gegend dienen soll. Er ruht auf einer Anhöhe vor der Gebirgskette des Ruhenden Drachen (Wolonggang) und folgt der Regel *"Zuoshi xiangxu"!* (Auf Solidem sitzend der Leere zugewandt!). Das Hauptgebäude hat sieben Buchten und kein oberes Stockwerk; entlang der fünf Mittelbuchten läuft eine Veranda, vor den seitlichen Buchten schließt eine Balustrade *(meirenkao)* an die Dachvorsprünge an. An der Rückseite liegt ein Blumengarten, der in ein üppig grünes Bambuswäldchen übergeht. Vorne führt zentral ein Weg auf das mit Backsteinen gelegte Haupttor zu. Es läßt keinen Durchtritt zu, da es auf dem hohen, mit Steinen gelegten Frontsockel steht. Ein liebevoll geschnitztes Gitter verschließt das Tor. Der Frontsockel ist anderthalb Meter hoch. Der Teich entlang des Frontsockels ist dreißig Meter lang und vier Meter breit. Eine Treppe führt vom Haupttor zum zweiten Tor an der rechten Seite, an das ein kleines, mit einer Balustrade geschmücktes Gebäude anschließt. Von diesem Tor führt der Weg zu dem Tempel des Luban, dem Gott der Zimmerleute, der die kunstfertig gearbeiteten Höfe beschützen soll. Die Häuser sind im *chuandou*-Fachwerk meist mit sieben, nie mit weniger als fünf und nie mit mehr als neun Dachpfetten gebaut. Die mittleren Dachsparren sind oft, Querbalken stützend, im *tailiang*-Stil gebaut (s. S. 114 links oben). Dieser Fachwerkstil ist besonders geeignet, Dachtraufen als Schutz vor Regen und Sonne vorzubauen. (Die Dörfer dieser Region sind derzeit vom sinkenden Grundwasserspiegel bedroht.)

Thus in Jiangnan houses used to be built leaning on embankments (sometimes with the back inclining towards the river) and facing the (riverside) alley in front (cf. pp. 78–83).

Villages and courtyards built in river areas followed the *fengshui* rule: *yixing jiushi, yangchang biduan!* (Power depends on the form, praise the long, avoid the short!) Thus settlements were established near the concave rather than near the convex bank of the river, to avoid filth and flooding. The villages in the middle reaches of the Nanxi river in Zhejiang offer some fine examples of this. Often a curved river borders a village, feeding water reservoirs, which are carefully laid with natural stones. The villages there have to be protected from fire and rainstorms, that is why the houses are built on high corbels and secured by stone walls immediately adjacent to the alleys. Walls and alleys are laid in different patterns with stones polished smooth by the water of the rivers. The courtyard called "Songfeng-Shuiyue (Pine-Wind-Water-Moon)" in Daitou, a village in the Yongjia district, is a special Ming Dynasty courtyard which can stand as an outstanding regional example of a courtyard built according to the rules of *fengshui*. It sits on a rolling rise of the Sleeping-Dragon-Ridge (Wolonggang), following the rule "*Zuoshi xiangxu* (sitting on the solid, facing the void)." The main building has seven bays and no upper storey; a veranda runs along the five middle bays, and a balustrade *(meirenkao)* sits below the eaves of the side bays. At the back, a beautiful flower garden forms a link with a luxuriant bamboo forest. At the front, the path leads to the main gate, which is laid with bricks. No one can pass through this, as it is set on the high front corbel. It is barred with a delicately carved wooden lattice. The front corbel is one and a half meters high. The pool accompanying the corbel is thirty meters long and four meters wide. A flight of steps leads from the middle gate to a gate on the right, which has a little building decorated with a wooden balustrade adjacent to it. The path from the side gate leads to the towering temple of Luban, the god of carpenters, and protector of the skilfully timbered courtyards of the village. The houses are usually constructed on the *chuandou* framework with seven purlins, but never fewer than five or more than nine. The middle truss was often constructed in the *tailiang* style, supporting cross beams (cf. p. 114 left above). This framework style was suitable for the addition of projecting eaves as a protection against rain and sunshine. (The villages in this area are under threat from the sinking ground water table.)

Weg entlang des Frontsockels mit Haupt- und Seitentor vor dem Kiefernwind-Wassermond-Hof
mit Blick über die Giebel des Luban-Tempels auf die Gebirgskette des Ruhenden Drachen
Daitou, Yongjia, Zhejiang

Way along the front corbel with middle and side gate of the Pine-Wind-Water-Moon courtyard
with view of the Sleeping-Dragon-Ridge over the gables of the Luban Temple
Daitou, Yongjia, Zhejiang

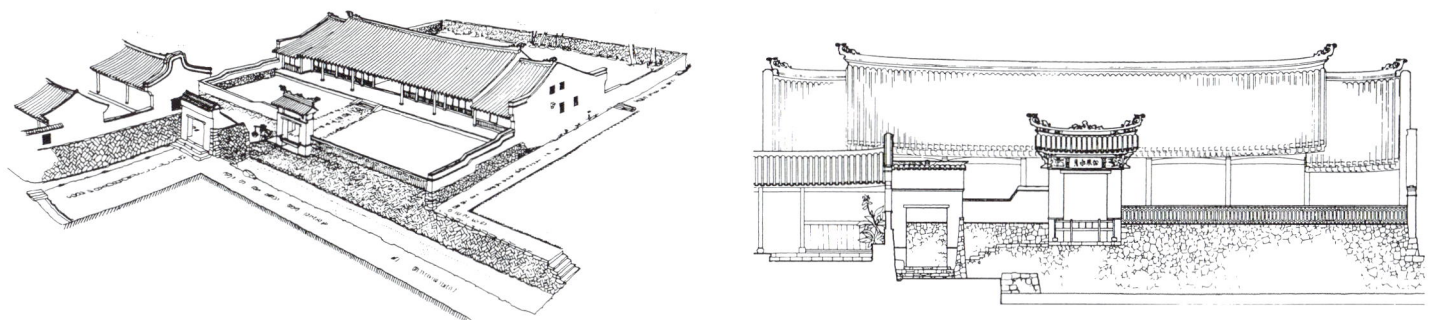

Skizzen des Kiefernwind-Wassermond-Hofes in dem Dorf Daitou, Yongjia, Zhejiang
Sketches of the Pine-Wind-Water-Moon courtyard in the village of Daitou, Yongjia, Zhejiang

Oben: Sogenannter Flaschenkürbisbrunnen *(huguajing)* vor dem Dorf Xian
Links oben: Höfe entlang einer mit Steinen gepflasterten Gasse in dem Dorf Langxia
Links unten: Wasserreservoir entlang den Hofmauern des Dorfes Pengxicun
Yongjia, Zhejiang

Above: So-called bottle-gourd well *(huguajing)* in front of the village of Xian
Left above: Courtyards along an alley paved with stones in the village of Langxia
Left below: View of courtyard walls across the water reservoir of the village of Pengxicun
Yongjia, Zhejiang

Baustile

In China unterschieden sich seit frühen Zeiten drei Hauptstile der Holzkonstruktionen: das Holzskelett mit tragenden Querbalken, genannt *tailiang*-Stil, das Fachwerk, genannt *chuandou*-Stil und der Pfahlbaustil mit Brunnenrumpf, genannt *jinggan*-Stil. Der *tailiang*-Stil war in der Frühlings- und Herbstperiode (770–476 v. Chr.) vollendet und wurde in den späteren Dynastien in Zentralchina bevorzugt. Die Holzsäulen wurden auf Steinsockeln aufgerichtet. Querbalken stützen die Längsträger. Gebäude in diesem Stil konnten dreieckig, rechteckig, rund und vieleckig mit rundem oder vieleckigem Dach konstruiert werden. Das Fachwerk im sogenannten *chuandou*-Stil war seit der Han-Dynastie vorwiegend im Süden Chinas verbreitet. Es wurde dort sowohl in den Ebenen für den Bau der Häuser mit überhängenden Dächern als auch in den gebirgigen Gebieten für die Konstruktion der terrassenförmigen überhängenden Häuser bevorzugt. Brunnenpfahlbauten *(jinggan)* wurden mit rundem oder ovalem Einlaß gebaut; Bronzefunde dieses Baustils im Südwesten Chinas datieren circa einhundert Jahre vor unserer Zeit. Blockhäuser und Pfahlbauten in diesem Stil werden derzeit von Minoritäten bewohnt, die in Gebirgs- und Waldregionen Yunnans leben.

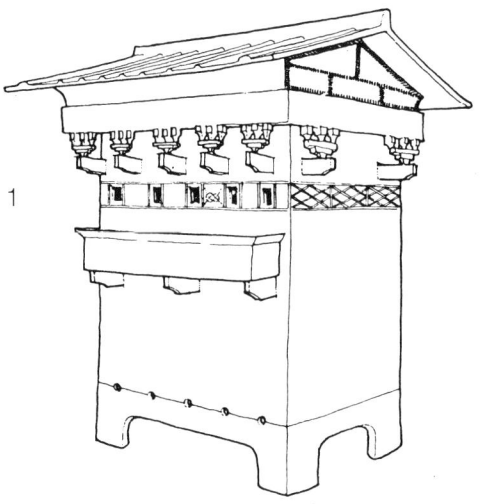

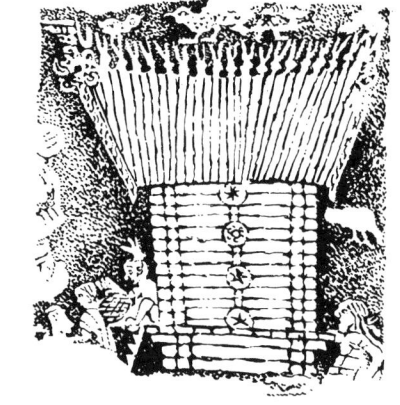

Blockhaus im Gebiet des Lugu-Sees in Yongning
Log cabin in the Lugu lake area in Yongning
Ninglang, Yunnan

Baustile der Han-Dynastie, dargestellt mit Grabbeigaben, Bronzen und Steinbasreliefs

1,4 Konstruktion im *tailiang*-Stil
  5 Fachwerk im *chuandou*-Stil
2,6 Pfahlbauten im *ganlan*-Stil
3,7 Brunnenpfahlbauten (*jinggan*-Stil)

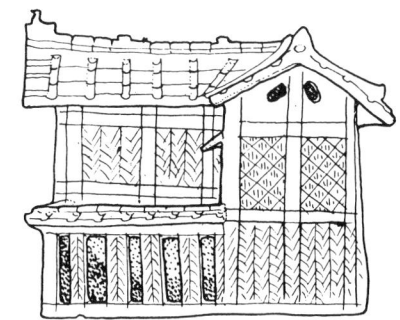

Architectural styles

In the earliest days, three styles of wood constructions were distinguished: the *tailiang* style, the *chuandou* style and the stilt-house style with posts, forming the shape of a well, called *jinggan* style. The *tailiang* style was completed in the Spring and Autumn Period (770–476 AD) and in later dynasties became favored in Central China. Wooden columns were set up on stone plinths, cross beams support the longitudinal beams. Buildings in this style were triangular, square, polygonal or round. Houses built in the *chuandou* style occurred mainly in the south of China. This style was preferred for the construction of overhanging houses on the plains as well as for the construction of terraced overhanging houses in mountainous areas. Stilt houses in the *jinggan* style were constructed with round, oval, square or hexagonal top openings. Houses in this style originate in the south-west of China, bronzes in this style date from a hundred years before our time. At the present time, log cabins and piled houses are inhabited by different minorities living in the mountainous and forest regions of Yunnan.

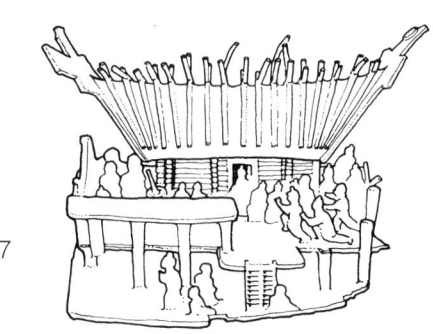

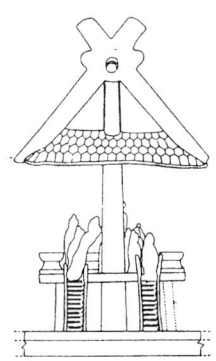 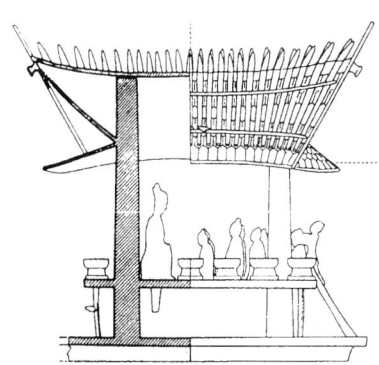

Architectural styles of the Han Dynasty depicted with burial objects, bronze ware and stone reliefs

1,4 Construction in the *tailing* style
 5 framework in the *chuandou* style
2,6 stilt houses in the *ganlan* style
3,7 well-stilt houses (*jinggan* style)

Struktur eines Brunnenpfahlbaus
Structure of a well-stilt house

117

Fachwerkhaus *(chuandou)*. *Zhejiang,* Langxia, Yongjia
Framework house *(chuandou)*. *Zhejiang,* Langxia, Yongjia

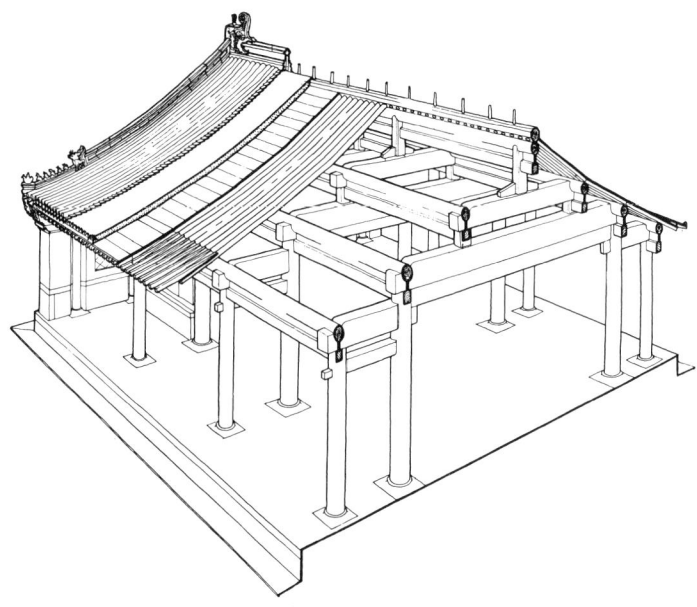

Haus im *tailiang*-Stil. Beijing
House built in the *tailiang* style. Beijing

Die Holzbauten im *tailiang*-Stil wurden in Buchten, genannt *jian*, unterteilt, die im Innenraum von vier Säulen markiert waren und zu Veranden an den Seiten durch je zwei Säulen ergänzt werden konnten. (Die Tiefe der Bauten im Stil der tragenden Balken wurde in Dachpfetten gemessen.) Die Dächer einfacher Häuser waren konkav geformt. In Residenzen und Palästen hatten die Dächer geschwungene Dachvorsprünge, die mit Gruppierungen von Ochsenkopfkapitellen gestützt wurden. Die kleinsten Häuser hatten drei Buchten. Diese Anordnung wurde in der Ming- und Qing-Dynastie *yiming, liangan* (ein heller, zwei dunkle) genannt. Die Bezeichnung leitete sich aus *yiming, ernei* (ein heller, zwei innen) für quadratische Gebäude früherer Zeiten mit vorderer Halle und zwei hinteren dunklen Räumen ab. Die Gebäude wurden symmetrisch zur Mittelachse der Zentralhalle angelegt und hatten deshalb grundsätzlich eine ungerade *(yang)* Zahl an Räumen. Seit der Tang-Dynastie wurden Baurichtlinien erlassen, die Maße und Unterteilungen der Baugerüste vorgaben, die Strukturen blieben dabei in den folgenden Epochen im wesentlichen gleich. In der Ming- und Qing-Dynastie waren zum Beispiel die Säulen im Vergleich zur Tang-Zeit breiter und höher; während die Kapitelle *(dougong)* graziler gearbeitet und folglich in vielgliedrigen Gruppierungen angelegt wurden.

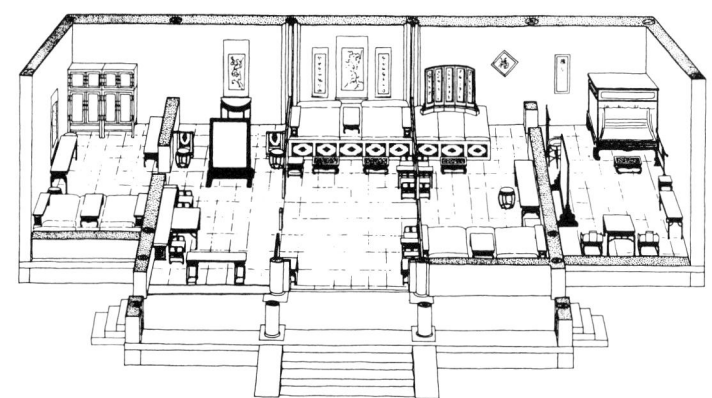

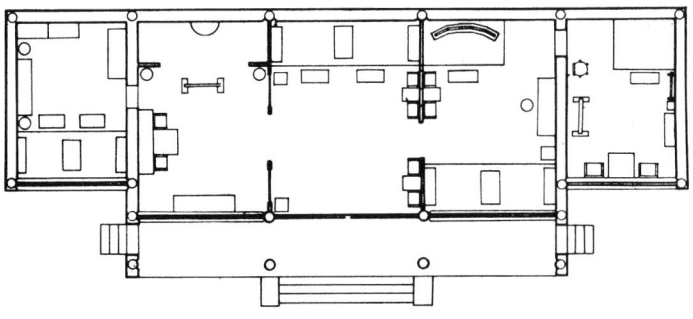

Innenansicht eines Hauptgebäudes mit fünf Buchten *(kaijian)*. Beijing
Inner decor of a main building with five bays *(kaijian)*. Beijing

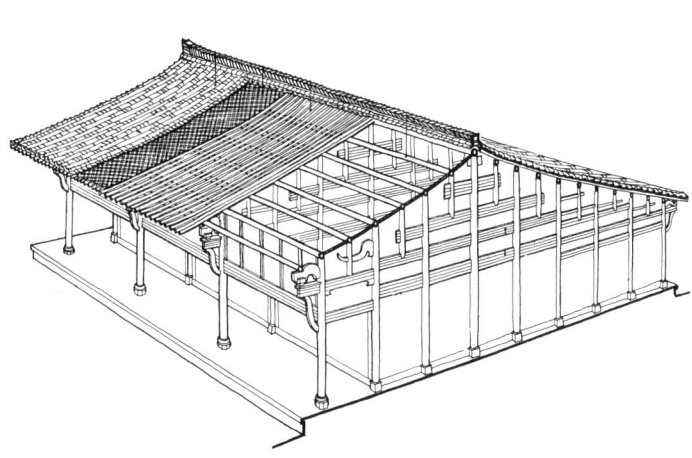

Haus im *chuandou*-Fachwerk
House built in the *chuandou* framework

Häuser im *chuandou*-Fachwerk. Sichuan, Fubao
Houses in the *chuandou* style. Sichuan, Fubao

Blick aus dem Raum an der Westseite in den Mittelraum des Hauptgebäudes eines *siheyuan*. Beijing
View from the room on the west side of the middle room in the main building of a *siheyuan*. Beijing

The independent framework of the houses in the *tailiang* style, built on earth foundations, was subdivided into bays called *jian,* marked by four columns in the inside room. If a gallery was added on one or both sides, the bays were extended, marked by two columns on each side. The depth of the framework in the *tailiang* style was measured in the number of purlins. The roofs in common houses are concave in shape. In residences and palaces the roofs were constructed with upturned eaves which were supported by ox-head capitals *(dougong)*. The smallest houses were subdivided into three bays, called *yiming, liangan* (one light, two dark). This name derives from the traditional square buildings with a hall and two symmetrical rooms behind, called *yiming, ernei* (one light, two inside). Since the residences were laid out symmetrically to the middle axis of the central room, the bays were counted in odd numbers, up to nine according to the *yang* system. From the Tang Dynasty onwards, guidelines were enacted for the construction of the framework. They changed only in terms of the size and proportion of the joined parts, while the basic design remained. In the Ming and Qing Dynasties, beams and columns were higher and broader than in the Tang Dynasty, while the supporting capitals *(dougong)* were more delicate and logically constructed in polynomial groupings.

Oben und links: Feuerschutzmauer genannt Pferdekopfmauer im Sperlingsschwanz-Stil *(queweishi matouqiang)*
Above and left: Fireproof wall called horse-head wall in the sparrow-tail style *(queweishi matouqiang)*
Fujian, Bandong, Minqing

Die traditionellen Freilichthöfe im *siheyuan*-Stil in Beijing 北京

Die Anlage der Altstadt Beijings datiert aus dem zwölften Jahrhundert, als die Stadt, genannt Dadu, zur Hauptstadt des vereinten chinesischen Kaiserreiches erklärt worden war. Sie wurde nach Jahrtausende alten Vorlagen auf rechteckiger Fläche mit dem Kaiserpalast im Zentrum symmetrisch zu ihrer in Richtung Nordsüd verlaufenden Achse angelegt. In der Ming-Dynastie ließ der Herrscher Yongle (1406–1425 n.Chr.) die nördlichen Stadtmauern 2,5 km nach Süden vorziehen und rekonstruierte die Stadt auf annähernd quadratischer Fläche. Bei der Planung soll er dem Astrologen Liu Bowen gefolgt sein. Wie eine Legende erzählt, hatte dieser die Stadt in Harmonie mit den fünf Elementen als Körper des taoistischen Helden und Premierministers des Himmels Necha entworfen. In den Jahren 1522–1566 n.Chr. wurde an die Innenstadt (Tartarenstadt) eine Außenstadt (Chinesenstadt) im Süden angeschlossen. Während der Qing-Dynastie wurde das architektonische Stadtbild mit Palästen und Parkanlagen vollendet.

Von Beginn der Ming- bis Ende der Qing-Dynastie war die Altstadt in Ost-, West-, Nord-, Süd- und Zentralbezirke aufgeteilt, die in Wohnviertel mit schachbrettartig angeordneten Straßen und Gassen *(hutong* – Bezeichnung mongolischen Ursprungs) untergliedert waren. Die Höfe entlang der Gassen orientierten sich an der Anlage des Kaiserpalastes. Ihre Zentralachse verläuft gewöhnlich in Richtung

The traditional open air courtyards in the *siheyuan* style in Beijing

The layout of the old town of Beijing dates from the twelfth century when the city named Dadu was declared the capital of the united Kingdom of China. The city was constructed on the ancient outlines, with the palace in the center, and symmetrically divided by the central north-south axis. In the Ming Dynasty the emperor Yongle (1406 to 1425 AD) shifted the northern walls 2.5 km towards the south and rebuilt the city on an almost square plan. He is said to have followed the astrologer Liu Bowen who, as legend tells, designed the city in accordance with the five elements as the body of the taoist hero and prime minister of heaven Necha with his head lying in the south. In the years 1522–1566 AD the outer city (Chinese town) was built south of the inner city (Tartar town). In the Qing Dynasty the architectural townscape was beautifully completed with palaces, gardens and parks.

In the Ming Dynasty and through to the end of the Qing Dynasty the city was partitioned into north, east, south, west and central districts, subdivided into quarters with streets and alleys *(hutong,* name of Mongolian origin) laid out as a grid. The courtyards along the alleys were modeled on the emperor's palace. Their central axis runs usually from north to south, the inner yard is square; the main gate lies at the south-east of the front wall. In ancient times the calendar house, called *mingtang* (bright hall), built on a square plan,

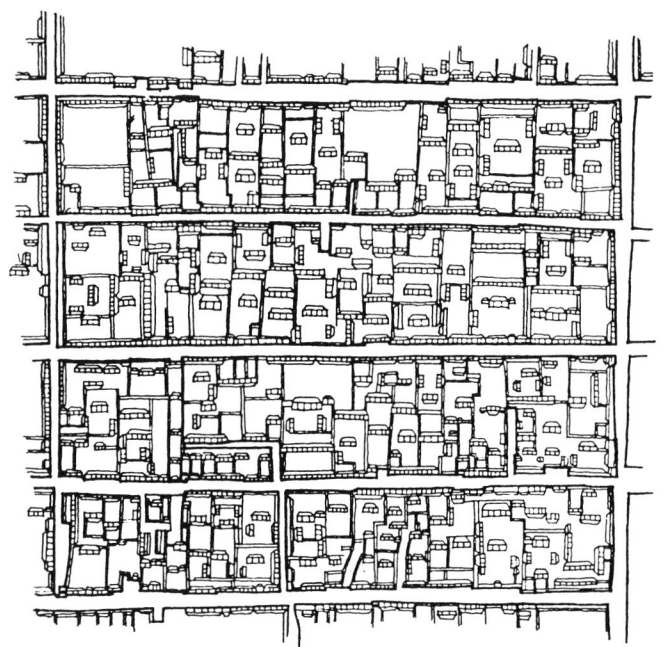
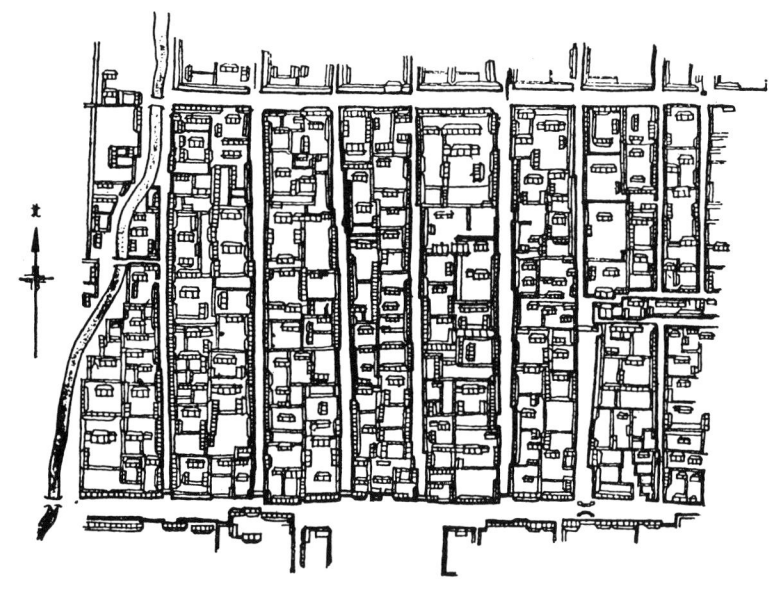

Stadtteile im Zentrum Beijings. Qing-Dynastie
Districts of Central Beijing. Qing Dynasty

Hof im *siheyuan*-Stil in der Dongchangbei-Gasse im Oststadtteil Beijings
Courtyard in the *siheyuan* style in the Dongchangbei alley in the East District of Beijing

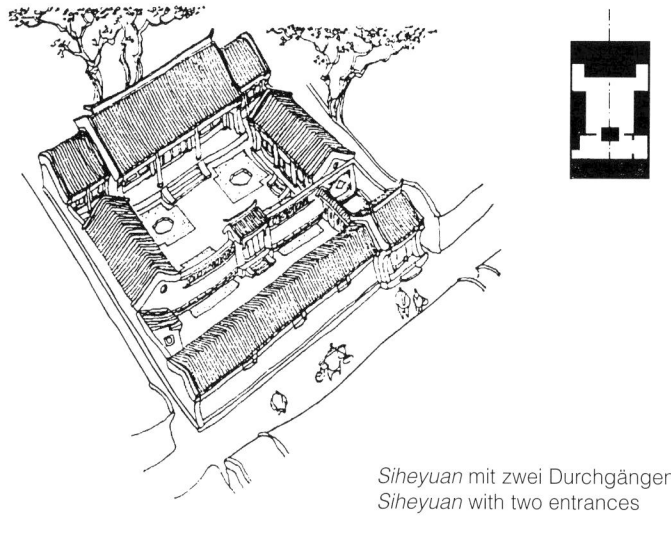

Siheyuan mit zwei Durchgängen
Siheyuan with two entrances

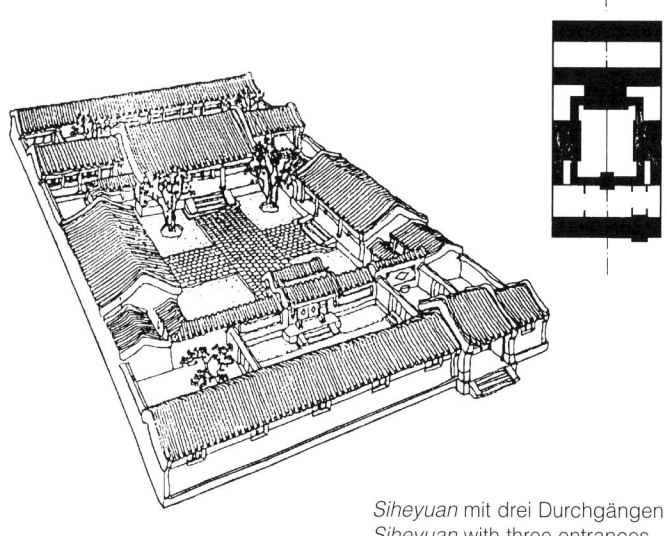

Siheyuan mit drei Durchgängen
Siheyuan with three entrances

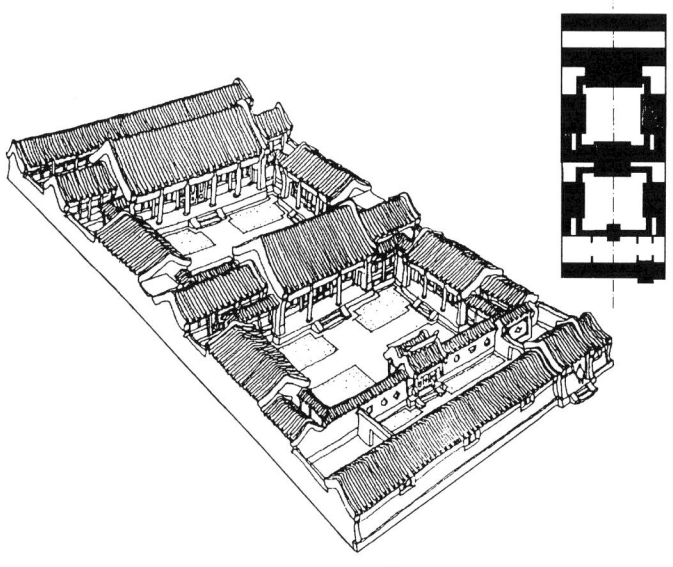

Siheyuan mit vier Durchgängen
Siheyuan with four entrances

Nordsüd, der Innenhof ist quadratisch, das Eingangstor liegt im Südosten. Zentrum der Kaiserpaläste war in frühen Zeiten das Kalenderhaus, genannt *mingtang* (helle Halle), das auf quadratischer, die Erde symbolisierender Terrasse gebaut und mit einem runden, den Himmel symbolisierenden Dach gedeckt war. Die Terrasse war in neun kleine, als Paläste bezeichnete quadratische Räume unterteilt, von deren zwölf Seiten der acht Außenquadrate der Herrscher, als Sohn des Himmels, die zwölf Monate eröffnete. Es bestand Einheit von Zeit und Raum. Diesem Prinzip folgend wurden die Höfe als Mikrokosmos gestaltet, deren Räume nach Sozial- und Familienstruktur des Konfuzianismus angeordnet waren. (Konfuzius hatte in einem Gespräch mit seinem besonders geschätzten Schüler Ran Yong Residenzhöfe mit der Front nach Süden blickend als Voraussetzung der Kaiserwürde definiert, welche dieser zu erlangen befähigt sei *[Yong ye, ke shi nan mian]*).

Die Räume wurden in Harmonie mit dem *yinyang*, den fünf Elementen, den acht Trigrammen, den Himmels- und Erdstämmen etc. angelegt. Der Spruch „*Kan zhai xun men (kan* entspricht der Residenz, *xun* dem Eingangstor)" beschrieb ihre Anordnung nach den acht Trigrammen, die Anordnung nach den zwölf Erdstämmen beschrieb der Spruch „*Zi shan wu wei* (Geschützt vom Berg blickt der erste Stamm [*zi* – Kind – Himmelssohn]" des Mittwinters, der Mitternacht und des Nordens in Richtung des siebten Stammes *wu* des Mittags, Mittsommers und Südens). Die Residenz (Haupthalle) im Norden war üblicherweise in drei Buchten *(jian)* unterteilt. In ihrem Zentrum lag die Ahnenhalle. An der Ostseite befand sich der Wohnraum der älteren Generation, an der Westseite wohnten die Eltern. Diese Anordnung beruhte darauf, daß nach dem *yinyang*-Prinzip die Auffassung bestand, daß das *Yang*, welches sich in das Reich der Toten zu den gelben Quellen des Winters zurückgezogen hatte, vom Wasser *(yin* – nordöstliches Trigramm) umschlossen, den Winter überdauerte und dort seine Kraft zurückgewönne, um neu zu erstehen. So wurden auch in den Höfen, deren Gasseneingänge in Nord-, West-, oder Ostrichtung lagen, die Haupthallen im Norden mit der Front nach Süden gebaut. In Richtung Ostwest verliefen kleine Gassen mit simuliertem Eingang im Südosten.

An den Seiten der Haupthalle waren sogenannte Ohrräume mit kürzerer Tiefe angeschlossen. Im Ostflügel des Hofes *(zhen*-Trigramm) pflegten die Söhne der Familie zu wohnen. Die Töchter des Hauses und die weiblichen Bediensteten nächtigten in den Räumen der Rückfront. Die Küchen lagen im Nord- oder Südosten der Seitenflügel. Die

symbolizing the earth, covered with a round roof, symbolizing heaven, formed the center of the palaces. The terrace was subdivided into nine square rooms, named as palaces with the turning point of time in the center. From the twelve sides of the outer square rooms the emperor, as the son of heaven, inaugurated the twelve months of the year. Time and space were an integrated whole. Following this principle, the courtyards were designed as microcosms with their rooms arranged according to the Confucian hierarchical system and family order. (In a discussion with his most appreciated disciple Ran Yong, Confucius had defined residences facing south as prior condition for the dignity of an emperor, which he thought him capable of achieving *[Yong ye, ke shi nan mian]*).

The rooms were arranged according to the *yinyang*, the five elements, the eight trigrams, the ten celestial and the twelve earth stems, etc. The proverb *"Kan zhai xun men (kan – residence, xun – gate)"* described their design following the eight trigrams; the proverb *"Zi shan wu wei"* (In the shelter of the mountain the first earth stem named as *zi* – heaven's son, assigned to the midnight, midwinter, and the north faces the seventh earth stem named as *wu* and assigned to the midday, midsummer and the south.)

The main hall, or residence, was usually subdivided into three bays. In the center was the ancestor hall. The older generation used to reside on the east side, while the living room for the parents of the family was set up on the west side. The rooms were set up this way for a reason: according to the *yinyang* belief the *yang* retired from the world to the kingdom of the dead and to the yellow sources of the winter, surrounded by the water (*yin* – north-west trigram), survived the winter there and restored its own power to rise again. Thus in those courtyards which faced the *hutong* in the north, west or east, little lanes running from east to west were arranged in front of the residences, and the yards were entered via a simulated gate in the southeast. On both sides of the main halls little rooms, called ear-rooms, shorter in depth, were added. The rooms in the east wings (*zhen* trigram) were favored as living rooms for the sons of the family. The daughters and the female servants lived in the rear rooms. Kitchens were located in the northeast or south-east of the wings. The rooms of the front wall faced the north.

On the east side of the main gate a little private study room was set up with a little garden in front; the male servants used to live in the middle room opposite the second gate. The toilet rooms were located at the west side, and

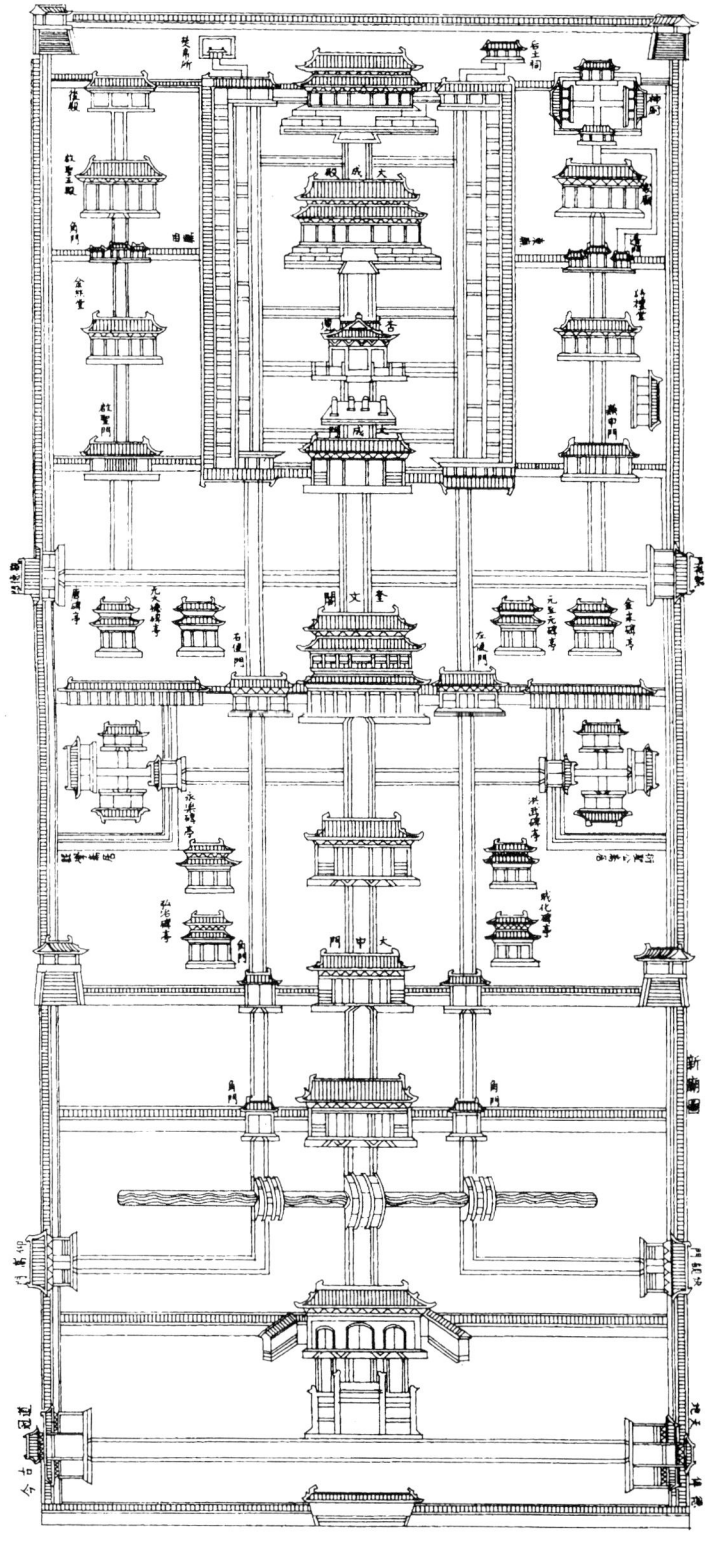

Skizze des Konfuziustempels in Beijing
Sketch of the Confucius Temple in Beijing

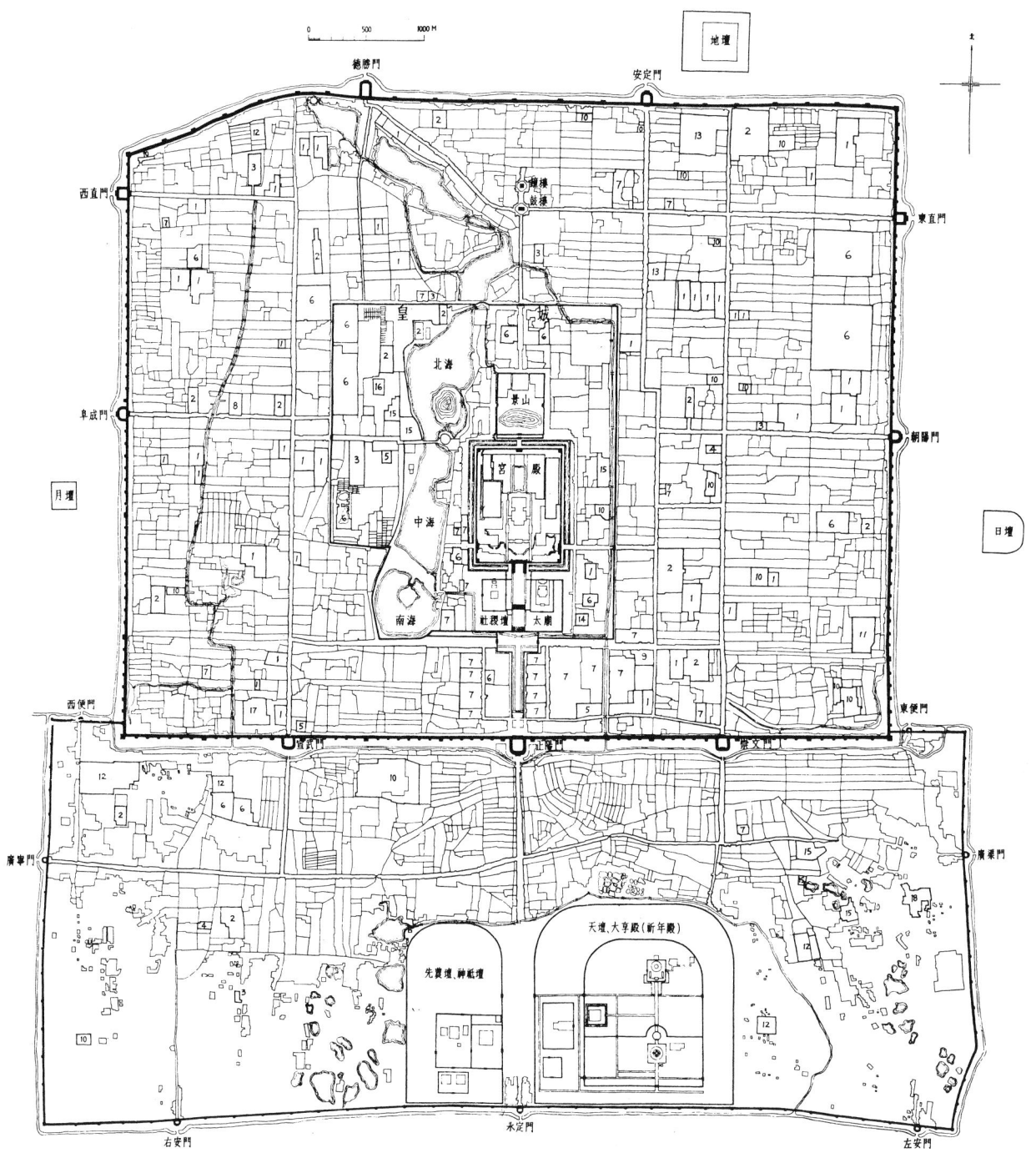

Beijing, Stadtplan der Qing-Dynastie
1 Kaiserfamilie – 2 Buddhist-Tempel – 3 Taoist-Kloster – 4 Moschee – 5 Katholische Kirche – 6 Speicher – 7 Gerichtshof – 8 Kaiserlicher Ahnentempel – 9 Mandschu-Tempel – 10 Handwerkskammer – 11 Steuerhof – 12 „Acht Banner" der Mandschu-Armee – 13 Kulturtempel – 14 Kaiserliches Archiv – 15 Pferdestall – 16 Ochsenstall – 17 Elefantendressurschule – 18 Rechtshof

Beijing, Cityplan of the Qing Dynasty
1 Emperor's Family – 2 Buddhist Temple – 3 Taoist Temple – 4 Mosque – 5 Catholic Church – 6 Granary – 7 Court – 8 Emperor's Ancestor Temple – 9 Manchu Temple – 10 Trade Corporation – 11 Tribute Court – 12 Eight Banners of the Manchu Army – 13 Culture Temple – 14 Emperor's Archive – 15 Horse Fold – 16 Ox Fold – 17 Elefant-Dressage School – 18 Court of Justice and Education

Räume der Frontmauer blickten nach Norden; neben dem Eingang an der Ostseite befand sich ein privater Schulraum mit einem kleinem Garten davor. In den Mittelräumen gegenüber dem zweiten Tor lebten die männlichen Bediensteten. An der Südwestseite befanden sich die Toilettenräume, die ebenso wie der Schulraum durch eine kleine Mauer abgetrennt waren. Frischwasser floß aus Südosten zu, die *yin*-Kanäle flossen im Südwesten ab.

Das Leben der Familien fand im Innenhof statt. Ihre Privatsphäre war durch das zweite sogenannte Tor der hängenden Blumen geschützt. An den Seiten führten Veranden den Innenhof entlang, den kleine Steingärten und Pflanzen schmückten. Die Gebäude waren einstöckig und mit konkaven Dächern überdacht, die nach Tradition im *yinyang*-Muster gedeckt wurden; in größeren Höfen waren an den Seiten schmale Höfe entlang einer in Richtung Nordsüd verlaufenden blinden Gasse angefügt. Innenhöfe, die an der Zentralachse des Hofes aufgereiht wurden, durften die höchste *yang*-Zahl neun nicht überschreiten.

Um den Kaiserpalast nach *fengshui*-Gesetzen anzulegen, war im Norden des Palastes ein Berg als Schutz aufgeschüttet worden. Die Höfe wurden durch Bäume vor den starken Winden geschützt, die im Winter aus Nordnordwest wehen. Beliebt waren japanische Schnurbäume, wie sie bis heute in einigen Gassen zu sehen sind. Wie der Spruch „Ein Himmelsdach, ein Fischbehälter, ein Granatapfelbaum; ein Herr, ein fetter Hund und ein dickes Dienstmädchen!" erzählt, symbolisierten Granatapfelbäume Glück und Wohlstand für die Familie. Dattelbäume versprachen die baldige Ankunft eines Sohnes. Unter Pinien und Zypressen pflegte man altehrwürdige Personen zu beerdigen; ebenso wurden Pappeln, durch die der Wind tobt, auf Friedhöfen gepflanzt. Maulbeerbäume waren tabu wegen des gleichen Klanglautes *sang* mit dem Wort für beerdigen.

Schlichte graue Backsteinmauern mit kleinen eingelassenen Fenstern trennten die Höfe von der Außenwelt ab. Mit den Mauern kontrastierten die Haupttore, die als Gesicht der Höfe betrachtet wurden, Statussymbol des Eigentümers waren und seinem Rang gemäß prachtvoll gestaltet wurden. Vorrangig war das *jinzhu*-(goldene Säulen)Tor, darauf folgten das *guangliang*-(glänzend), das *manzi*-(Bewohner des Südens) und das *ruyi*-(Glückssymbol)Tor. In kleinere Höfe führte der Weg zu ebener Erde durch schmale, mit geschnitzten Steinblöcken *(dunmen)* dekorierte Tore.

Die Ausstattung der Höfe in Größe, Farben und Dekoration sowie ihre Benennung folgten hierarchischen Regeln, die im folgenden kurz skizziert werden.

they were separated like the study room by a little wall running from north to south. The *yin* channels usually leave the yards at the south-west side, while the fresh water runs into the yards from the south-east.

Family life took place in the inner yard. Their privacy was protected by the second gate, which is the size of a little room and covered with a double roof resting on hanging columns decorated with carved flowers. On both sides of the door, little verandas lead along the yard, which were decorated with little rock gardens, flowers and trees. The buildings were single storeyed, with an independent timber framework, subdivided into three bays and covered with single layered roofs, concave in form and traditionally tiled in the *yinyang* pattern. In larger courtyards, side yards along a blind alley were added, according to the highest *yang* number. A maximum of nine inner yards were lined up along the central axis as in the Confucius Temple, one of the layouts on which common courtyards were modelled.

To protect the emperor's palace from bad energy a hill was thrown up in the north, while the courtyards were protected against the wind, which blows strongly from the north-north-west in the winter, by *fengshui* trees. Scholar trees were the preferred trees. The pomegranate symbolizes the family's good fortune and wealth as in the proverb: "A heavens' roof, wa fish bowl, a pomegranate; an old gentleman, a fat dog, a stout slave girl!" A date tree promises the imminent birth of a son. Old and venerable persons were buried under pines and cypresses. Poplars, through which the wind whistles, were only planted in cemeteries, and since the word for mulberry tree *(sang)* sounds like the word for to die and mourn, those trees were taboo for family courtyards.

Grey brick walls, broken with little windows, divide the courtyards from the outside world. The main gates, as the faces of the courtyards and status symbols of the owner, were decorated in different styles to make them contrast with the front walls. The *jinzhu* (gold-column) gate was the most splendid, followed by the *guangliang* (light and bright), *ruyi* (symbol for happiness) and the *manzi* (southerners) gate. To pass the gates, stairs have to be climbed; in smaller properties the way into the yard leads at ground level through a gate decorated with little ornamented stone blocks *(dunmen)*.

The arrangement of the courtyards in size, color and decoration as well as their names were ordered according to hierarchical rules, and laws were enacted throughout history as described briefly below.

Haupttor im Stil der goldenen Säulen des Militärdepartements der späten Qing-Dynastie in der Lishi Gasse im Oststadtteil Beijings, erworben, umgebaut und als Privatresidenz genutzt von Li Songju, Sohn des Salzkaufmanns Li Shan

Main gate designed in the golden-columns style of the government's military department of the late Qing Dynasty in the Lishi alley in the east quarter of Beijing, bought, reconstructed and used as private residence by Li Songju, son of the salt merchant Li Shan

Hierarchy of the residences

Before the Qin (221–207 BC) and Han Dynasty the residences of the emperor (di) as well as the houses of ordinary people were called gong (today: palace) or gongshi. In the document Yixici of the Zhou Dynasty (1122–255 BC) it says: "In primitive times men lived in the wilderness and dwelled in caves, later sages (shengren) transformed them into palaces."

In a document of the Warring States Period (475 to 221 BC) (Zhanguoce–Qin) it says: "Su Qin approached the way to Luoyang, the parents heard about it, cleaned the palace (gong), swept the path, put up drink and a welcome was provided along 30 li." (Su Qin, son of a lower ranking official, in the capital of Dongzhou, member of the Zonghengjia – Vertical-horizontal school, mediated between the feuding states and fell victim to a political assessination attempt.) This document shows that in past ages houses of ordinary people were called palaces (gong).

People's houses were called palaces, and the centers of the houses were called gongting 宮廷, or 宮庭 palace court. The philosopher Xun Zi, a follower of the doctrine of Confucius, wrote: "It is incumbent upon the nobleman to care with great zeal for the altar of the house and the palace court (shi junzi zhi suo yi cheng zhi yi yu tan zhai, gong ting ye)." He further said "The house is called palace; inside behind the gate and screen there is the court. (Gong wei zhi wu; ting, men ping zhi nei ye.)" Later the term gongting was only used for the residence of the emperor, no ordinary person dared to call his yard gongting, or he would have been sentenced to death. (Note: In the Zhou Dynasty the meaning of the terms ting 廷 and ting 庭 was the same, after the Han Dynasty the first was used for the emperor's courtyard, the second for the official government's courtyard.)

In the early Qin Dynasty not only people's houses were called palaces (gongshi), as well as this their ancestor halls were called temples (miao). In the Shi (jing) Daya Siqi (chapter 59) it says: "Harmony, harmony in the palace, honor and worship in the temple (Yong yong zai gong, su su zai miao)." From the Qin and Han Dynasty onwards, only the emperors' families had the advantage of calling their ancestor halls temples (miao), as for example the Taimiao in Beijing. Ordinary people had to make do with the term ancestor hall. The halls for honoring the sages were also called temple, such as the Confucius Temple, or the Sage of Healing Art Temple.

The kings' residences were called gongshi at that time; the residences of the aristocracy were called dizhai. During the Han Dynasty the following regulation was in force:

Ferner wurde seit jener Zeit der Begriff *gongshi* nur für die Residenzen der Könige verwendet, die Residenzen der Aristokratie wurden *dizhai* (Residenzwohnhaus) genannt. In der Han-Dynastie galt folgende Bestimmung: Die Wohnsitze hoher Beamter, die ihr Gehalt von mehr als 10 000 Haushalten bezogen, wurden Residenz *(di)* genannt; waren es weniger als 10 000 Haushalte, welche die Pfründe dieser Honoratioren abdeckten, so nannte sich ihr Wohnsitz *she* (Haus, Behausung).

Der Begriff Volkshaus *(minju)* erschien zuerst in den Zhou Li (Gesetze der Zhou-Dynastie). Hier wurde er, im Gegensatz zu den kaiserlichen Residenzen, als einheitliche Bezeichnung der Häuser des Volkes verwendet; dazu gehörten auch die Residenzen und Gärten hoher Beamter und Honoratioren. Heute fassen Architekturhistoriker Paläste, Residenzen, Tempel und kaiserliche Grabgewölbe unter dem Begriff Palastbauten zusammen und bezeichnen alle anderen als Volkshäuser.

Im alten China schrieb die Verwaltung nicht nur die Benennung der Häuser vor, auch die Dimensionen und Dekorationen der Gebäude mußten mit der gesellschaftlichen Stellung des Hausherrn im Einklang zu sehen sein. Seit der Han-Dynastie erließen alle Kaiserhöfe Verfügungen dazu. Laut historischer Dokumente der Qin-Dynastie durften Schutzmauern nur bei Kaiserpalästen vor dem Haupttor aufgestellt werden, Fürsten und Prinzen hatten sie innen vor dem Tor aufzustellen. Bei Würdenträgern und Gelehrten schützten Vorhänge den Eingang. Den Kaiserpalast schmückten Walmdächer mit schweren Traufen. Die Säulen waren rot, die Kapitelle und Stuhlsäulen mit bunten Bildern verziert. Nur Prinzen, Fürsten und offizielle Gelehrte durften sich doppelt gedeckte Dächer leisten, die Ziegel waren nach ihrem Status lichtblaugrün oder gelb glasiert oder naturbelassen.

Zu Beginn der Tang-Dynastie wurden folgende Bestimmungen erlassen: Das Maß der Zentralhallen Beamter über dem fünften Rang war auf fünf Buchten *(jian)* festgelegt, doch waren Anlagen im 工 *(gong* – Arbeit)-Muster mit zwei Hauptgebäuden, die durch einen überdachten Korridor verbunden waren, erlaubt. Die Giebel der Walmdächer ihrer Residenzen wurden mit dekorierten Windbrettern geschützt. Für Beamte unter dem fünften Rang maßen die Zentralgebäude drei Buchten und vier Konsolen in der Tiefe. Ihre einfachen Dächer wurden nicht geschmückt. Seit der Song-Dynastie waren überhängende, auf Säulen einer Galerie gestützte Walmdächer den kaiserlichen Palästen vorbehalten.

Domiciles of high officials who drew their income from more than 10000 households were called residence *(di)*, in cases where less than 10000 households had paid their wages, their dwelling houses were called *she* (house, shed, hut).

The term folk house is noted for the first time in the document Zhou Li (Zhou Dynasty). In contrast to the emperor's residences, it was used as a standard term for ordinary people's houses including residences, gardens and dwellings of high officials and men of distinction. Architectural historians now sum up all the palaces, residences, monasteries and royal tombs under the term palaces and call all the other buildings folk houses *(minju)*.

In former times ordinary people were prohibited from using terms like *miao* and *gong,* and the dimension and form of the buildings, as well as their decoration, also had to be laid out and designed according to the official rank of the owner. From the Han Dynasty onwards, regulations were issued by the royal court. According to historical documents of the Qin Dynasty only royal palaces had screen walls in front of the main gate outside the yard. Princes had to put up the screen walls inside the yard. In the houses of scholars and dignitaries curtains were used instead. Hipped roofs with heavy eaves decorated the royal palaces. The columns were painted red, the capitals embellished with colored pictures. Only princes, officials and scholars were allowed double roofs. The columns of their houses had to be painted, according to their rank, in black, blue or yellow.

At the beginning of the Tang and Song Dynasty the following regulations were issued: The central halls of officials, of higher rank than the fifth, measured five bays *(jian)* in

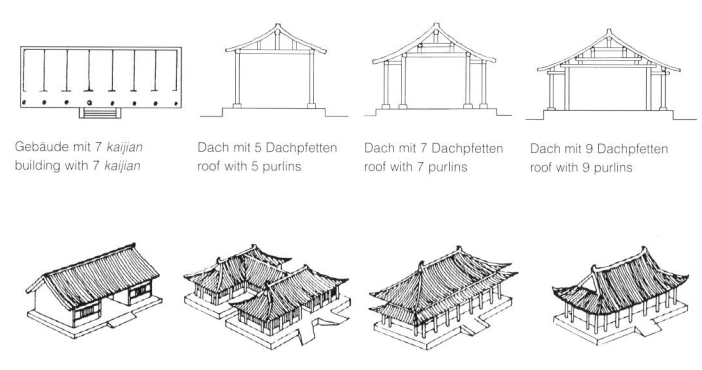

Gebäude mit 7 *kaijian* / building with 7 *kaijian*

Dach mit 5 Dachpfetten / roof with 5 purlins

Dach mit 7 Dachpfetten / roof with 7 purlins

Dach mit 9 Dachpfetten / roof with 9 purlins

Dach einfacher Häuser / roof of simple houses

工字 Hallen (Tang-Zeit) / *gongzi* halls (Tang period)

doppeltes Walmdach / hipped double roof

gegiebeltes Walmdach / gabled and hipped roof

Gedenkbögen zu errichten, war Privileg hoher Beamter. In Shanxi sind jedoch mehr Gedenkbögen aus der Qing-Dynastie zu finden, als Beamte dort in jener Zeit gelebt haben. Das Recht, Gedenkbögen als Statussymbol aufzustellen, war zu jener Zeit käuflich zu erwerben, sie durften jedoch nur im Hof aufgestellt werden, um keine Verwirrung über den Rang der Eigentümer zu stiften.
Oben: Gedenkbogen vor einer Schutzmauer im Innenhof eines Hofes Shanxi, Dingcun, Xiangfenxian

High ranking officials were privileged to build memorial arches, but in Shanxi far more of these arches remain from the Qing Dynasty than high officials lived there in those days. The right to set up memorial arches as status symbols could be bought, but only inside the courtyards, to avoid any confusion concerning the ranks of the owners.
Above: Memorial arch in front of a screen wall inside a courtyard Shanxi, Dingcun, Xiangfenxian

In der Ming-Dynastie (1368–1644 n.Chr.) änderten sich die Bestimmungen wiederum. Jetzt durften die Haupthallen der Prinzen und der beiden obersten Adelsränge sieben Buchten messen, die Beamten über dem fünften Rang residierten in Haupthallen, die fünf Buchten maßen, Beamte der unteren Ränge bewohnten Hauptgebäude mit drei Buchten. Die Dächer der kaiserlichen Paläste wurden mit gelb glasierten Ziegeln gedeckt, während die Residenzen der Prinzen mit grün glasierten, Dächer der Beamten und der übrigen Bevölkerung mit einfachen Ziegeln gedeckt werden mußten.

Zuwiderhandlungen wurden bestraft. Dem Tanglü, (Gesetzbuch der Tang-Dynastie) zufolge wurden hundert Stockschläge erteilt, wenn den Anordnungen nicht Folge geleistet wurde, und der Betreffende wurde gezwungen, sein Haus abzureißen. Kam es wegen einer Imitation des kaiserlichen Palastes zur Anklage, so wurde die Todesstrafe verhängt.

In Zeiten chaotischer Hofpolitik brandmarkte die Gesellschaft bei Zuwiderhandlungen den Betreffenden und hielt sich an die bestehende Gesetzgebung. Satirische Dokumente zu diesem Thema lassen sich seit der Frühlings- und Herbst-Periode finden. Weithin bekannt ist der Fall He Shen der Qing-Dynastie. Seine Beamtenposition war aus dem Erbrecht hervorgegangen. Zu Beginn seiner Regierungszeit hatte der Herrscher Qian Long (1763–1796 n.Chr.) ihn mit mehreren Ministerposten betraut, und in den letzten Jahren seiner Regierungszeit, als er selbst vorwiegend dem luxuriösen Dasein frönte, überließ er He Shen nahezu uneingeschränkte Entscheidungsbefugnis. Bei der Finanzierung der Bekämpfung der Bailianchao (1796 n.Chr.) füllte He Shen seine eigenen Taschen; die Rebellion kam nicht zur Ruhe, und die Staatskassen waren leer. Unmittelbar nach dem Tode des Qian Long proklamierte sein Nachfolger Jia Qing (1796–1821 n.Chr.) zwanzig Anklagepunkte gegen He Shen. Darunter wurde aufgeführt, daß He Shen in seiner Residenz Phöbenholz zur Dekoration verwendet und in seinem Park eine Imitation des kaiserlichen Yuanmingyuan angelegt hatte. He Shen wurde zum Tode verurteilt und gezwungen, Selbstmord zu begehen. Sein Besitz wurde beschlagnahmt. Der Kommentar im Volksmund lautete: „He Shen fiel, Jian Qing ißt sich satt *(He Shen diedao, Jia Qing chibao)*". Zu den eindrucksvollen Anlagen des He Shen, die von Jia Qing konfisziert wurden, gehörte die Residenz Gong Fu in Beijing, Baujahr 1777 n. Chr. (s. S. 133). Später übernahm der Prinz Guang Xu (1875–1908 n.Chr.) die Residenz in seinen Besitz.

width; but constructions designed in 工 (*gong* – work)-form, with two such cross-buildings connected by a narrow gallery were common. Their hipped roofs *(xieshan)* were protected by wind boards, decorated with carvings. Central halls of officials ranked below the fifth rank measured three bays *(jian)* in width and four consoles in depth. The ordinary roofs *(xuanshan)* were not decorated. From the beginning of the Song Dynasty onwards double and hipped roofs, supported by the columns of a gallery, were only allowed in the emperors' palaces and temples.

In the Ming Dynasty different regulations were again issued. The central halls of princes and of the two highest ranking officials measured seven bays (*jian*) in width, officials of the fifth rank and higher measured five bays and of lower ranking officials three bays in width. The roofs of the royal palaces were tiled with yellow glazed tiles, the residences of princes with light blue-green glazed and the roofs of officials and ordinary people with unglazed tiles.

Any contravention was penalized. According to the Tang Lü (Law of the Tang), hundred strokes with a cane were administered in case of contravention, and the person concerned had to pull his house down. If someone was charged with imitation of a royal palace, he was sentenced to death.

Even in times of utterly chaotic court politics there was no way to circumvent these regulations, since the person concerned was denounced by society. Satirical documents kept from the Spring and Autumn Dynasty record such cases.

One of the most popular cases is the He Shen affair. He Shen was an official by law of inheritance; he held several ministerial posts, and he was favored by the emperor Qian Long (1736–786 AD), who, in his last years, allowed him unlimited decision-making powers. While financing the resistance to the Bailianchao rebellion, He Shen filled his own pockets, the rebellion dragged on and the state coffers were emptied. After the death of Qian Long his son and successor Jia Qing (1796–1821 AD) proclaimed twenty charges against He Shen. Among these charges the imitation of the royal park called Yuanmingyuan and the use of phoebe wood for furnishing were itemized. He Shen was sentenced and forced to commit suicide, and his property was confiscated. "He Shen fell, Jia Qing ate his fill (*He Shen diedao, Jia Qing chibao*)". was the common commentary. One of the many impressive complexes, which were confiscated by Jia Qing, is the beautiful prince's court called Gong Fu in Beijing, built 1777 (cf. p. 133). Later this residence became the property of the Emperor Guang Xu (1875–1908 AD).

Blick durch das Tor der hängenden Blumen *(chuihuamen)* in den Hof der Residenz Gong Fu in Beijing
View through the hanging flower gate *(chuihuamen)* into the central yard of the Residence Gong Fu in Beijing

Traditionelle Höfe in Shanxi 山西

歡 歡 喜 喜 份 河 灣
哭 哭 啼 啼 呂 梁 山
湊 湊 乎 乎 晉 東 南
死 也 不 去 雁 門 關

An der Biegung des Fen-Flusses Freude und Glück
im Luliang-Gebirge Weinen und Wehklagen
nach Süd-Ostjin gelegentlich einmal
Sterben sicher – nach Yanmenguan – nie

An der Biegung des Flusses Fenhe, südlich von Taiyuan, im Zentrum Shanxis, liegt die Bezirksstadt Qi. Sie ist repräsentativ für den Reichtum der Provinz und wurde in früheren Dynastien Zhaoyu (heller Überfluß) oder Qize (gewaltig, Prunk) genannt. In der Frühlings- und Herbstperiode (770 bis 476 v. Chr.) gehörte der Bezirk Qi zu dem Königreich Jin. Im Jahre 556 v. Chr. gab Ping Gong, der Herrscher Jins, dem Beamten Ji Xi den Bezirk Zhaoyu zu Lehen. Dieser nannte die Stadt Qi, gab sich denselben Namen und wurde in der Geschichte unter dem Namen Qi Huangyang (Prunk, das Gelbe Schaf) bekannt.

Qixian (*xian* – Bezirk) hat Handelstradition. Seit der Ming-Dynastie gewann der Außenhandel zunehmend an Bedeutung, und in der Qing-Dynastie unter der Regentschaft des Dao Guang (1821–1851 n. Chr.) und Xian Feng (1851–1862 n. Chr.) war eine Zeit der Hochkonjunktur erreicht. In der Stadt sowie in den benachbarten Marktflecken des Bezirks reihten sich Läden und Privatbanken aneinander. Mehr als die Hälfte der Familien betrieb Außenhandel und dies mit so großem Erfolg, daß „Im ganzen Land fließt Gold aus dem Ohr des (Opfer) Büffels" als gängiges Sprichwort zutreffend den Reichtum des Bezirkes beschreiben konnte.

Mehr als vierzig Großhöfe aus jener Zeit sind in Qixian erhalten. Der bekannteste ist der Großhof Qiao. Er er-streckt sich über eine Fläche von 8724,8 qm. Der bebaute Boden umfaßt auf 3870 qm sechs Höfe mit 20 kleinen Höfen und 313 Zimmern; die Außenmauern sind drei bis vier Stockwerke hoch. Die Anlage wurde im Jahre 1756 gegründet, nachdem Qiao Quanmei und seine Brüder den Familienbesitz aufgeteilt hatten. Der erste Hof liegt im Nord-Ost-Winkel der Anlage. Neben dem Tor steht die Ahnenhalle, genannt Fünf-Wege-Tempel (Wudaoci). Wie eine Legende erzählt, plante Qiao Quanmei eine Ahnenhalle ohne jeden Baum zu errichten. Daraufhin erschien ihm im Traum ein Geist im goldenen Panzerkleid und sagte, daß Bäume das Leben und Tempel den Reichtum beeinflussen, und beide

Traditional courtyards in Shanxi

*Huan, huan, xi xi fen he wan
ku ku ti ti lü liang shan
cou cou hu hu jin dong nan
si ye bu qu yan men guan*

Joy and happiness at the Fen River bend
Sobbing and weeping in the Luliang-mountains
Once in a while to south-east Jin
Death is certain, do not to go to Yanmenguan

The county of Qi lies south of Taiyuan in the center of Shanxi at the bend of the Fen River. The town was representative of the wealth of the province and used to be called Zhaoyu (abundance) or Qize (brilliance) in earlier periods. In the Spring and Autumn Period (770 – 476 BC) the county belonged to the Kingdom of Jin. In the year 556 BC Ping Gong, the Emperor of Jin, invested the official Ji Xi (Ji family name of Huang Di) with the county. Ji Xi renamed the county Qi, called himself after the city, and became famous in history by the name Qi Huangyang (Abundance, The Yellow Sheep).

Qixian (*xian* – district) has a trading tradition. In the Ming Dynasty foreign trade began to gain in importance, and in the Qing Dynasty, in the reign of Dao Guang (1821–1851 AD) and his successor Xian Feng (1851–1862 AD), the economy flourished and boomed to such an extent that the common proverb "Gold is flowing out of the buffalo's ear all over the country" described the evolution of the county very accurately. Private banks and shops sprang up in the streets in the city of Qi as well as in the neighbouring small market towns, and more than half of the families were in business.

More than forty grand courtyards of that time still remain. The best known courtyard is the Qiao great court. It covers an area of 8724.8 sq m, the built-up land includes six courtyards with 20 small inner courtyards and 313 rooms, covering an area of 3370 sq m; the outer walls are three to four storeys high. The courtyard was established in 1756 AD, after Qiao Quanmei and his brothers had shared out the family property between them. The first courtyard is located in the north-east corner of the great court. Beside the main gate is the ancestor hall, named Five-Ways-Temple (Wudaoci). As legend tells, Qiao Quanmei originally planned to build an ancestor hall without any tree at all. Then a spirit, dressed in a coat of golden mail, appeared to him in a dream and told him that trees influence life and

Schutzmauer des hundertfachen langen Lebens vor der Mittelgasse der Qiao-Höfe
Hundredfold long life screen wall in front of the middle alley of the Qiao courtyards

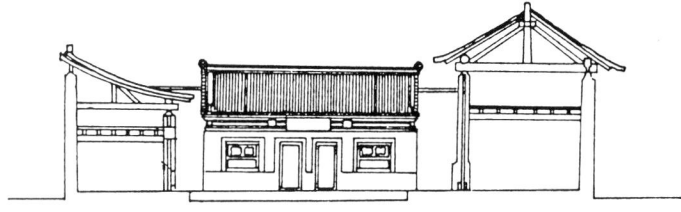
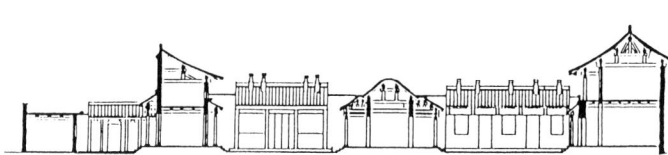

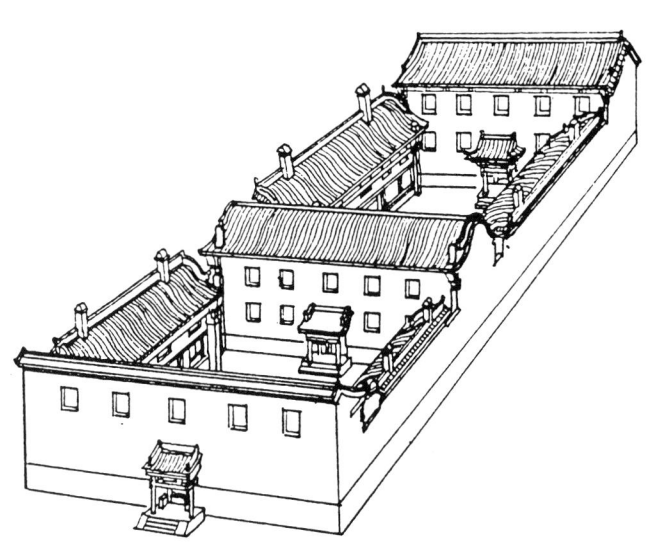
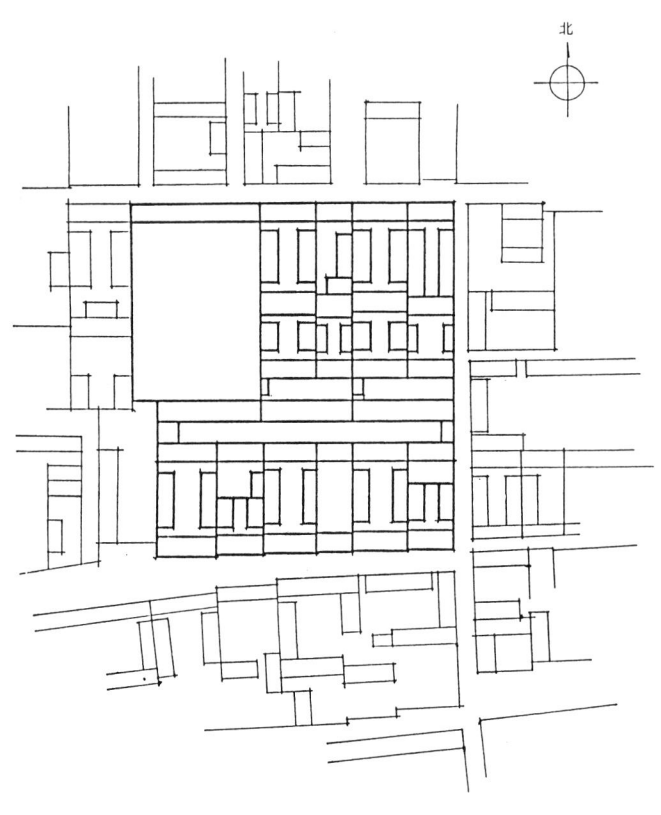

Skizze eines Hofes im Stil „innen fünf, außen drei im Zentrum von einem Gebäude durchtrennter Hof" 裏 五外三 穿心 樓 院

Sketch of a courtyard in the style "inside five, outside three subdivided in the center by a building courtyard *(li wu wai san chuanxin louyuan)*"

Skizze des 喬家 大院 Großhofes Qiao
Sketch of the Qiao great court

von gleicher Bedeutung seien. Fünf Schritte möge er in Richtung Osten gehen, wo ein Baum erblühe. Würde ein Tempel errichtet, und stürbe dabei ein Baum, so blieben die Menschen ohne Reichtum. Qiao Quanmei fürchtete die Strafe des Geistes, doch als er an den im Traum gezeigten Ort ging, war der Baum, der vor kurzem kaum mehr geatmet hatte, wieder in voller Pracht erblüht. Heute stehen zwei als Geistbäume bezeichnete Schurbäume vor der Halle (s. S. 149). Aus jener Zeit datiert auch die Schutzmauer im ersten Hof, deren Dekoration diese Legende widerspiegelt (s. S. 150). In der frühen Qing-Zeit baute Qiao Zhiyong (1818 – 1907) für seine sechs Frauen drei Höfe; in der Mitte der Qing- und während der Minguo-Zeit wurde die Anlage nochmals von seinen Söhnen erweitert. Die Hofherren residierten im Zentralgebäude (s. S. 144) und wurden deshalb Zai Zhongtang (das Oberhaupt des Clans in der Zentralhalle) genannt. Mit Ausnahme des sechsten Hofes, der während der japanischen Invasion (1937/38) zerstört wurde, sind die Gebäude gut erhalten. Nachdem bei Unruhen in den Jahren 1966 und 1967 Ausstattungen beschädigt wurden, stellte die Regierung den Hof unter ihren Schutz und gestaltete ihn als Museum. Im Jahre 1990 begannen die Dreharbeiten des preisgekrönten, in der Minguo-Zeit spielenden Filmes „Die rote Laterne" mit dem Originaltitel „Hauptfrau und Nebenfrauen in Gruppe (Qi qie chengyun)".

Gemäß einem alten Brauch wurde vor den Toren, die ungeordnete Luftströmungen auslösenden Bewegungskräften ausgesetzt waren, eine Steinstele mit dem sogenannten Taishan Steinwächter (Taishan: Heiliger Berg in Shandong) aufgestellt. So stehen an der Mündung zweier Straßen vor der Frontmauer des Qiao-Hofes zwei Steinstelen, von denen die eine in die Schutzmauer vor dem Haupttor eingelassen ist (s. S. 138). Der Hof wird von einer Gasse umsäumt, die so schmal ist, daß der Betrachter das imposante Tor nicht mit einem Blick erfassen kann und unwillkürlich zum Torbogen aufsieht. Über dem Tor fällt der Blick auf eine Holztafel mit der Aufschrift: „Sei das Glück wie ein Ring edler Jade (*Fu Zhong Langhuan*)". Die Tafel war vom Gouverneur der Provinz Shanxi als Dankgruß dafür übersandt worden, daß die Prinzessin Cixi auf ihrer Flucht von Beijing nach Xian in Shaanxi im Jahre 1900 hier ein Geschenk von 100000 Silbermünzen erhalten hatte. Hinter dem Haupttor steht eine Schutzmauer und versperrt den Blick in den Mittelweg des Hofes. Hundert mit Goldfolie bedeckte Siegelschnitzereien des Schriftzeichens *shou* 壽 (langes Leben) verzieren die Schutzmauer. Sie stellen Vögel und Pflanzen dar, und es wird erzählt, ein

temples wealth and both are equally important. He was to take five paces towards the east where a tree would flourish. If a temple were built, while a tree was going to die, then people would have no wealth throughout their lives. Thereafter Qiao Quanmei, in fear of the spirit's punishment, went to the place that had been described in the dream. There a tree, which a little while ago was on the brink of death, had now revived in its full splendour. Today two scholar trees, called spirit trees, stand in front of the Five-Ways-Temple (cf. p. 149). A screen wall in the first courtyard with decorations, reflecting this legend, also date from this time (cf. p. 150). Qiao Zhiyong (1818 – 1907 AD), who lived there with his six wives, enlarged the court by three courtyards. In the later Qing and during the Minguo Period his sons again extended the complex. The owners resided in the central building (cf. p. 144) and therefore were called Zai Zhongtang (the-main-one-of-the-clan-in-the-central-hall). With the exception of the sixth court, which was destroyed during the Japanese invasion (1937/38), the buildings have survived in good condition. Some interiors were damaged in the disturbances of 1966 and 1967. After this the estate was placed under government protection and used as a museum. Shooting started on the award-winning film "The Red Lantern", with the original title called "Spouse and consorts in group (Qi qie chengyun)", set in the Minguo Period.

Since earlier times it has been a custom to position stone steles with the Tai Mountain Stone Guard (Tai Mountain: holy mountain in Shandong) in places of energetic turbulence. Two Tai Mountain stone guards are set up in front of the main gate, where two alleys fork. One of them is set in a screen wall facing the main entrance (cf. p. 138). Brick walls, colossal like medieval city walls, surround the grand courtyard. The alley running along the walls is so narrow that the viewer, standing in front of the high main gate, cannot take it all in at once, but looks up to the arch of the gate spontaneously. Above the arch the eye lights on a wooden board, with the compliment "Let the fortune be like a ring of finest jade (*Fu Zhong Langhuan*)" inscribed. The Governor of Shanxi sent this board as a note of thanks on behalf of the Dowager Cixi, who, on her flight from the Boxer Rebellion in Beijing to Xian in Shaanxi in the year 1900 had received a gift of 100000 silver coins. Behind the main gate, a screen wall protects the middle alley of the courtyard. The wall is decorated with the character *shou* 壽 (long life), carved in hundred different patterns, covered with gold leaf. It is told that a son-in-law of Qiao Zhiyong carved the wall as a paean of praise to the spring.

Schwiegersohn des Qiao Zhiyong habe sie als Hymne an den Frühling geschnitzt. Das Spruchpaar: *sun ren yu yi fu tianli, xu daode er neng wenzhang* an den Seiten der Schutzmauer preist die Beherrschung der menschlichen Wünsche im Einklang mit den himmlischen Gesetzen zugunsten der Ethik und des literarischen Schaffens.

Zu beiden Seiten des von Ost nach West verlaufenden Mittelweges führen je drei Tore in die Höfe, die entsprechend den *fengshui*-Regeln versetzt angeordnet sind. Die Höfe an der Nordseite sind in dem Stil „innen fünf, außen drei, im Zentrum von einem Gebäude durchtrennter Hof (*li wu wai san, chuan xin louyuan*)" angelegt. Das Licht fällt nur von den Innenhöfen in die Räume; die Außenmauern haben keine Fenster. Die Seitenflügel sind einstöckig, während die Hauptgebäude zwei Stockwerke haben. Die Höfe an der Südseite sind im Stil genannt *sihedouyuan* (vier verbunden zu einem kleinen Hof) angelegt. Die Seitenflügel werden über Treppen vom Dachgeschoß der beiden Quergebäude erreicht. An der Westseite wohnten die Familienmitglieder, an der Ostseite waren die Räume für die Bediensteten und Gästehallen eingerichtet.

Die Gebäude der Vorhöfe haben mit Lehm, Reisschleim und Zucker befestigte Flachdächer. Die Dächer der Haupthöfe sind einfach mit Ziegeln gedeckt und verlaufen vom Dachfirst schräg geneigt zum Innenhof. Ihr Profil, das einer umgekehrten Schiffsseite gleicht, gilt als lokale Besonderheit (s. S. 145). Auf den Dächern führt ein mit Brüstungen geschützter Wachweg um die Höfe, der nur über einen Aufgang neben dem Haupttor zu erreichen ist. Von den Wachtürmen, die gleichzeitig den Wächtern als Unterkunft dienten, konnten die Innenhöfe und die Umgebung beobachtet werden. Im Hauptgebäude war eine Fußbodenheizung eingebaut, während in den Wohnhöfen mit Backsteinen gelegte Ofenbetten *(kang)* für eine ausgeglichene Temperatur sorgten. Die Schornsteine sind als Häuschen modelliert und schmücken die Dachfirste der Seitenflügel (s. S. 147).

Steinschnitzereien mit traditionellen Motiven dekorieren Dachfirste, Eingangstore, Schutzmauern und Brüstungen der Höfe (s. S. 150/151). Wandtafeln, Bilder und Holzschnitzereien schmücken die Räume. Sehr reizvoll wirkt eine Tafel über der Tür eines Empfangsraumes, die als ein mit Tautropfen bedecktes Lotusblatt modelliert ist (s. S. 148).

Viele der mit großer Kunstfertigkeit gebauten Höfe in Qixian sind leider dem Verfall überlassen, doch widerspiegeln sie noch heute den kulturellen Reichtum jener Zeit. Als Beispiel werden hier einige Bilder des Hofes der Beamtenfamilie Liu gezeigt (s. S. 152–156).

All the *shou* characters are designed as flowers and birds. The couplet: *sun ren yu yi fu tianli, xu daode er neng wenzhang* on both sides of the screen wall, praises resistance to human inclination in harmony with divine justice and the cultivation of ethics and talent for literary creativity.

On each side of the middle alley, which runs from east to west, three entrances lead to the six private courtyards, symmetrically staggered according to *fengshui* rules. The courtyards on the north side are designed in the style "inside five outside three in the center subdivided by a building courtyard (*li wu wai san chuan xin louyuan*)". The rooms are lit only from the inner courtyards, there are no windows in the outer walls. The main buildings are two storeys high, the wings only one. The courtyards on the south side of the middle alley are designed in the style *sihedouyuan* (four connected to a small courtyard). The wings are linked via steps from the upper storeys of their two transverse buildings. The family members lived on the west side, while the rooms for the servants and the guest halls were located on the east side.

The buildings in the front yards have flat roofs, paved with clay, rice slime and sugar. The roofs in the main yards are single, and shaped like a ship's bow turned inside out (cf. p. 145). On the roofs a guard path runs around the inner yards, which is accessible by one set of steps only, beside the main entrance. It is protected by parapets, decorated with stone carvings (cf. p. 148). The guards lived in little sentry boxes, which enabled them to look out and provide security. In the main building a floor heating was installed. In the residential wings brick laid oven beds *(kang)* balanced the temperature in the living rooms. Little chimneys let out the smoke (cf. p. 147). They decorate the ridges of the wings very attractively modelled with little houses on top, each individual in design.

Beautiful stone carvings of common motifs decorate the ridges, the entrances, and the screen walls of the courtyards (cf. pp. 150/151). Pictures, scrolls, and wooden carvings decorate the rooms. A very special feature is a wooden board above the entrance of a guest room, carved as a lotus leaf covered with dew drops (cf. p. 148).

Many other courtyards in Qixian were built with great artistic skill. Although most of them have fallen into disrepair, they still reflect the wealth of those days. A further grand courtyard, which belonged to the official Liu, is shown here (cf. pp. 152–156).

Tai Shan-Steinwächter auf der Schutzmauer vor dem Haupttor des Qiao-Großhofes
Tai Shan stone guard set in the screen wall in front of the Qiao great court

Die Schutzmauer des hundertfachen langen Lebens hinter dem Haupttor des Qiao-Großhofes
The hundredfold long life screen wall behind the main gate of the Qiao great court

Mittelallee der Qiao-Höfe mit versetzt angeordneten Eingangstoren
Middle alley of the Qiao courtyards with symmetrically staggered gates

Oben: Innenhof mit Blick auf das Hauptgebäude im ersten der sechs Höfe des Qiao-Großhofes
Links oben: Freistehende Durchgangstür des ersten Hofes. Auf beiden Seiten der Charakter *shou* als Ornament eingeschnitzt
Links unten: Blick von außen auf die obige Durchgangstür

Above: Inner yard with view of the main-hall entrance in the first courtyard of the Qiao great court
Left above: Standalone partition door with the character *shou* below the window of the wings carved as an ornament
Left below: View from outside the entrance hall

Hauptgebäude des Qiao-Großhofes
Main building of the Qiao great court

Blick über die Dächer des zweiten Hofes des Qiao-Großhofes
View from the roofs of the second yard of the Qiao great court

Blick über die Dächer des Qiao-Hofes mit durch Brüstungen geschützten Wachgängen. Links ein kleiner Wachpavillon
Guard path on the roofs of the Qiao great court framed with parapets. To the left a little sentry box

Schornstein als Häuschen modelliert, am Giebel verziert mit dem Zeichen *shou*
Chimney, constructed as a little building, decorated with a *shou* character at the gable end

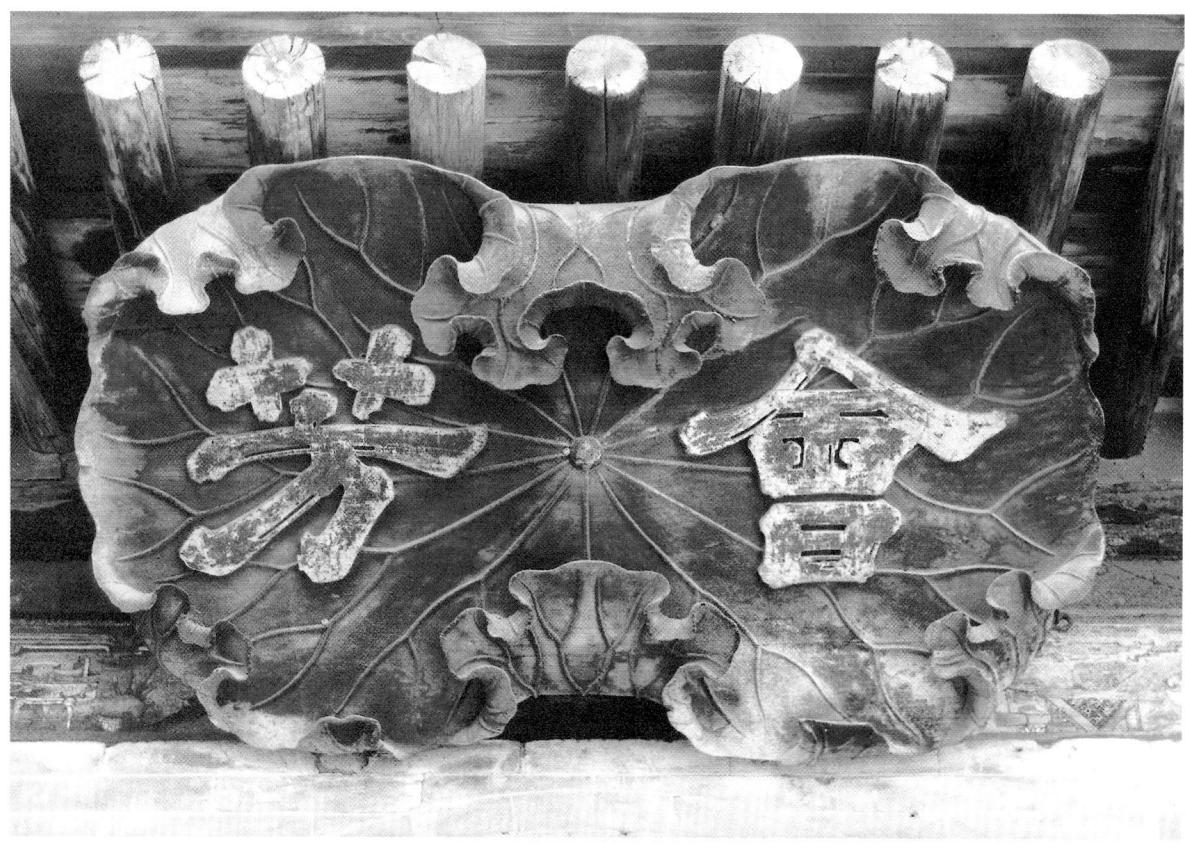

Lotusblatt über der Tür eines Empfangszimmers mit der Aufschrift *huifang* (Zusammenkunft von Düften)
Wooden lotus leaf above the entrance of a guest room with the carving *huifang* (fragrance meetings)

Blick auf die Fünf-Wege-Halle (Wudaoci) zwischen den Haupteingängen in den ersten und sechsten Hof
View from the Five-Ways-Hall (Wudaoci) between the main gates of the first and sixth courtyard

Oben: Schutzmauer des ersten Hofes mit der Aufschrift *fudeci* (Wohlstand-und-Ethik-Tempel) auf einer Holztafel unter dem Dachvorsprung. Darunter an der Kopfleiste Schnitzereien von vier Löwen und einem *ruyi*-Ornament, Glück in den vier Jahreszeiten symbolisierend *(si shi ruyi)*. Der eingelassene Schrein für den Erdherrscher eingefaßt mit Schnitzereien eines Phönixbaumes und Wohlstand symbolisierendem Rotwild, Paar für Paar angeordnet, nach dem Motiv „Sechs unzertrennlich vereint *(liu he tongshun)*", darüber ein Kraut der Unsterblichkeit kauender Hirsch mit einem Kitz

Rechts: Einer von zwei einander gegenüberliegenden Durchgängen im dritten Hof, gerahmt mit Steinschnitzereien von Ziergeräten, überschrieben mit dem Spruchpaar *guangjing, tongda,* den Zutritt in friedvolle Gemächer an der Ost- und Westseite des Hofes bezeichnend

Above: Screen wall in the first courtyard with a wooden board below the eaves showing the inscription fortune ethic temple *(fudeci)*. Below on the head-piece stone carvings of four lions and a *ruyi* ornament symbolizing luck in all the four seasons *(si shi ruyi)*. Surrounding the shrine of the earth ruler a stone carved Phoenix tree and deer arranged in couples according to the saying "Six together inseparable *(liu he tongshun)*", above a stag chewing a plant of immortality and a fawn

Right: One of two facing doors in the third courtyard framed with stone carvings of ornamental tools and the couplet *jingguan, tongda* carved above, signifying entry into peaceful rooms on the east and west side of the courtyard

Bilder des Großhofes des Beamten Liu und seiner Familie in Shanxi, Tuwo, Qinshui
Oben: Trommelsteine *(baogushi)* und Löwen zu den Seiten zweier Haupttore
Links: Ein Haupttor mit Holzaufbau und Ochsenkopfkapitellen

Pictures of the grand courtyard of the official Liu and his family in Shanxi, Tuwo, Qinshui
Above: Drum stones *(baogushi)* and lions on the side of two main gates
Left: Main gate of a courtyard

Säulensockel mit steingeschnitzten Löwen und Peonien
Stone pedestal with chiseled lion cubs and peonies

Galerie in einem Innenhof der Familie Liu
Gallery in a yard decorated with wooden carvings of the Liu family

Oben: Torflügel dekoriert mit Eisenbeschlägen, unter den Türringen Fledermäuse als Glückssymbol. Shanxi, Dingcun, Xiangfen
Unten: Eingangstor im einem Hof der Familie Liu. Eisenbeschläge mit Swastika, Torringe als Seidenraupen geformt, im Rahmen auf dem linken Flügel einer der beiden Torhüter. Shanxi, Tuwo, Qinshui
Rechts: Haupttor mit der Tafelinschrift: Angenehmes Wohnen. Eisenbeschläge: Meanderring als Einfassung der Türschlösser, auf den Flügeln je zwei *shou*-Symbole, Türringe dekoriert mit Löwenköpfen. An den Seiten ein Löwenpaar auf Steinsockeln. Shanxi, Dingcun, Xiangfen
S. 158/159: Dachlandschaft in Shanxi, Hebianzhen, Dingxiang

Above: Main door decorated with iron mounting below the door handles bats symbolizing good fortune. Shanxi, Dingcun, Xiangfen
Below: Gate in a courtyard of the Liu family. Metal-work decorated with swastikas, the door handle shaped like silk worms, on the left wing one of the two door guards in a frame. Shanxi, Tuwo, Qinshui
Right: Main door with iron mounting of meander rings circling the lock, lion heads on the door handles and two *shou* characters on each wing. Compliment above the door: comfortable living. Stone pedestals with a pair of lions framing the door. Shanxi, Dingcun, Xiangfen
pp. 158/159: View of roof scenery. Shanxi, Hebianzhen, Dingxiang

Traditional Chinese architecture and its special features in Anhui

Anhui is called a treasure chamber of traditional architecture and a miniature of Eastern culture. The beauty of the buildings is further emphasized by the beautiful landscape of the Yellow and White Mountains in the border area of the provinces Zhejiang and Jiangxi. "A fragrant veil, interwoven with peach blossoms, covers the valleys for a hundred miles," described the atmosphere of this scenery. In this region Xiuning, Xixian, Qimen, Wuyuan, Jixi and Yixian, the counties of the Huizhou district, are spread. The name which means Emblem District, was given to the district in 1121 AD under Xuan He of the Northern Song Dynasty.

The architecture in Huizhou is an offspring of the traditional architecture in Central China, which stands out due to special features. The courtyards, called water from four sides towards the hall *(si shui gui tang)*, are laid out in the *siheyuan* style in central China, while the construction of the buildings is local in origin. The history and development of this combination is described below.

In primeval times, when humans lived in caves, the center was kept open for the light and to let the rain water flow away. In the work 'Explanation of names and palaces/residences *(Shiming – Shi gongshi)*' it says that this center was called flow *(liu)*. Later people built their houses with the center kept open. The center with the *tianjing* and the hall was holy and became tradition. According to the work 'Culture of Asia' by Zhang Mingyuan, the construction of the *tianjing* originated from the prehistoric tribes of China, who originally built caves with the open center called water flowing from heaven *(tianliu)*. In the course of time the courtyards, at first constructed below called heaven-hall-yard *(tiantingyuan)*, later above the surface called four-connected-in-one-yard *(siheyuan)*, were developed. Courtyards designed as *siheyuan* can already be traced in the Shang Dynasty (16 – 11th C.), and since the end of the Shang Dynasty they spread over wide areas with different climatic conditions. The work 'Chinese Architecture in the early epochs' makes it clear, that the *siheyuan* look back on a history of some thousand years.

Cave-frescos in Dunhuang offer beautiful impressions of the Tang Dynasty's courtyards. The royal tombs in Xian, imitating the earthly residences, demonstrate that such constructions were common in this period. In the tombs of Yi De's wife and children (860 AD) *tianjing* seven in number, in the tomb of the princess Yong Feng (765 AD) six, and below eight constructions with four *tianjing* are laid out.

In Huizhou courtyards in this style, rooted in Central China, are mentioned for the first time in clan documents of

Straße mit Kanalisation entlang des Ortes Yuliangba, Yixian, Huizhou.
Baubeginn Ende der Sui-Dynastie, Fertigstellung in der Song-Dynastie

Street above a water channel leading along the village Yuliangba. Yixian, Huizhou.
Construction began in the Sui Dynasty and was completed in the Song Dynasty

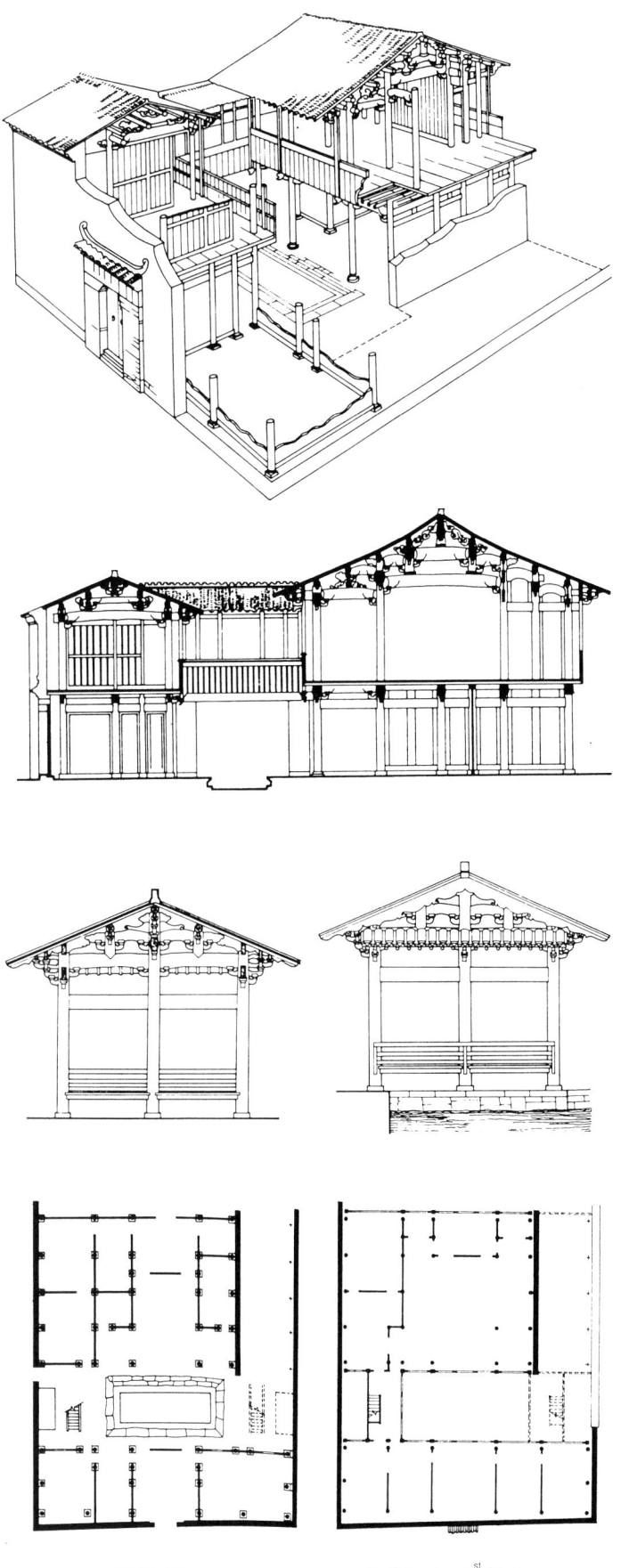

Parterre · 1. Etage – 1st floor

In Huizhou sind seit der Song-Dynastie (960 – 1279 n.Chr.) Anlagen mit *tianjing* als Zentrum in Sippendokumenten zu lesen. Heute sind nur Höfe aus der Ming- und Qing-Dynastie erhalten. Als Besonderheit fällt auf, daß ihre *tianjing* tiefer in die Erdoberfläche eingegraben wurden als in Zentralchina, um Überschwemmungen zu vermeiden und das Wasser über *yin*-Kanäle abzuleiten.

Bis Ende der Ming-Dynastie wurden die Wohnräume in Huizhou im oberen Stockwerk eingerichtet, das auf Palisaden gestützt wurde. Die unteren Stockwerke blieben meist unbewohnt. Anders als in Zentralchina gab es in den Höfen in Huizhou keine einstöckigen Gebäude. Im Gegensatz zu der Entstehung der *tianjing* hat diese Bauweise lokalen Ursprung. Viele Historiker und Architekten haben sich mit der Entwicklung und Wandlung des Brauches, die Hallen im oberen Stockwerk anzulegen, beschäftigt. Dabei kam es hin und wieder zu recht skurrilen Spekulationen. So wurde vermutet, daß dieser Brauch in der Yuan-Dynastie (1271 bis 1368 n.Chr.) entstanden sei, als in jedem Haus ein Soldat stationiert wurde. Die Tartaren *(dazi)*, so pflegte der Volksmund die Soldaten zu nennen, seien im unteren Stockwerk untergebracht worden, und daraufhin hätten die Hausherren in ihren Häusern die oberen Stockwerke höher angelegt und komfortabler ausgestattet als die unteren. Aus Dokumenten jener Zeit geht jedoch hervor, daß „in zehn Familien ein Soldat stationiert war", und es ist kaum anzunehmen, daß die Minderheit der Betroffenen die traditionellen Bräuche der Allgemeinheit verändert hat. Selbst wenn zu jener Zeit das untere Stockwerk niedrig gebaut worden wäre, weil Soldaten darin lebten, so wäre in den folgenden dreihundert Jahren der Ming-Dynastie dieser Brauch sicher nicht beibehalten worden.

Der Brauch, die Hallen in den oberen Stockwerken anzulegen, hat eine lokale Entstehungsgeschichte. In frühester Zeit wurden im Süden Anhuis Pfahlbauten konstruiert. In den 7000 Jahre alten Ruinenstätten an der Furt des Mu-Flusses sind bei Ausgrabungen Strukturen von Pfahlbauten entdeckt worden. Nach der Ost-Jin-Dynastie (317 – 414 n.Chr.) verlegten die dortigen Sippen ihre Wohnorte nach Shanyue. Daraufhin wurden die Häuser der dort lebenden Völker auf Palisaden eingerichtet. Im Laufe der Zeit veränderten sich die Umweltbedingungen, und infolgedessen wurden die Wohnräume in die unteren Stockwerke verlegt.

Links: Skizze der Wu-Residenz. Huizhou, Xidi Nancun. Ming-Dynastie
Rechts: Skizze der Cheng-Residenz. Huizhou, Chengcunxiang. Qing-Dynastie

the Song Dynasty (960–1279 AD). Only courtyards of the Ming and Qing Dynasties have been maintained until today. Their *tianjing* were more deeply excavated than those in Central China to avoid any flooding. The rain water, collected in the well, is drawn off along subsurface channels.

In contrast with the *tianjing*, the halls and living rooms arranged in the upper floor are of local origin. No houses in Huizhou were ever constructed single-storeyed or flat-roofed, as is common in Beijing, or to an extent in other districts of Central China. In the Ming Dynasty the halls were set up in the larger and higher upper floors, which were supported by palisades. The lower floors were usually kept empty. Many historians and architects were anxious to know why in the Ming Dynasty the central hall was set up in the upper floor and later changed to the lower floor. Curiously enough some of them assumed that the custom of residing in the hall on the upper floor originated in the Yuan Dynasty when soldiers, who popularly were called *dazi* (Tartar), were stationed in Huizhou, and each family had to accommodate one of them. The owners, so they thought, had settled the problem by putting the *dazi* in the lower floor, and had comfortably arranged a residence for themselves on the upper one. According to documents only "one soldier was stationed to watch ten households" during this time, and it is rather unlikely that the minority of affected families had changed a custom that had been a tradition through the ages. Even if in those days the houses had been constructed with a lower floor to accommodate Tartars, it is improbable that this custom would have prevailed in the following 300 years of the Ming Dynasty. That is why those statements turn out to be purely speculative. Though the custom of setting up the hall on the upper floor appears to be a characteristic of the Ming Dynasty, it is safe to say that this custom has a local origin. Stilt houses were built in the south of Anhui in primeval times. Along the River Mu remains of stilt houses were discovered in archeological excavations, dating back to primitive times 7000 years ago. After the East Jin Dynasty (317–414 AD) the local people migrated to the Shanyue Mountains, transferred their style of architecture and the houses there were supported on palisades. In the course of time the environmental conditions changed, and consequently the hall and the living rooms were transposed to the ground floor.

Left: Sketch of the Wu Residence. Huizhou, Xidi Nancun. Ming Dynasty
Right: Sketch of the Cheng residence. Huizhou, Chengcunxiang. Qing Dynasty

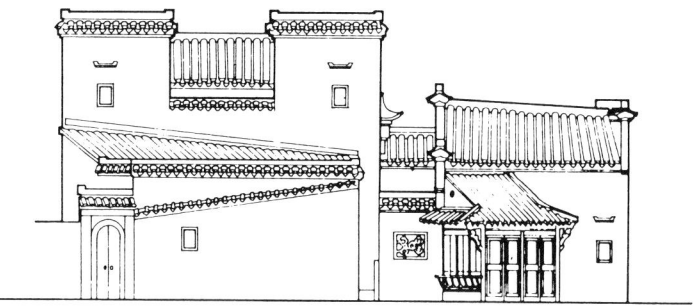
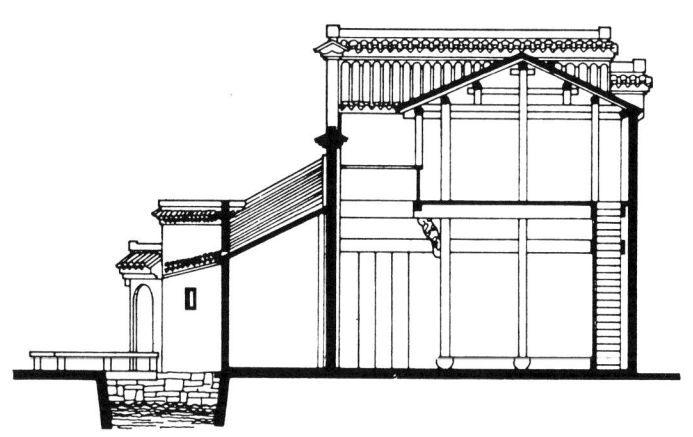
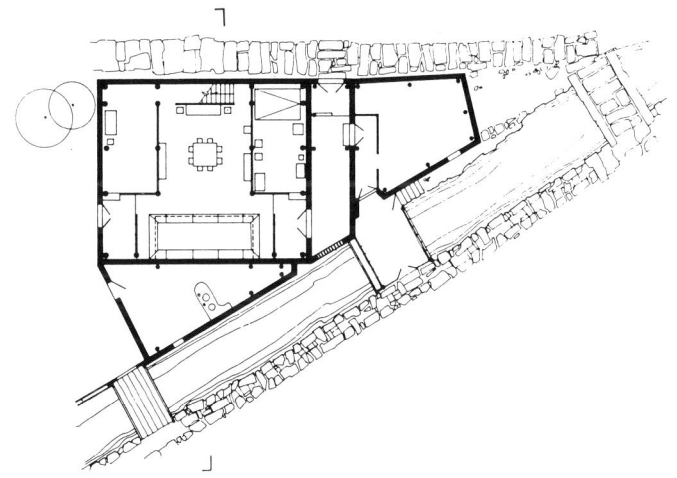
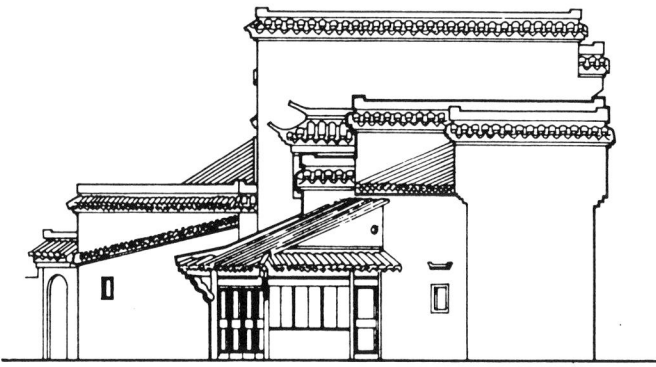

Eingang der Cheng-Residenz über eine von Steinbalken getragene Brücke. Qing-Dynastie
Entrance to the Cheng residence across a little bridge supported by stone beams. Qing Dynasty
Huizhou, Chengcunxiang, Yixian

Blick vom *tianjing* auf das obere Stockwerk, verkleidet mit einer Holztäfelung im *yi ban yi ci* (eine Platte, eine Leiste)-Stil unter verstellbaren Gitterfenstern in der Residenz der Familie Wu. Ming Dynastie. Huizhou, Xidi-Nancun, Yixian

View from the upper floor coverd with wood paneling in the *yi ban yi ci* (one panel one trim) style supporting partition windows in the residence of the Wu family. Ming Dynasty. Huizhou, Xidi-Nancun, Yixian

Zur Geschichte der alten Dörfer in Süd-Anhui

In frühen Zeiten lebten drei Miao-Völker in Huizhou, die von den Han-Völkern, wie die Landschaft, Shanyue genannt wurden. Nach der Han-Dynastie in der Zeit der Drei Reiche (220–263 n. Chr.) unterwarf Sun, der Herrscher des Reiches Wu, Shanyue und öffnete damit den Zugang in dieses Gebiet. Wie aus der Xinan Chronik der Song-Dynastie (420–479 n. Chr.) hervorgeht, siedelten sich daraufhin Klans aus Zentralchina an und erschlossen ihre neue Heimat (Xinan–Neue Siedlung). Das kleine Gebiet hat in der

On the history of the old villages in South Anhui

In primeval times, three Miao tribes lived in the narrow mountain pass of Huizhou, which were, like the area, called Shanyue. After the Han Dynasty, at the time of the Three Kingdoms (210–263 AD), Sun conquered Shanyue and opened the way to it. In the course of this and throughout the following centuries, clans from Central China moved there and opened up a new homeland, which they renamed Xinan (New Settlement). Three times, in the Jin (265 to 420 AD), Tang (618–907 AD) and in the Song Dynasty

Jin- (265–420 n.Chr.), zu Ende der Tang- (618–907 n.Chr.) und in der Südlichen Song-Dynastie (1127–1279 n.Chr.) Übersiedlungen aus dreizehn Provinzen aufgenommen, und durch den Zusammenfluß der verschiedenen Kulturströmungen bildete sich die Kultur des späteren Huizhou.

Überreste der Shanyue-Bauten sind nicht mehr erhalten. Die ältesten Brücken, Pagoden und Schulen datieren aus der Song- und Yuan-Dynastie, die ältesten Höfe aus der Ming-Dynastie.

Im Verlauf von mehr als 1500 Jahren veränderten sich die Dörfer in ihrer Anlageform. Die Sippen, die ihre Heimat verlassen hatten, um den Kriegswirren zu entkommen, mußten sich zuerst vor den Gefahren der Wildnis schützen und gegen die Attacken der Shanyue absichern. Deshalb wählten sie Schluchten, die leicht zu verteidigen waren, und es entstanden zu Festungsdörfern angelegte Landgüter. Dichtgedrängte Höfe, eingefaßt von hohen Mauern, umsäumt von schmalen Gassen, geschützt durch Stadtmauern und -gräben, bestimmen ihr Bild. Orte dieser Anlageform sind bis heute erhalten.

In den dreihundert Jahren von der Südlichen Song- bis Beginn der Ming-Dynastie entfalteten sich Wirtschaft und Kultur. Die übergesiedelten Sippen lebten in Frieden und konnten ihren kulturellen Interessen nachgehen. Zufolge einer Huizhou-Residenzchronik der Ming-Dynastie unter Hong Shi (1488–1506 n.Chr.) wurde die Kultur noch verfeinert, hohe Beamte der Song in der Funktion kaiserlicher Schriftverwalter taten sich hervor, und viele Gelehrte der Logik, genannt Dongnan Zhou Lü (Ost-Süd-Konfuzius-Mencius) folgten der Lehre des Zhu Xi. „Ein Tor führt zu neun Beamten, zwei von ihnen sind kaiserliche Schriftverwalter höchsten offiziellen Ranges", ist ein Zitat, das auf eine administrativ bestimmte Bevölkerungsstruktur hinweist. Schulen und Ahnenhallen prägten das Bild der Dörfer, die sich harmonisch in die Landschaft einfügten. Im Umkreis lebten einfache Bauern, die als Unfreie den Boden bestellten, in Hütten. Fischer wohnten in Hausbooten am Ufer der Flüsse Xinan, Heng, Chang und Heshui.

Von Mitte der Ming- bis Ende der Qing-Dynastie wandelten sich die Dörfer zu Kaufmannssiedlungen. „Von zehn Menschen sind drei Bauern und sieben Kaufleute" oder „wenige Felder, Menschen wachsen dicht wie Korn, auf zehn von ihnen kommen neun Kaufleute" sind Sprichwörter jener Zeit, die den wirtschaftlichen Umschwung und seine Ursachen erklären. Als Folge des finanziellen Überflusses wurden die Häuser prunkvoller ausgestattet; Opiumhöhlen und Spielhallen sorgten für Pläsier. Nach dem Ende der Qing-Dynastie gerieten die Dörfer langsam in Verfall.

(1127–1279 AD) the small area experienced migrations from thirteen provinces whose different cultures were transferred, intermingled, and the new culture of the later Huizhou developed.

No remains of the Shanyue have survived. The oldest bridges, pagodas and schools that do remain were built in the Song and Yuan Dynasties. The oldest courtyards are those dating from the Ming Dynasty.

In the course of fifteen centuries the villages changed in layout and style. The clans, who had left their native country to shake off the chaos of war, had to protect themselves from the danger of the wilderness, and from sudden attacks by the Shanyue. Consequently they chose hidden valleys to settle, which were easy to defend, and feudal estates in the style of fortress villages were developed. Moated city walls with watch towers, surrounding the courtyards built next to each other, enclosed by high walls, and narrow alleys characterize the townscapes. Villages in this style have survived until today.

The Huizhou culture and economy developed in the three hundred years from the Southern Song until the beginning of the Ming Dynasty. The clans who had emigrated lived in peace and pursued the cultural interests of their native country. According to a Huizhou residence document of the Ming Dynasty under Hong Shi (1488–1506 AD) the culture was still being refined; statesmen, celebrated by the Song, emerged in large numbers; many of them were imperial counselors; and many scholars followed the school of Zhu Xi, called Dongnan Zhou Lü (East-South-Confucius-Mencius). "One entrance leads to nine scholars, two of them are of the highest literary degree" is one of the quotations, which refers to a population ruled by bureaucracy. The villages were laid out in harmony with nature, their features include schools and ancestor halls. In the neighbourhood of the villages huts were set up for the peasants, who, in thrall of the clans, tilled the fields; fishermen lived in boats at the banks of the Heshui, Xinan, Heng, and Chang rivers.

From the middle of the Ming until the end of the Qing Dynasty the villages changed due to an economic boom and became rich merchant villages. Proverbs like "three peasants, seven merchants", or "few fields, people are growing closely like grain, nine out of ten are merchants", describe the situation of those days. The houses were decorated magnificently, opium dens and gambling halls took care of pleasure. The prosperity of the villages was maintained until the end of the Qing Dynasty, thereafter they fell into decay.

Häuser entlang einer Wasserstraße in dem Dorf Likeng, Wuyuan, Jiangxi
Houses along a water channel in the village of Likeng, Wuyuan, Jiangxi

Blick von dem *tianjing* auf die Ahnen- und Gästehalle eines Hofes. Trenntüren im Eismuster geschnitzt
View from the *tianjing* of the ancestor and guest hall of a courtyard. Partition doors carved in the ice pattern
Huizhou, Xidi, Yixian

Tianjing mit Blick durch ein mit Holzschnitzereien verziertes Tor in den Hausgarten
View from a *tianjing* of a gate decorated with wooden carvings leading into the yard
Huizhou, Bingshan, Yixian

Anlage und Dekoration der Höfe

Die Höfe in Süd Anhui wurden nach dem Vorbild der Höfe in Zentralchina angelegt. Die Höfe wurden dort, wie für Shanxi und Beijing beschrieben, symmetrisch im *siheyuan*-Stil gestaltet. Die Gebäude waren in Buchten *(kaijian)* unterteilt. Die Seitengebäude hatten eine helle Mittel- und zwei dunkle Seitenbuchten *(yiming, liangan)*. Die Buchten der Hauptgebäude hatten gleichen Lichteinlaß. Die Hofanlagen ließen sich wie Bilder oder Schriftzeichen lesen. Die einfachste Form der Höfe 囗 gleicht einem kaiserlichen Siegel und wird Jadesiegel genannt. Die nächste Anlageform entspricht dem Zeichen für Rückkehren 回 *hui,* darauf folgen das Zeichen für die Sonne 日 *ri* mit zwei und das Zeichen Auge 目 *mu* mit drei Quergebäuden. Diese Anlageformen wurden bis zu neun Quergebäuden erweitert.

In den Dörfern in Huizhou mußten die Höfe der Topographie des Gebirges angepaßt werden. Deshalb wurden sie auf dreieckiger, halbkreisförmiger oder polygonaler Grundfläche angelegt. Geschützt von hohen Mauern auf engem Raum lebend, konnten sich die Bewohner geborgen fühlen, doch stellte sich dabei auch ein Gefühl der Abgeschiedenheit von der freien Natur ein. Um diese Stimmung aufzulockern, gestalteten sie die Seitenhöfe nach dem Vorbild der Höfe in Jiangnan als Landschaftsminiatur und schmückten sie mit Steintischen und -stühlen, Pflanzen und Springbrunnen (s. S. 176/177).

Die Haupteingänge werden von einem Steinlager aus Steinpfeiler, Querbalken und Schwelle getragen. Ihr Bild simuliert oft den Charakter *kai* 開 (öffnen). Die Aufsätze wurden im Stil der horizontalen Aufschriften, der hängenden Blumen oder im Prachtbogenstil dekoriert. Der prächtigste Stil ist der Fünf-Phönix-Stil, der in der Qing-Dynastie beliebt war; fünf Aufsätze unter fünf Dachvorsprüngen, jeweils zwei von beiden Seiten zum mittleren ansteigend, sind unterteilt von vier tragenden Steinpfeilern. Über den Aufsätzen dekorierten auf Ochsenkopfkapitellen ruhende Dachvorsprünge den Eingang. In der Ming-Dynastie wurden die Türflügel innen mit Ziegelplatten belegt, die mit Metallpickeln befestigt wurden (s. S. 184). Später kamen Metallbeschläge in Mode.

Die Eingangshallen dienen als Korridor. Eine freistehende Flügeltür im Zentrum schützt vor Wind und Rauch und dem Einblick der Passanten. Vom Innenhof grenzt eine Trenntür ab, deren einzelne Flügel auf einer hohen Schwelle montiert wurden und verstellbar sind. Zu alltäglichen Zeiten wurden nur die Seitenflügel geöffnet. Nur bei offiziellen Anlässen pflegten die Besucher durch die Mitteltür einzutreten.

Layout and decoration of the courtyards

The courtyards in South Anhui were modelled on the courtyards in Central China. There the courtyards were laid out exactly symmetrically as described for Beijing and Shanxi. The wings have three bays *(kaijian)* in the one (room) light, two (rooms) dark *(yiming, liangan)* style. The main halls have three (or five) bays in the three (rooms)light style. They layout of the courtyards can be read like pictures and Chinese characters. The simplest layout 囗 looks like an Emperor's seal and is called jade seal. The first following this layout is the sign for return 回 *hui,* the next, in which two cross buildings are lined up along the central axis is called sun 日 *ri,* the next has three cross buildings and is called eye 目 *mu.* This kind of layout could be extended up to nine cross buildings, which ascended step by step up to the main hall.

In the villages of Huizhou the courtyards were modified depending on the topography of the mountains, and laid out on triangular, polygonal or semicircular plans. The fortress-like courtyards afforded safety, but also made the inhabitants feel isolated. Consequently the side yards were arranged as a miniature of the outside nature. Beautiful details, plants, stone tables and stone chairs decorated the yards and even little fountains were set up (cf. pp. 176/177).

The main entrance is supported by a natural stone support, consisting of crossbeam, threshold and side uprights. The entrance, as an overall picture, often simulates the character *kai* 開 (open). The top part of the gate is usually decorated with horizontal board inscriptions, also common were the hanging flower and the memorial arch style. Above the top part, roof shades supported by ox-head capitals complete the main entrance. The most magnificent style, favored in the Qing Dynasty, is called Five-Phoenix style. This style is made up of five top parts, decorated with roofshades, two ascending from each side to the central top part, subdivided by four columns. The wooden doors were covered with metal foil or, in former times, tiled with adobe bricks, fixed with metal spikes (cf. p. 184).

The entrance hall is used as a corridor. From outside, the hall is closed off by the main gate and separated from the inner yard by a partition door. An independent screen, set up in the center, offers protection against wind, smoke and the curiosity of passers-by. The partition door, which faces the *tianjing,* stands on a high threshold. On normal days only the side gates are open, the central door is only open for official feasts and ceremonies.

Aufsatz eines Haupteinganges, modelliert in *kai*-Form, dekoriert mit narrativen Schnitzereien
Top of a main entrance simulating the character *kai*, decorated with narrative carvings

Links: Traditionelles Arrangement einer Ahnentafel in einem Hof in Huizhou, Xidi, Yixian

Oben: Ahnentafel in der Galerie entlang des *tianjing* in der Chengzhi-Halle geschützt mit einer Holzbalustrade
Huizhou, Hongcun, Yixian

Left: Traditional arrangement of an ancestor wall in a courtyard in Huizhou, Xidi, Yixian

Above: Ancestor wall in the gallery running along the *tianjing* in the Chengzhi hall protected by a wooden lattice balustrade
Huizhou, Hongcun, Yixian

Der Brunnen des *tianjing* ist mit Steinplatten abgedeckt. Das Wasser wird von den Ecken des Bassins entlang der *yin*-Kanäle abgeleitet. Steinplatten, meist im Münzmuster perforiert, decken die Kanäle ab, um sie vor dem Verschlammen zu schützen. Die Maße des *tianjing* bestimmten sich durch die Größe der Haupt- und Seitengebäude.

Die Hauptgebäude sind in Ahnenhalle, Gästehalle und Räume der älteren Generation unterteilt. Im Zentrum der Ahnenhalle steht die Wand des höchsten Gelehrten *(taishibi,* Bezeichnung aus der Zhou-Dynastie), die mit Verspaaren und entrollten Bildern dekoriert wurde. Vor der *taishibi* steht auf einem Tisch zentral eine Uhr, die in Homophonie für langes Leben und Glück tönt. An den Seiten der Uhr stehen Opfergefäße. Daneben steht auf der Westseite ein Spiegel, in dem sich eine Vase reflektiert, die auf der Ostseite neben dem Opfergefäß aufgestellt ist. Das Wort für Vase *(ping)* klingt wie das Wort für Frieden *(ping)*, und das Wort für Spiegel *(jing)* klingt wie das Wort für Ruhe/ Frieden *(jing)*. Daraus erklärt sich das etymologische Symbol dieser Anordnung. Der längliche Tisch ist von zwei Stühlen der höchsten Gelehrten eingerahmt. Ein Tisch mit Stühlen für die acht Unsterblichen vervollständigt das Arrangement.

The well of the *tianjing* is covered with natural stone slabs. The water drains from the corners of the basin below, along the *yin* channels. To stop mud building up, the channels were also covered with stone slabs, pierced with holes, mostly designed in coin patterns. The size of the *tianjing* is determined by the size of the main building and the wings.

The main hall is subdivided into three rooms: the ancestor hall, the room for the older generation and the guest hall. The wall of the highest scholar (*taishibi,* name dating from the Zhou Dynasty) is positioned in the center. According to custom antithetical couplets and unrolled pictures decorate the wall. On a longitudinal table in front of the *taishibi* a clock chimes in homophony for long life and fortune. On both sides of the clock offertory pots are placed, and a vase on the east side is reflected in a mirror standing on the west side. Since the word for vase *(ping)* sounds like the word for peaceful/calm *(ping)*, and the word for mirror *(jing)* sounds like the word for calm/quiet *(jing)*, the etymological symbol is obvious. The longitudinal table is framed by two chairs for the highest scholars *(taishiyi)*. In front, a table with chairs for the eight immortals furnished the hall and completed the arrangement.

Blick über den von einer Galerie mit Holzgeländer umlaufenden *tianjing* auf die Trenntüren und Fenster der Empfangshalle eines Hofes. Jiangxi, Tuochuan, Wuyuan

View of an entrance into a guest hall with partition doors and windows, across the *tianjing* and the framing gallery in a courtyard. Jiangxi, Tuochuan, Wuyuan

Oben: Mit Pflanzen geschmückter Innenhof, geschnitztes Steinfenstergitter mit vierblättrigen Blüten in den Kreuzungspunkten der Quadrate eine oktagonale Struktur bildend.
Huizhou, Xidi, Yixian
Rechts: Blick auf eine mit Holzschnitzereien verzierte Veranda in einem vielfältig geschmückten Innenhof. Huizhou, Hongcun, Yixian

Above: Yard decorated with plants, window with stone lattice of four-leafed flowers in the cross points of the squares, forming an octagonal pattern. Huizhou, Xidi, Yixian
Right: View of a veranda decorated with wooden lattice in a picturesque yard.
Huizhou, Hongcun, Yixian

Feingearbeitete, auf Holzschwellen installierte Trenntüren grenzen die Wohnräume vom *tianjing* ab. Sie sorgen für Licht, für Luftzirkulation, schützen gegen Wind und Staub und grenzen Innen- und Außenraum voneinander ab. Sie sind verstell- und abnehmbar und lassen somit den freien Raum vergrößern. Früher waren die Trenntüren in den Höfen ein wesentlicher Bestandteil der dekorativen Holzausbauten. Seit in der Qing-Dynastie die Wohnräume im hohen unteren Stockwerk eingerichtet wurden, waren auch die Trenntüren sehr hoch. Ihre schmalen, verstellbaren Flügel verglich der Volksmund mit der Gestalt eines hübschen jungen Mädchens. Die mittlere, mit Schnitzereien verzierte Querplanke der Türen wurde Taille schnüren *(shuyao)* genannt, das Brett darunter Rockbrett *(qunban),* und die untere Planke hieß Schuhe schnüren *(shujiao).* Die Trennfenster wurden in der dortigen Mundart mit dem Begriff *jianta* bezeichnet. Die kunstfertig geschnitzten Fensterflügel sollten, als Kleider der Gitterfenster *(jiantayi),* die Blicke einfangen und die Blöße verdecken.

Separate Eingänge führen in die Seitengebäude. Ihre Trenntüren sind auf Holzdielen mit einer Stufenhöhe Abstand von der Grundfläche der Gästehallen eingerichtet. Für die Luftzirkulation sind ihre tragenden Steinschwellen mit Löchern perforiert, die im Münzmuster geschnitzt wurden (siehe Bild). Ein Korridor umläuft den *tianjing* in □ *(kou*- Mund)-Form (s. S. 173).

Blick in den Innenhof der Chengzhi-Halle
View of the inner yard of the Chenzhi hall
Hongcun, Yixian, Huizhou

Tragende Steinschwelle
Supporting stone threshold
Doushanjie, Yixian, Huizhou

Skillfully crafted partition doors, fitted on wooden thresholds, which are often higher than a step, protect the living rooms from wind and dust and keep the air circulating. They can be turned and removed, and thus the open air space can be enlarged. From the Qing Dynasty onwards the ground floor changed into the living center. The high, slim shape of the door wings was popularly compared with the figure of a beautiful girl. The cross-board in the middle is called lacing up the waist *(shuyao)*, the part below named skirt board *(qunban)* and the lowest part tie up the shoe *(shujiao).* The partition doors originate in Central China, but in Huizhou they are timbered and carved. The partition windows are another outstanding feature of the interior decor. They are decorated with cross boards, which are finely carved with popular narratives. The lattice windows are called *jianta* and the skillfully timbered and carved wings lattice-window clothing *(jiantayi),* since they attract the eye but protect from view.

The wings of the courtyards have separate entrances to bypass the main hall. The partition doors are constructed on wooden planks, one step higher than the surface of the guest halls. The supporting stone thresholds are pierced with air circulation holes, which are usually have brick carvings, patterned like coins (see left). A corridor in □ form *(kou* – mouth) surrounds the *tianjing* along the wings (cf. p. 173).

Trenntürflügel und ein Fenster, bedeckt mit einer geschnitzten Querplanke, im *tianjing* eines Hofes
Partition door wing and a window covered with a carved wooden traverse board in the *tianjing* of a courtyard
Huizhou, Xucun, Yixian

Die Dächer sind in Richtung *tianjing* geneigt und mit Drachenschuppenziegeln überlappend konkav–konvex gedeckt, um Rinnen für das Regenwasser zu bilden. Auf den Dachfirsten imitieren vertikal gereihte Ziegel das Rückgrat *(jijie)* eines Drachen. In der Ming-Dynastie wurden die Firste oft mit Durchbrucharbeit im Blumenmuster dekoriert.

Drei verschiedene Ziegel schützen und dekorieren die Dachtraufen. Der Tropfwasserziegel hat die Form eines Persimonblütenblattes und schließt im Winkel von 30 Grad an den Kopfziegel an. Dieser hat die Form eines Katzenkopfes, der gern mit Menschengesicht modelliert wird. Er trägt einen Kappenziegel mit der Form eines gefalteten Blütenblattes (hier mit einem *shou*-Symbol verziert), verschließt zwei Rinnen und versperrt so Mäusen den Durchschlupf. An den Seiten sind die Dächer durch Pferdekopfmauern geschützt, die zu den Dachfirsten aufragen. Eine Variante dieser Mauern mit geschwungenen Giebeln wird Pferdekopfmauer im Sperlingsschwanz-Stil genannt (s. S. 120/121).

Drei Gassen sichern gegen Feuer. Die erste trennt die Seitengebäude in Querrichtung voneinander ab, die zweite verbindet die einzelnen Gebäude miteinander, die dritte führt an den Seitengebäuden entlang. In diesen Gassen gingen die Gattinnen, in Sänften getragen, durch das sogenannte tausendfach goldene Tor ein und aus. Von einem Pavillon über dem Tor wurden die Gassen bewacht.

The roofs are tiled in overlapping convex–concave lines to form gutters to let the rain run down to the *tianjing*. The tiles are called dragon-scale tiles. On the ridges the tiles are lined up vertically, to imitate the spine *(jijie)* of a dragon. In the Ming Dynasty it was common to decorate the ridges with open brickwork in flower patterns.

Three different tiles protect and decorate the eaves. The gutter-head tile imitates the head of a cat, often modelled with the face of a human being to prevent mice from getting in. A cap tile shaped like a leaf, folded like a fan (here decorated with a *shou* symbol), covers the gutter-head tile. The drip tile, which is shaped like the leaf of a persimmon flower symbolizing luck, tilts at an angle of 30 degrees downwards from the gutter-head tile. Fireproof walls, called horse-head walls, adjoin the roof on both sides of the building and extend to the height of the ridge. A variant of this kind whose gables are turned upwards is called horse-head wall in the sparrow-tail style (cf. p. 120/121).

Three different alleys protect against fire. Transverse fire alleys intersect the wings of the courtyards. The second alley serves as protection against the neighbouring buildings. The third alley leads to the so-called thousand fold golden door through which the women went in and out, carried in armchairs by the servants. A guard pavilion looks down from above the thousand fold golden door.

Kennzeichen der Hofanlagen in der Ming- und Qing-Zeit

Wie beschrieben, blicken die Höfe in Süd Anhui auf eine Jahrtausende lange historische Entwicklung zurück. In der Ming- und Qing-Zeit erfuhren die Provinz einen starken wirtschaftlichen Aufschwung, der sich in Ausstattung der Höfe reflektiert. Im folgenden werden die wesentlichen Charakteristika im Wandel der beiden Dynastien aufgeführt und mit Fotos historisch bedeutender Orte dargestellt.

Characteristics of the courtyards in the Ming and Qing Period

The courtyards in South Anhui look back on a historical development of some thousand years as described above. In the course of the Ming and Qing Dynasties the province experienced a major economic boom, which is reflected in the changing design of the courtyards. The main characteristics of both dynasties are described below and shown with some pictures of historically important villages.

Hofanlage mit schmalen Seitenhöfen und Feuerschutzmauern im Pferdekopf-Stil mit Fünf-Stufen-Profil
Courtyard with narrow side yards, protected by fireproof walls in the horse-head style with five-step profile
Huizhou, Xidi, Yixian

Ming-Dynastie

- Die Höfe waren rechteckig, eingeschlossen von hohen Ziegelsteinmauern. Das zweite und dritte Stockwerk der Gebäude war in fünf Räume unterteilt. Die Wohnräume lagen im zweiten, höheren Stockwerk.
- Die Mauern wurden in 一 (*yi* – eins)-Form gedeckt. In der Mitte der Ming-Dynastie wechselte sie zur 凹 (*ao* – konkav)-Form. Die seitlichen Giebel hatten meist 人 (*ren* – Mensch)-Form (s. S. 78), später wurden Pferdekopfmauern üblich.
- Wie in der Song- und Yuan-Dynastie wurde Holz als Baumaterial verwendet. In der frühen Ming-Dynastie wurden die Querbalken aus einem Eichenstamm geformt. Ochsenkopfkapitelle waren Tradition (s. S. 187).
- Die Außenmauern hatten keine Fenster. Alle Fenster blickten in den *tianjing* und waren mit Holzgittern verkleidet.
- Die Korridore wurden im Stil *yi ban yi ci* (eine Platte, eine Leiste) getäfelt. Alle dekorierenden Schnitzereien waren schlicht. Schilfwände unterteilten die Räume.
- Die Holzsäulen waren massiv und glatt; die Relation des Durchmessers zur Länge betrug $1 + 9 = 10$. Nur Silberbarren dienten zur Stabilisierung der verzapften Querbalken und Säulen.
- Die Dachgewölbe wurden im vollständig offenen Stil (*toukong xingshi*) konstruiert.

Ming Dynasty

- The surfaces of the yards were rectangular, enclosed by high brick walls, the second and the third floor were subdivided into five rooms. The living rooms were placed on the second floor.
- The brick walls were tiled in 一 (*yi – one*)-form. In the middle of the Ming Dynasty they changed to 凹 (*ao* – concave)-form, the gables were shaped like a 人 (*ren* – human being) (cf. p. 78), later the horse-head walls were common.
- As in the Song and Yuan Dynasty wood was the only material used for scaffolding. In the early Ming Dynasty a whole oak trunk was made into one crossbeam (cf. p. 187). Oxhead capitals were common.
- The outer walls had no windows. The windows faced the *tianjing* and were covered with wooden lattice. The wainscoting of the corridors was designed in the style *yi ban yi ci* (one panel one trim). The carvings looked unpretentious and smooth. The rooms were separated by reed screens.
- The wooden columns were solid and polished smooth; the ratio diameter + length equaled $1 + 9 = 10$. Only silver ingots were used for joining crossbeams and columns.
- The vaulting of the roofs was constructed in the fully-open style *(toukong xingshi)*.

Hof des höchsten Beamten in Qiankou, Huizhou. Ming-Dynastie
Links oben: Blick aus einem Gitterfenster in den *tianjing*
Links unten: Blick auf die Ahnentafel des *tianjing*
Oben: Blick auf die obere Etage mit verstellbaren Gitterfenstern in *tianjing*

Courtyard of the highest official in Qiankou, Huizhou. Ming Dynasty
Left above: View of the *tianjing* from a window in the ground floor
Left below: View of the ancestor hall with the grand tutor's wall
Above: View of the upper floor with partition windows and wooden carvings

Oben: Holzsäulen auf Steinsockeln in der Ahnenhalle Sanhuaitang in Xiuning. Huizhou
Links oben: Aufgang zu dem Ahnentempel in Qiankou, Yixian, Huizhou. Ming-Dynastie
Links unten: *Tianjing* des Ahnentempels, Türflügel bedeckt mit Lehmziegeln, befestigt mit Metallpickeln

Above: Wooden columns on stone pedestals in the ancestor hall Sanhuaitang in Xiuning. Huizhou
Left above: Front of the ancestor temple in Qiankou, Yixian, Huizhou. Ming Dynasty
Left below: *Tianjing* of the ancestor temple, doors covered with adobe bricks fixed with spikes

Löwenpaar der Ming-Zeit transponiert von dem Ahnentempel des Dorfes Chengkan vor den Eingang des Ortes Qiankou in Yixian, Huizhou

Pair of lions of the Ming Period transposed from an ancestor temple in the village of Chengkan to the entrance of the village of Qiankou in Yixian, Huizhou

Offenes Dachgewölbe *(toukong xingshi)* mit aus Eichenstämmen geformten sogenannten Mondbalken in einer Ahnenhalle. Huizhou, Yixian, Tangyuecun. Ming-Dynastie

Vaulting in the fully-open-style *(toukong xingshi)* in an ancestor hall, cross beams formed with one oak trunk each. Huizhou, Yixian, Tangyuecun. Ming Dynasty

Qing-Dynastie

- Die hohen Pferdekopfmauern hatten drei oder fünf Stufen-Profil. Giebel in Bogenform waren selten.
- Die Monomer- der Ming-Dynastie hatte sich zur Polymer-Architektur gewandelt. Die Längsachsen der Innenhöfe verliefen nicht grundsätzlich parallel.
- Die Mauer der Haupteingänge war in 八 (ba – acht)-Form gedeckt, ihre Mitteltüren waren täglich geöffnet.
- Gästehallen und Wohnräume waren im jetzt höheren unteren Stockwerk eingerichtet. Die Treppen führten hinter der Ahnentafel in das obere Stockwerk.
- Für den Ausblick aus Seitenräumen der oberen Stockwerke wurden Fenster in die Außenmauern eingelassen.
- Der schlichte Stil der Ming- war dem prächtigen Stil der Qing-Dynastie gewichen. Die Gitter der Fenster und Türen wurden in vielfältigen Mustern geschnitzt. Neben traditionellen Motiven waren Opern und Erzählungen als narrative Themen in Mode.
- Die Holzsäulen wurden länger und dünner gearbeitet, ihr Querschnitt war oft quadratisch, das Verhältnis des Durchmessers zur Länge betrug 1 + 14 = 15. Kassettendecken waren Mode. Silberbarren wurden nicht mehr verwendet.
- Die Gärten wurden nach dem Vorbild der Gärten in Jiangsu angelegt und erschienen als Landschaftsminiatur.

Qing Dynasty

- The style of the fireproof walls had changed to 3-step or 5-step horse-head walls. Arch forms were rarely seen.
- The monomer- of the Ming had changed to polymer-architecture. The inner yards with their axis running in different directions formed one complex.
- The center of the main entrance was open daily. The entrance wall was 八 (ba – eight)-shaped.
- The guest halls and living rooms were transposed to the ground floor, which was now higher than the upper floor. Stairs to the upper floor ascended behind the ancestor wall.
- Little windows in studies looked out through the outer wall
- The unpretentiousness of the Ming was replaced by the magnificence of the Qing Dynasty, and the geometric style of the wooden lattices had changed to multiform style. Narratives like opera scenes and folktales were favored motifs for the wooden carvings. Traditional motifs and symbols as well as narratives were retained but shaped variously.
- The columns were longer and thinner, diameter + length equaled 1 + 14 = 15. Their cross section was often square. Coffered ceilings were favored. Silver ingots were gone.
- The yards were decorated in the style of the parks in Jiangsu, looking like a miniature of nature outside.

Oben: Dachgewölbe der Ahnenhalle Baolunge. Huizhou, Yixian, Chengkancun. Späte Ming-Dynastie
Unten: Dachgewölbe der Ahnenhalle der Familie Yu in Jiangxi, Wuyuan, Wangkoucun. Qing-Dynastie

Above: Vaulting in the ancestor hall Baolunge. Huizhou, Yixian, Chengkancun. Late Ming Dynasty
Below: Vaulting in the ancestor hall of the family Yu in Jiangxi, Wuyuan, Wangkoucun. Qing Dynasty

Holzschnitzereien eines Fensters mit *ruyi* (Glückssymbol) und *hui* (Rückkehr)-Ornamenten und Blumen. Im Ring zwei Vögel, das Zeichen *fu* (Glück) bildend, im Rahmen eine Szene aus der Liebesgeschichte 'Pfirsichblütenfächer' geschrieben in der Yuan-Dynastie. Huizhou, Yixian, Hongcun

Wooden carvings of a window with *ruyi* (symbol of fortune) and *hui* (return) ornaments and flowers. Two birds forming the character *fu* (good fortune) framed in a ring, below a scene of the love story 'Peach Blossom Fan' written in the Yuan Dynasty. Huizhou, Yixian, Hongcun

Oben: Holzschnitzereien in einem *tianjing:* narrative Darstellungen und spielende Löwen an der Verknüpfungsstelle eines Querbalkens und einer tragenden Säule der oberen Galerie, Fenstergitter geformt von Kakiblüten und Ornamenten. Huizhou, Yixian, Xidi
Rechts: Hängende Blumensäule und Stützsäule mit Holzschnitzereien eines Hirsches, verziert mit Kakiblüten, eine Pflanze der Unsterblichkeit kauend, unter einer mit Pflaumenblüten verzierten Stützplanke. Huizhou, Yixian, Guanlucun

Above: Wooden carvings in a *tianjing:* narrative depictions and playing lions decorating the supporting beam and column of the upper gallery, persimmon flowers and ornaments forming a window lattice. Huizhou, Yixian, Xidi
Right: Hanging flower column and a supporting pillar with wooden carvings of a deer, engraved with persimmon flowers, chewing a plant of immortality, under a wooden board carved with plum blossoms. Huizhou, Yixian, Guanlucun

Der östliche Geist in der traditionellen Baukunst

Die Baukunst vermittelt in ihrer rhythmischen Sprache den Geist der Ästhetik des Ostens. Die alten Dörfer des Bezirkes Yi sind in der Song- und Ming-Dynastie gegründet worden, und in der Zeit des Yang Li (1403–1424), einer kulturellen Blütezeit, wurde Yi Metropole. Die Dörfer dieses Bezirkes dürfen daher als repräsentativ für die Ästhetik der traditionellen chinesischen Baukunst betrachtet werden. Im folgenden werden vier Grundprinzipien vorgestellt.

The Eastern mind in traditional architecture

The rhythmic language of architecture conveys the spirit of the eastern aesthetic. The villages in Yi county in Huizhou were founded in the Song and in the Ming Dynasty and under Yang Li (1403–1424 AD), when culture and economy were flourishing, Yi became the capital. The villages in this district can be considered as representative of the traditional Chinese architectural aesthetic. In the following four main aspects are introduced.

Schlichtheit im Einklang mit der Natur

Die chinesische Ästhetik beruht auf den Theorien und Thesen der taoistischen Philosophen Laozi und Zhuang Chou. Laozi hatte zu Ende der Frühlings- und Herbst-Periode (ca. 500 v. Chr.) seine Anschauung zur Ästhetik seiner Zeit wie folgt formuliert: „... Fünf Farben machen den heutigen Menschen blind, fünf Töne machen den heutigen Menschen taub ..." und ferner „... lauter Ton hat keinen Klang, großer Umfang hat keine Form ...". Zhuang Chou (3. Jh. v. Chr.) brachte sein Ästhetikideal mit den Worten „Natürliche Schlichtheit kann der Welt die Schönheit nicht streitig machen" zum Ausdruck. Der Legalist Han Fei (3. Jh. v. Chr.) stellte seine philosophische Einstellung zur Ästhetik sehr konkret dar, indem er sagte: „Wie ein Emblem der Jade soll eine schöne Frau nicht geschmückt werden, wie eine Perle soll der Marquis Sui nicht mit Gold und Silber geschmückt werden. Dies ist das Prinzip der Schönheit der Natur, die nicht geschmückt werden darf." In Süd-Anhui folgten Zhu Xi (1133 bis 1200 n. Chr.) und später seine Schüler ihrer Theorie. Sie prägten das ästhetische Empfinden der Menschen und hatten entscheidenden Einfluß auf die Kunst und Bau-

Laozi auf einem Ochsen reitend
Laozi riding a buffalo

Unpretentiousness in accordance with nature

The aesthetic theory is based on the theories and well-known propositions of the Taoist philosophers and scholars Laozi and Zhuang Chou, who emphasized the simplicity of nature. At the end of the Spring and Autumn Period (500 BC) Laozi expressed his opinion concerning the aesthetic of his time with the proposition: "... Five colors make men of today blind, five sounds make men of today deaf ..." and "... loud tone has no timbre, huge dimension has no shape ...". Zhuang Chou (3rd C. BC) said: "Unadorned nature cannot be in dispute with the world's beauty." Very concretely the Legalist Han Fei (3rd C. BC) expressed his aesthetic principle with the proposition: "Like (an emblem of) jade the beautiful woman shall not be adorned, like a pearl the Marquis Sui shall not be adorned with gold and silver. This is the beauty of nature, which shall not be adorned." In South-Anhui, the philosopher Zhu Xi (1133–1200 AD) and later his disciples followed their theory. As they were respected, they shaped the people's aesthetic sensibilities, and had a formative influence on art and architecture. No matter whether they belonged to wealthy merchants,

kunst. Gleich, ob es sich um einfache Bauten, Großhöfe der Kaufleute oder Residenzen höherer Beamter handelte, wurde nur naturbelassenes Material verwendet. Die Dachziegel wurden nicht glasiert, und auch die feinsten Dekorationen nicht im Fünf-Farb-System bemalt. Dadurch heben sich die Bauwerke in ihrer schlichten Schönheit von der kaiserlichen Palastarchitektur in Zentralchina ab. Erst gegen Ende der Qing-Dynastie wurde es in Kaufmannshäusern üblich, die Holzschnitzereien mit Goldblatt auf einem dem Holzton ähnlichen Rot zu kolorieren. Doch blieb das Gefühl für Schlichtheit maßgebend in der Gestaltung.

Für den Reichtum des Landes verantwortlich galt der Ochse, und er wurde als unsterblich geehrt; er war Symbol des Frühlings und der Erde, und er erschien immer wiederkehrend in vielfältigen Motiven der darstellenden und narrativen Kunst Chinas. Sehr anschaulich kommt er als Motiv an dem Dorf Hongcun in Yixian zur Darstellung, dessen Anlage die Gestalt eines Ochsen nachbildet und das den Beinamen Ochsendorf trägt. Im Norden schützt ein *fengshui* Berg mit dem Namen Donnerberg *(leigangshan)* den Ort; gegenüber fließen der Abendflutfluß *(xijiang)* und der Schaftavernenfluß *(yangzhanjiang)* zusammen. Von einem Stausee in den Hügeln werden die als Ochsendarm bezeichneten Wasserkanäle gespeist, die in neun Richtungen und achtzehn Biegungen entlang der Dorfwege durch den Ort ziehen. Sie haben Verbindung zu den Bassins am Fuß der Mauern in den Höfen und sind mit Steinplatten bedeckt. Im Zentrum des Ortes liegt der Mondteich. Im Süden wird ein etwas größerer, wie ein Magen geformter und Ochsenbauch genannter Teich mit Frischwasser gespeist. Über den Fluß führen vier Brücken, die als Beine des Ochsen bezeichnet werden. Die dicht an dicht liegenden Höfe bilden den Ochsenkörper. Im Süden des Ortes erstrecken sich die Felder. Natur und Lebensraum waren in Harmonie verbunden.

high officials or ordinary people, all the buildings were constructed of pure materials like wood, bricks, tiles and stones. The tiles of their roofs were not glazed, and all the decorations, even the finest, were kept unpainted in the five-color-system. Thus the buildings in their unadorned beauty were distinct from the Royal Palace Architecture in Central China. Only at the end of the Qing Dynasty, in just some merchants' properties, the wooden carvings were refined with gold leaf, but very sparingly on red paint, imitating the color of the wood. Unpretentiousness remained as a formal principle.

Zhu Xi (1183–1200) Gugong Bowuyuan, Taipei

The ox, as the beast of burden, was regarded responsible for the wealth of the country and thus he was worshipped as an immortal creature. As a spring and earth symbol and in other different motifs he recurrently appeared in the Chinese narrative and visual arts. An outstanding example of this is offered by the village of Hongcun in Yixian, laid out as the picture of an ox and called Ox Village. According to the *fengshui,* in the north a mountain, called Thunder Hillock *(leigangshan),* gives shelter to the village. Opposite, two rivers, the Sheep-Inn River *(yangzhanjiang)* and the Night-Tides River *(xijiang),* join. The water channels in the village are described as ox bowels. They are fed from a water reservoir in the hills and curve in nine directions with eighteen loops along the alleys through the village. They are covered with stone slabs and connected with the pools in the yards. In the center of the village, a little pool, called Moon Lake, and in the south a little larger pool, shaped like a stomach, and described as ox belly, are fed with fresh water for common use. The courtyards, laid out close to each other, form the body of the ox, and the four bridges crossing the river are his legs. South of the village paths criss-cross the fields. Nature and lebensraum were joined in harmony.

Hongcun, das sogenannte Ochsendorf (Niuxingcun) in Huizhou
Hongcun, the so-called Ox Village in Huizhou

Der Mondsee *yuetang* 月塘 im Ochsendorf
Moon lake in the so-called Ox Village

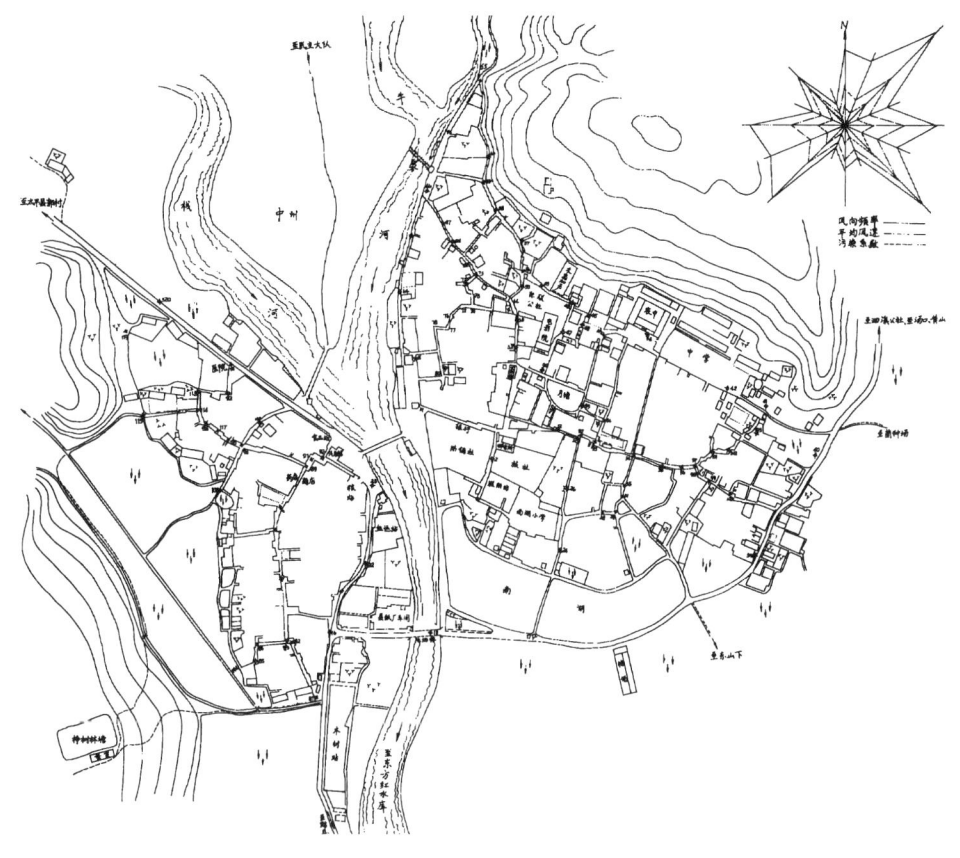

Huizhou, Yixian, Hongcun

Linienführung in der Ästhetik

Die chinesische Baukunst beschritt mit Holzkonstruktionen ihren Weg. Vergleichbar mit der Kalligraphie bildeten hier gezimmerte Komponenten als Linienkompositionen eine Schriftsprache, mit der die Menschen ihre Gedankenwelt zum Ausdruck brachten. Somit reflektieren die Strukturen der Häuser Philosophie und Ästhetik der östlichen Kultur in den verschiedenen Epochen.

Wie in der Fünf-Elementen-Lehre gezeigt, wird die Erde als Quadrat und der Himmel als Kreis abstrahiert dargestellt. Die Konstruktionen der Häuser simulieren diese Formen mit anmutig geführten Linien. Konkav geneigte Dächer und an den Ecken himmelwärts geschwungene Dachvorsprünge, harmonieren mit den flächigen, waagerecht gedeckten Mauern. Dächer und Dachvorsprünge werden von Kapitellen getragen, die aus rechteckigem *(gong)* und geschwungenem *(dou)* Teil bestehen. In Gruppen angeordnet, bilden sie eine Komposition kurzer Linien mit kraftvollem Rhythmus (s. S. 30).

Für den Innenausbau der Häuser ist Sanftheit das Prinzip. Geschwungene Querbalken, genannt Mondbalken, der Dachgewölbe kontrastieren mit geraden Säulen. Ihre Form erinnert an eine chinesische Laute, und sie wurde auch mit einem Wachskürbis verglichen. Die Säulen der Ming-Dynastie sind rund und massiv, an den Enden schmal zulaufend und gespalten, und sie werden deshalb Webschiffchensäule genannt. Ästhetiker, wie zum Beispiel Wang Chaowen, verglichen die Säulen der Ahnentempel in ihrer optischen Eleganz mit den antiken griechischen Säulen (s. S. 183).

In der Ming-Dynastie waren Holzverkleidungen aus schlichten, schmalen Holzplatten mit in gleichen Abständen parallel eingelegten Holzleisten üblich. Dieser Stil, genannt eine Platte, eine Leiste *(yi ban yi ci)*, entsprach dem aufrichtigen Verhalten der Menschen, einem Ideal der Zeit.

Die Böden der Hallen wurden mit Platten ausgelegt, die mit Goldlinien *(jintiaoge)* strukturiert waren. Die Linien liefen gerade auf den Eingang zu, um die Besucher willkommen zu heißen. Doch hatte dieser Linienverlauf auch die Konnotation, das Herz zu durchstechen. Deshalb laufen die Linien der Bodenmuster in den dahinter liegenden Wohnräumen diagonal auf die Ecken der Räume zu. Die Ecke öffnen *(kaijiao)* klingt wie das Haus öffnen *(kaijia)*, und dies trug wiederum die Bedeutung Wohlstand zu erlangen. Diagonal verlaufende Karos, wie sie als Muster für Balken und Träger der frei einsehbaren Dächer zu sehen sind, bringen diese Widersprüche in Einklang (s. S. 186).

Drawing lines

Traditional Chinese architecture started as timber frame architecture. As in the written characters, in architecture the timber patterns created their own language as a combination of lines. In this way people expressed the world of their thoughts and feelings, and the structure of the buildings reflect the eastern philosophy and the Zeitgeist of different epochs.

The construction of the buildings shows a great delicacy of line. As shown in the Five Element Theory *(wu xing)* the earth is depicted as square and heaven as a circle. Concave lines of the roofs and eaves turned up at the corner, a special feature of traditional Chinese architecture, contrast with the straight lines of the horizontally layered walls. The so-called oxhead capitals, combined from rectangular *(gong)* and round sections *(dou)*, support the roofs and eaves. Arranged in groups of short lines they offer a composition full of vigorous musical rhythm (cf. p. 30).

For the inner decor of the houses softness is the ideal. Vaulting in the fully open style are supported by curved crossbeams, called moon beams, contrasting with straight columns. In the Ming Dynasty the shape of the crossbeams was reminiscent of the Chinese lute, and they were also compared with pumpkins. The columns were round and solid, tapered towards the end, split like shuttles, and called shuttle columns. Aestheticians, as for instance Wang Chaowen, compared the wooden columns in the ancestor temples in their visual elegance with ancient Greek columns (cf. p. 183).

In the Ming Dynasty the wainscoting were timbered with plain and thin wooden planks, inlaid with parallel trims at equal intervals. This style, called one panel, one trim *(yi ban yi ci)*, stands for people's sincerity, a characteristic which was at a premium in that time.

The floors in the halls were laid out with tiles patterned with gold lines *(jintiaoge)*, which run straight towards the entrance to welcome the visitors. The bad connotation given to this pattern is that straight lines pierce the heart, and consequently the pattern lines in the living rooms behind the guest hall run diagonally to open the corner. Opening the corner *(kaijiao)* sounds like opening the house *(kaijia)*, which signifies acquiring wealth. Squares running diagonally solve the problem and are favored as patterns for beams for instance, supporting the vaulting in the fully open style (cf. p. 186).

Die Einheit im Gegensatz

Die philosophische Idee der Einheit der Gegensätze war bereits in frühen Zeiten ein Ideal der Kunst und Baukunst. Kontraste wie Punkt – Fläche, hell – dunkel, leer – voll, licht – dicht in Harmonie zu arrangieren, war üblich. Hohe weiße Festungsmauern mit ihren winzig kleinen Fenstern bieten die Einheit im Kontrast von Punkt und Fläche. In den Gebäuden kontrastieren mit den hellen Gästehallen die dunklen Räume der Seitenflügel, in denen die Schlafräume lagen. Dunkelheit sammelt Reichtum an, so hieß es. An den weißen flächigen Mauern dekorieren fein gearbeitete Aufsätze die Tore. Sie leben in dem Kontrast licht – dicht, der in der Kunsttheorie mit dem Spruch „Ein Pferd sprengt durch Lichtes, kein Wind zieht durch Dichtes *(shu neng qi ma, mi bu tou feng)*" beschrieben wird. Die Ornamentgitter der Fenster und Falttüren zeigen den Kontrast leer – voll. Ihre Konstruktion entspricht dem Prinzip der Gartenkunst, genannt den Anblick leihen *(jiejing)*, der äußere Anblick lockt den inneren an und umgekehrt. „Stärke verbirgt sich in der Erscheinung der Sanftheit" entspricht dem ästhetischen Empfinden der chinesischen Menschen. In der Baukunst wurde dieser Kontrast als Kunstmittel in der Dekoration und im Design verwendet. Starke Mauern umschließen die aus biegsamem Holz gezimmerten Gerüste der Häuser. In der Ming-Dynastie umkleideten geschnitzte Holzschalen die Steinsockel der Säulen. Die Dachvorsprünge über den Eingängen werden von Kapitellen getragen, deren stabile *gong*- und biegsame *dou*-Teile sich gegenseitig be- und entlasten.

Fengshui, die Basis der chinesischen Baukunst, lebt mit Kontrasteinheiten. In den Gebirgen sollte nach dem Drachenberg gesucht werden, dessen Quellen in die Täler münden. Die Lehre des *yinyang* und der Fünf Elemente sind im *fengshui* verflochten. Die Elemente Holz, Feuer, Erde, Metall, Wasser, als Pentagon betrachtet, entstehen in genannter Reihenfolge auseinander, sind reziprok und kontrastieren in den Diagonalen.

Unity of contrast

The philosophical idea of unity of contrast has been the ideal of Chinese art and architecture since primeval times. Contrasts such as point – plain, light – dark, vain – full, thin – dense are artificial means which make the constructions appear in harmony. Point and plain is the contrast offered by the huge white fortress walls with their tiny little windows. The top parts of the entrances appear in contrast to the white and empty walls and show the contrast thin – dense, resembling written Chinese characters. This contrast is described in Chinese art with the proverb "A horse leaps through sparseness, no zephyr penetrates density *(shu neng qi ma, mi bu tou feng)*." Inside the houses the light guest rooms, where feasts are celebrated, contrast with the dark rooms in the wings, where the bedrooms are placed, darkness aquires wealth one used to say. Solid stone walls surround the soft wooden frameworks of the houses. The stability of the eaves is guaranteed by the supporting capitals, with their pliable *dou* part and their firm *gong* part, which load and relieve each other. "Strength is hidden under the appearance of gentleness" is a principle of Chinese etiquette, which reflects this contrast. In the Ming Dynasty the stone pedestals of the columns used to be enclosed by wooden bowls. The partition doors and windows thrive on the contrast of void – full, and they resemble the garden art principle called borrow the sight *(jiejing)*, since outer sight attracts inner sight and vice versa.

Unity of contrast is also the basic of *fengshui*. For the location of the settlement in mountainous areas the protecting dragon mountain must be looked out for, and in contrast the best water rivers are to be found in the valleys. The theory of the Five Elements, which is interwoven with *fengshui*, reflects the harmony of contrast as well. The elements fire, earth, metal, water, wood, imagined placed at the corner of a pentagon, give birth to each other, are reciprocal, and contrast with the diagonal of the pentagon.

Qiankou, Yixian, Huizhou

Giebelwand mit kleinem Fenster, verziert mit narrativer Malerei eines kindlichen Boten mit dem Spruchband: Möge der Himmelsmandarin Glück bringen *(tianguan ci fu)*; Verschluß der Traufe mit als Katzenkopf geformten Ziegeln mit Kappe zwischen Tropfwasserziegeln in der Form eines Persimonblattes. Am Giebel Verzierung mit Swastika.
Huizhou, Yixian

Gable wall with a little window and a narrative picture of a child offering a scroll with the compliment: May the divine official bring good luck *(tianguan ci fu)*; capped cat gutter tiles and dripping water tiles shaped like persimmon leafs closing the eaves of the roof. Swastika decorating the corner of the fireproof wall.
Huizhou, Yixian

Konfuzianische Charakteristika in der Ästhetik

Die Lehre des Konfuzius (551 bis ca. 479 v. Chr.) beeinflußte entscheidend die Theorie der Ästhetik.

In den Höfen wurden die Räume so angeordnet und aufgeteilt, daß sie als Emblem der konfuzianisch hierarchischen Stufenordnung betrachtet werden können. Die Seitengebäude stiegen Schritt für Schritt zum Hauptgebäude an, in dem die Ahnenhalle, die Repräsentationsräume und die Wohnräume der älteren Generation lagen.

Diese Anordnung wurde mit dem Sprichwort: „Vorn tief, hinten hoch, Kinder und Kindeskinder hervorragende Persönlichkeiten *(qian di, hou gao zisun yinghao)* beschrieben."

Die konfuzianischen Prinzipien der Moral und Ethik wurden oft in Volksmärchen und historischen Anekdoten erzählt, die in Bildern und Schnitzereien zur Darstellung kamen, mit denen die Höfe ausgeschmückt wurden. So wurde die Tugend der moralischen Integrität *(jie)* zum Beispiel in der historischen Geschichte „Su Wu hütet Schafe (Su Wu mu yang)" (Bild links unten) thematisiert, in welcher der Held, einer hoher Beamter, während eines militärischen Konfliktes im Land des Feindes festgehalten wird, dort ehelicht und bis zur Rückkehr in sein Land der bescheidenen Schäfertätigkeit nachgeht. Die Geschichte mit dem Titel „Schwiegermutter sticht Zeichen (Yuemu ci zi)" (Bild rechts unten) erzählt von einer Großmutter, die ihrem Enkel Zeichen auf den Rücken graviert, um sein loyales Verhalten *(zhong)* zu bestimmen.

Characteristics of Confucianism

The teachings of Confucius (551 to approx. 497 BC) have a crucial influence on aesthetic theory.

The rooms in the courtyards were arranged and divided up in such a way that they can be seen as an emblem of Confucian hierarchical principles. The side buildings rose step by step towards the main building, which contained the ancestor hall, ceremonial rooms and accomodation for the older generation.

This arrangement was described in the proverb "Low at the front, high at the back, sons and grandsons will be heroes *(qian di, hou gao zisun yinghao)*".

Confucius' moral and ethical principles were often narrated in folk tales and historical anecdotes. Scenes from these stories appeared in the pictures and carvings with which the courtyards were decorated. Thus the virtue of moral integrity *(jie)* was for instance the subject of the story called "Su Wu keeps sheep (Su Wu mu yang)" (picture left below). Here the hero, a high official, was taken prisoner in enemy territory during a military conflict, married there and modestly spent his life tending sheep, until he was set free to return to his native country. The story "Yuemu ci zi" (picture right below) tells how a mother-in-law carves characters on the back of one of her grandsons to ensure his loyal behavior *(zhong)*.

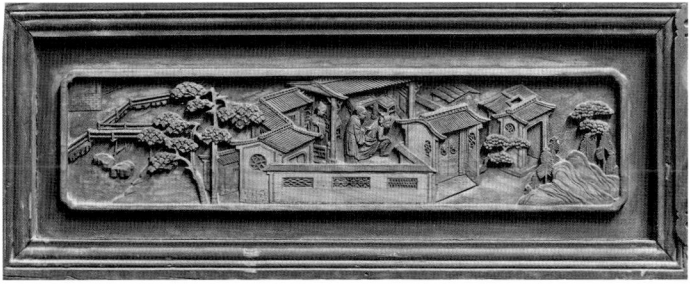

Links: Holzbrücke über einen Seitenarm des Wu-Flusses auf eine Ahnenhalle zuführend. Wangkoucun, Wuyuan, Jiangxi
S. 200/201: Blick durch eine Gruppierung von Pappeln auf fünf Gedenkbögen mit drei Aufsätzen über drei Zwischenräumen *(san zu san men san lou chong tian pailou)* auf dem Weg in den Ort Tangyuecun (Heckenkirschenbaumschattendorf) in Huizhou. Ming-Dynastie

Left: Wooden bridge traversing a branch of the Wu River to an ancestor hall. Wangkoucun, Wuyuan, Jiangxi
pp. 200/201: Wild plum trees in front of five memorial arch trees *(san zu san men san lou chong tian pailou)* on the way to the village of Tangyuecun (Wild-plum-tree-shadow-village) in Huizhou.
Ming Dynasty

Erdgestampfte Festungsbauten in Fujian 福建

Die Erdgebäude *(tulou)* 土樓

Die historische Entwicklung der *tulou*

Die Erdgebäude in Fujian werden meist von den Kejia (Kejia – Hakka – Gästefamilien) bewohnt. In der Yuan-Dynastie (1271–1368 n. Chr.) wanderten sie gleichzeitig mit den Helaoren, die ebenfalls zu den Han-Sippen gehören, auf verschiedenen Routen von Zentralchina nach Fujian. Die *tulou* werden oft als charakteristische Gebäude der Kejia angesehen, doch haben sie ihren Ursprung in den Festungen der lokalen Bevölkerung.

In Fuyue, im Grenzgebiet zu Guangdong, kam es während der Tang-Dynastie im ersten Regierungsjahr des Zong Zhang (688 n.Chr.) zu Aufständen des Volkes gegen die lokalen Behörden. Erst im folgenden Jahr, nach Übernahme der Truppen durch Chen Zheng, dem obersten Heerführer der Tang, wurden die Aufständischen besiegt und in die Berge vertrieben. Neun Jahre später, im zweiten Regierungsjahr des Yi Feng, eroberte der Sohn und Nachfolger des Chen Zheng, Chen Yuanguang, Nanshao (heutiger Shaoan-Bezirk) und zog in Fuzhou ein. Wie in Dokumenten belegt, hatten sich die Rebellierenden in Bergfestungen zurückgezogen. Chen Zheng folgte ihnen, ließ ebenfalls Festungen bauen und konnte ihnen Paroli bieten. Bis zum Beginn der südlichen Song-Dynastie (1127–1279 n.Chr.) wurden die Festungen zu Wohnbezirken. Aus Annalen des Bezirks Zhangtai geht hervor, daß es während der Song-Dynastie fortgesetzt zu Unruhen kam, denen zufolge sich die Landsleute in die Berge zurückzogen und in Festungen verbargen. Die Festungen waren Vorläufer der *tulou*. Aus dem Volk sind die ersten Dokumente der *tulou* aus der Yuan-Dynastie (1271–1368 n.Chr.) überliefert, und aus den frühesten offiziellen Dokumenten der Ming-Dynastie geht ebenfalls hervor, daß *tulou* bereits in der Yuan-Dynastie gebaut wurden.

In der Ming-Dynastie drangen japanische Banditen nach Zhangzhou ein, mordeten und plünderten. Die Menschen, die in der Nähe des Meeres wohnten, zogen sich in *tulou* zurück. Annalen des Bezirkes Zhangtai zufolge entstanden in der Zeit des Jia Jong (1522–1567 n.Chr.) viele Erdgebäude, von denen bis heute mehrere erhalten sind. Während der Qing-Dynastie kamen Attacken der Japaner nicht mehr vor, doch herrschten jetzt Unruhen in der Gesellschaft. Vertraute Familien zogen sich gemeinsam zurück und bauten *tulou* zur Abwehr. In der Zeit der Kulturrevolution fanden die Kejia Schutz in den *tulou*.

The rammed earth fortresses in Fujian

The rammed earth buildings *(tulou)*

Historical development of the rammed *tulou*

The *tulou* are usually inhabited by Kejia people (Kejia – Hakka – guest families). During the Yuan Dynasty (1271 to 1368 AD) the Kejia migrated, simultaneously with the Helaoren, following different routes, from Central China to Fujian. The *tulou* are often seen as the characteristic buildings of the Kejia, but history tells us that they originated as local peoples' fortresses built in the mountains.

The development of the *tulou* can be traced back to the Tang Dynasty. After the accession of Zong Zhang (688 AD) rebellions against the authorities took place in Fuyue, the border area north of Guangdong. Only one year later Tang troops under the command of Chen Zhang succeeded in turning the rebels away into the mountains. Nine years later in the second year of Yi Feng, Chen Yuanguang, the son and successor of Chen Zhang, conquered Nanshao (Shaoan district) and entered Fuzhou. He followed the rebels, concentrated troops in the mountains, built fortresses to defend the country against them, and achieved his aims. Until the Song Dynasty the *tulou* were used as residential buildings. According to documents of Zhangtai in the Song Dynasty (1127–1279 AD) rebellions occurred continuously, and they made local people flee to the mountains and build fortresses for defense. These fortresses are precursors of the *tulou*. The first records of *tulou* architecture are handed down from local people of the Yuan Dynasty. In the first official documents, dated in the Ming Dynasty, *tulou* are mentioned which were previously constructed in the Yuan Dynasty.

In the Ming Dynasty the Japanese invaded Zhangzhou. They plundered and murdered, and local people concentrated in the mountains and settled in their earth rammed fortresses. Local documents of Zhangzhou list quite a number of *tulou* built in the decades from 1522–1567 AD under

Rechts: Tianluokeng 田螺坑 Erdgestampfte Gebäude, angelegt nach der Fünf-Elementen-Lehre, mit einem quadratischen, die Erde symbolisierenden *tulou* im Zentrum. Minguo-Zeit. Shuxiang, Nanjing
S. 204: Innenhof des Shunyulou 順裕樓 Shiqiao, Shuxiang, Nanjing

Right: Tianluokeng. Five rammed earth buildings with a square *tulou* in the center symbolizing the earth according to the five element theory. Minguo Period. Shuxiang, Nanjing
p. 204: Inner yard of the rammed earth building named Shunyulou Shiqiao, Shuxiang, Nanjing

Die Besonderheiten der runden *tulou* in Fujian

In der Form ähneln die *tulou* den Bergfestungen, die auf den Gipfeln der Berge gebaut wurden. Das Regenschirm-Gebäude (Yusanlou) ist ein *tulou*, das wie eine Festung auf einem Berggipfel liegt. Zwei Rotunden mit leicht konkav geneigten Dächern umkreisen den Gipfel. Die innere überragt die äußere Rotunde, und aus der Ferne betrachtet wirkt die Anlage wie ein aufgespannter Regenschirm, der den Berggipfel bedeckt.

Die *tulou* liegen größtenteils in Gebirgsregionen mit schlammigem Boden und Reisfeldern. Deshalb müssen ihre Fundamente mit besonderer Sorgfalt trockengelegt und befestigt werden. Dem Gesetz „Der Wind bläst ewig über die Föhre, Wasser tränkt ewig die Kiefer!" folgend, werden sie mit öligen, prallen, alten Kiefernstämmen gesichert, die – meist im Kreis – nebeneinander gereiht werden. Darauf wird der Sockel der Mauer in einer Breite von etwa drei Metern mit Natursteinen gelegt. Das Fundament wird breiter angelegt als der größte Durchmesser der Mauern, um ihr Eigengewicht proportional zu vermindern. Auf dem Steinsockel ruht die Mauer, die aus Erde gestampft wird. Die Technik des Stampfens folgt dem Prinzip „eine Schalung – ein Sieb". Spießtannen, genannt Mauermuskeln, und Bambus, genannt Mauerknochen, bilden das Flechtwerk des Siebes. Üblicherweise liegen die *tulou* der Sonne zugewandt. Dadurch werden die Mauern ungleichmäßig ausgetrocknet, und durch ihr enormes Eigengewicht wird dabei ein so starker Druck ausgeübt, daß es zur Vorwölbung in Richtung der später austrocknenden Seite kommt. "Die Sonne wird die Mauer stoßen" sagt ein Sprichwort. Demzufolge werden die Mauern schräg, in Richtung des höchsten Sonnenstandes gestampft, und danach von der Sonne beim Austrocknen in die Vertikale aufgerichtet.

Die Mauern der *tulou* haben eine starke Abwehrfunktion. Nur ein Haupttor, das besonders abgesichert werden kann, führt in den Hof. Das Steinlager besteht aus Granitstein, die Torflügel sind vier *cun* (1 *cun* = ca. 3,23 cm) dick. Sie werden mit einem Balken verriegelt; außen überzieht eine Eisenfolie mit Wasserrinnen das Tor. Aus einem Wassertank im oberen Stockwerk kann Wasser herabgelassen werden, um einen Vorhang zum Schutz gegen Feueroffensiven zu bilden. Im Hof sind Brunnen zur Versorgung mit Frischwasser gegraben. Vorratsräume werden mit Getreide gefüllt. So können die Familien in den *tulou* abgesichert in Frieden zusammen leben. Im Zentrum ist ein Tempel zur Verehrung ihrer Ahnen eingerichtet.

Jia Jing. During the Qing Dynasty no further Japanese invaded, but local mutinies took place, and close families built their *tulou* for defense. Later, at the time of the cultural revolution, the Kejia constructed their *tulou* for defense.

The *tulou* and their special characteristics

The *tulou* resemble the old mountain-top fortresses. But only a few *tulou* were built on mountain tops. The Umbrella Building (Yusanlou) is one of those. Two rotundas circle the peak of the mountain, the inner rotunda is higher than the outer. From the distance this building looks like an open umbrella, covering the top of the mountain.

Most of the *tulou* are built in mountainous areas with narrow valleys, which are often wet and muddy. Therefore they have to be constructed with good, well-drained foundations. "Thousands of years the wind is blowing over the fir, thousands of years the water is soaking the pine!" According to natural law, old and oily pine stems were chosen to reinforce the foundations of the *tulou*. They are laid out, most of them in circles, next to each other, broader than the greater diameter of the walls, to diminish their proportional weight. On these foundations the bases are built with natural stones. On the base the walls, made up of rammed earth, are added. They reach the height of five to six storeys. The construction of the rammed earth walls works on the principle: "one formwork – one sieve". The sieve is woven with wall muscles (pines) and wall bones (bamboo). According to traditional *fengshui* laws the buildings face the sun, and the walls dry out unevenly. "The sun will push the wall!" a proverb says. This was taken for granted, and the walls are built to slope towards the sun's highest point. Consequently they are pushed upright by the sun as they dry out.

The massive outer walls were constructed as a defense to withstand any offense. Only the main gate, which was specially secured, leads into the yard. The wooden planks of the door wings usually measured four *cun* in diameter (1 *cun* = 3.23 cm). The door was closed with a huge beam, and from outside covered with a corrugated iron sheet. In case of fire attacks they let water run down from tanks above the gate to cover the door with a water curtain. Wells, and store rooms with harvest products helped people to survive when under siege. The families were enclosed and protected and able to live in peace together. An ancestor hall was built on the first floor, facing the main door, or set up as a little building in the center of the yard.

Skizze des Erdgebäudes Eryilou 二宜樓
Sketch of the rammed earth building named Eryilou. Dadi, Xiandu, Huaian

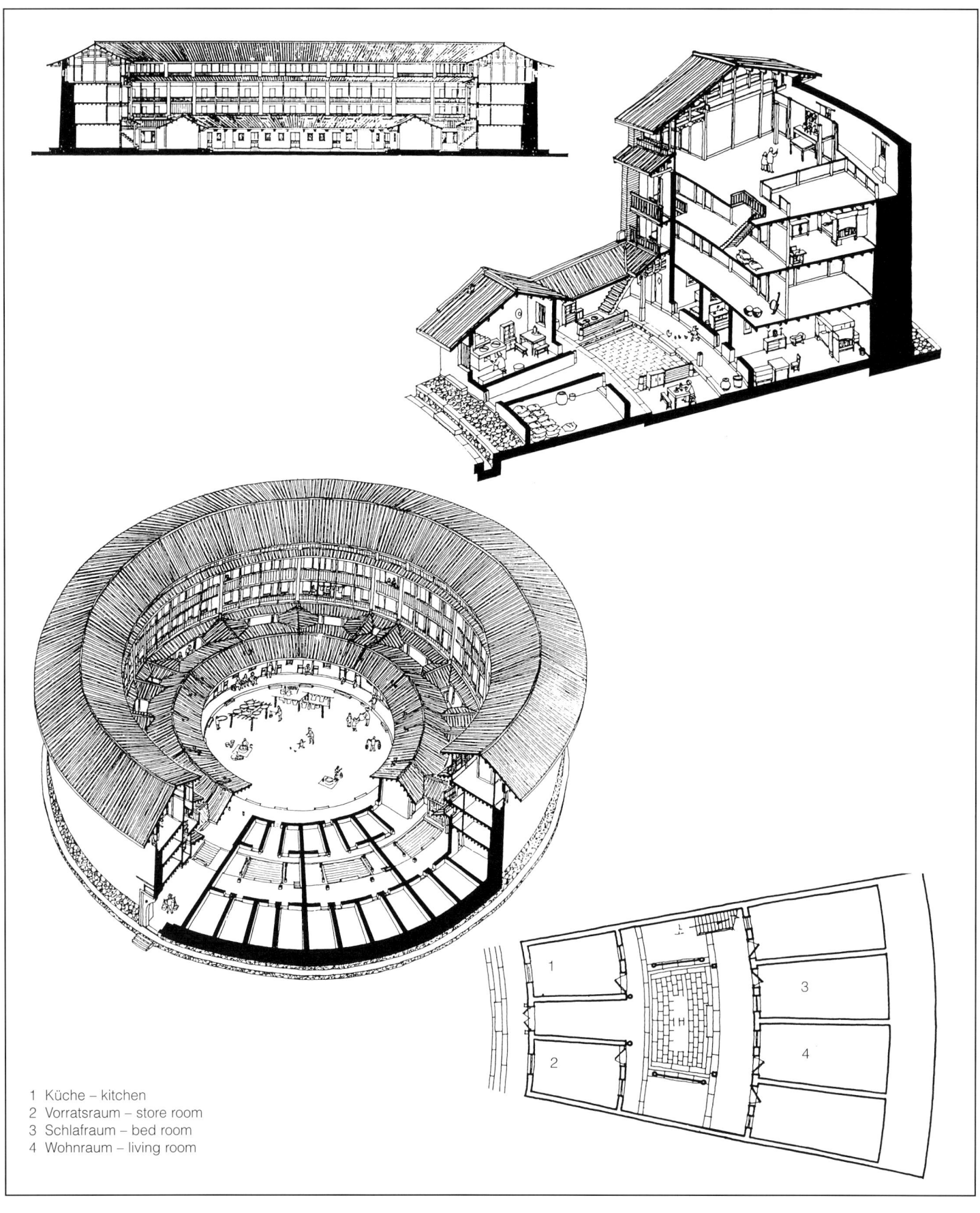

1 Küche – kitchen
2 Vorratsraum – store room
3 Schlafraum – bed room
4 Wohnraum – living room

如升樓 Rushenglou, das kleinste Erdgebäude *(tulou)* in Fujian
Rushenglou, the smallest rammed earth building *(tulou)* in Fujian
Yongding, Hukeng, Hongkeng

Oben: Innenhof mit Brunnen in einem Erdgebäude *(tulou)*
Links oben: Außenansicht des *tulou* mit Spiegelung im davor angelegten Teich
Links unten: Ausblick durch das Haupttor des *tulou*
Fujian, Xiuzhuan, Zhaoan

Above: Inner yard of a rammed earth building *(tulou)* with a well
Left above: Front view of the *tulou* reflected in the pool in front of the main entrance
Left below: View out of the main entrance, facing beautiful scenery
Fujian, Xiuzhuan, Zhaoan

Die Fünf-Phönix-Gebäude
(wufenglou) 五鳳樓

Drache, Phönix, Schildkröte und Einhorn sind die bedeutendsten Kreaturen in der Mythologie Chinas. Der Phönix symbolisiert den Süden und steht für Frieden. Deshalb wird er wie das Einhorn, welches ebenfalls nicht auf Beutejagd geht, im Buddhismus verehrt. Fünf ist die magische Zahl des Phönix. Er erscheint in fünf verschiedenen Arten, er mißt fünf Ellen an Höhe und seine Federn sind fünffarbig.

Die Fünf-Phönix-Gebäude waren beliebt bei den Kejia. Ihre Anlagen imitieren die Haltung eines Phönix vor dem Abflug. Die Gebäude sind symmetrisch im *siheyuan*-Stil gegliedert und steigen in drei Stufen zum Hauptgebäude an, das entsprechend der Höhe des Phönix fünf Stockwerke hat. Die Grundflächen der Seitengebäude liegen üblicherweise höher als die Grundfläche des Zentrums. Das hier gezeigte Fünf-Phönix-Gebäude mit dem Namen Fuyulou (Sei das Glück im Überfluß) in Hongkeng, Hukeng, Yongding entspricht der idealen Grundstruktur bei geographisch bedingter Modifikation. Die Fünf-Phönix-Gebäude können als Vorläufer der Erdschlösser bezeichnet werden, wie im folgenden gezeigt wird.

The Five-Phoenix-Buildings
(wufenglou)

Dragon, Phoenix, Turtle and Unicorn are the four most popular mythological creatures in China. The phoenix symbolizes the south, he stands for peace and is worshipped in Buddhism, since he, like the unicorn, does not prey on other creatures. Five is his magic number, he measures five cubits, appears in five different forms and his feathers have five colors.

The construction of the Five-Phoenix-Buildings was favored in Fujian by the kejia. The design imitates a phoenix, just raising his wings, ready for takeoff. According to traditional architecture the inner courtyards are symmetrical and designed in the style of the *siheyuan*. The wings climb in three steps up to the main building, which has five floors, to simulate the height of the phoenix. The surface of the outer wings is usually higher than the surface of the centre. Here the Fuyulou (Fortune in Abundance Building) in Hongkeng, Hukeng, Yongding is shown, which offers an ideal example of this kind of construction. The Five-Phoenix-Buildings in Fujian can be considered as forerunners of the earth castles in Fujian described below.

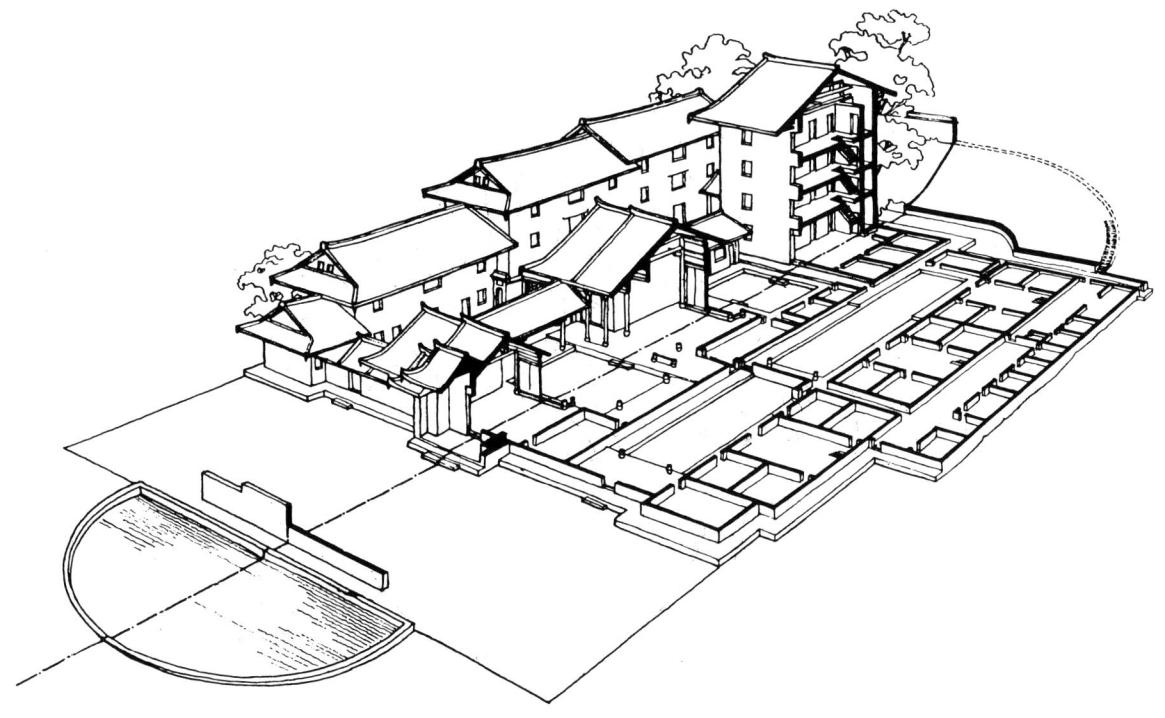

Das Fünf-Phönix-Gebäude Fuyulou 福裕樓
Oben: Räumliche Skizze mit Grundriß
Rechts oben: Eingangstor im Süd-Osten
Rechts unten: Gesamtansicht

The Five-Phoenix-Building named Fuyulou
Above: Three-dimensional outline
Right above: Southeast gate of the front yard
Right below: Overall view

Die Erdschlösser (tubao) 土堡

Die Erdschlösser *(tubao)* in Fujian dienten vertrauten Sippen als Schutzburgen. In der Art ihrer Anlage und Konstruktion können sie als Fusion der Fünf-Phönix-Gebäude und der Erdgebäude *(tulou)* betrachtet werden. Die Innenhöfe sind symmetrisch im *siheyuan*-Stil angelegt und steigen meist in drei Stufen zum Zentralgebäude an. Die aus Erde gestampften Außenmauern verlaufen nie als Rotunden, sondern umschließen die Innenhöfe im Rechteck mit abgerundeten Kanten für ungehinderte Luftzirkulation. Sie haben keine tragende Funktion für die Gebäude der Innenhöfe; üblicherweise wurde ein Wachkorridor zur Verteidigung wie ein Stockwerk eingelassen. Sie werden deshalb mit Stadtmauern verglichen. Einige Erdschlösser der Minguo-Zeit sind mit gleichförmigen Einzelhöfen angelegt und haben tatsächlich den Charakter kleiner Siedlungen, die von einer Stadtmauer umgeben sind.

Hier werden zwei traditionelle Erdschlösser der Ming- und Qing-Dynastie vorgestellt. Das Schloß der Ming-Dynastie gehörte der Familie Zhao, die bereits in der Yuan-Dynastie in Fujian siedelte. Das Schloß wurde in der Regierungszeit des Herrschers Wan Li (1573–1620 n. Chr.) gebaut und im Jahr 1600 fertiggestellt. Anlage und Gestaltung entsprechen traditionellen Herrschaftsgütern jener Zeiten.

The earth castles (tubao)

The earth castles *(tubao)* in Fujian were used as fortresses by the Kejia clans. In their conception the *tubao* can be considered as a fusion of the rammed earth buildings *(tulou)* and the Five-Phoenix-Buildings. According to traditional rules of architecture the inner courtyards are laid out in the *siheyuan* style, symmetrical to the central axis and also similar to the Five-Phoenix-Buildings, the wings rise in three steps to the central hall. The colossal walls are constructed with rammed earth. They surround the yards in a rectangle with the edges rounded off for better air circulation. Unlike the walls of the *tulou* they do not support the buildings of the inner yards, but only protect the yards like city walls with a watch corridor, constructed as a storey, let in for defense. Some earth castles, built in the Minguo Period, are laid out like little villages with uniform courtyards.

Two traditional earth castles, built in the Ming and Qing Dynasties, are shown here. The castle of the Ming belonged to the family Zhao, a clan, who settled in Fujian as early as in the Yuan Dynasty. The castle, built in the reign of the Emperor Wan Li (1573–1620 AD), was completed in 1600 AD. Layout and arrangement are characteristic of the manors of those days.

Eingänge in die Hofanlage der Familie Zhao in Huxi, Zhangpu
Oben: Südtor mit Rundbogen, darüber Steinaufsatz des verfallenen oberen Stockwerkes. Yuan-Dynastie
Rechts: Osttor mit Rundbogen, dahinter eine Schutzmauer mit eingelassenem Schrein des Erdherrschers. Ming-Dynastie

Entrances into the farmyard of the Zhao family in Huxi, Zhangpu
Left: Arched south gate with the top of the dilapidated upper floor. Yuan Dynasty
Above: Arched east gate, behind a screen wall with a shrine for the earth ruler let in. Ming Dynasty

Ansicht des Erdschlosses der Familie Zhao. Ming-Dynastie
The earth castle of the Zhao family. Ming Dynasty

Seitenhöfe des Erdschlosses der Familie Zhao. Ming-Dynastie
Outhouses of the Zhao family earth castle. Ming Dynasty

Haupteingang des Erdschlosses der Familie Zhao. Ming-Dynastie
Main entrance of the Zhao family's earth castle. Ming Dynasty

Tianjing des Erdschlosses der Familie Zhao. Ming-Dynastie
Tianjing of the Zhao family's earth castle. Ming Dynasty

Das Erdschloß Anzhenbao 安貞堡

Das Schloß des Friedens und der Beständigkeit (Anzhenbao) in Huainan, Yongan diente einer Sippe als Schutzburg. Seine Bauzeit, die fünfzehn Jahre in Anspruch nahm, war im Jahre 1885 beendet. Im Norden schützt der Berg Tianma als *fengshui* Berg die Burg, im Westen liegt der Berg Qihu. Die Burg blickt nach Süden, der Haupteingang des Vorhofes öffnet sich nach Südosten. Hohe, massive Mauern, mit einem Durchmesser von vier Metern, umschließen die Anlage. Die Grundfläche mißt 10 000 Quadratmeter. Mit dieser Zahl gilt die Beständigkeit des Schlosses als besiegelt.

Die Innenhöfe sind symmetrisch im *siheyuan*-Stil angelegt und steigen den Berghang in drei Stufen hinauf bis zum Zentralgebäude an, deren Dächer die gesamte Anlage überragen. Die Dächer der ansteigenden, zweistöckigen Seitengebäude überlappen sich und lassen dabei Zwischenraum für Luftzirkulation. Bilder, Holzschnitzereien und glasierte Keramik im Stil der Qing-Dynastie dekorieren die Innenhöfe. Das Schloß hat 320 Räume, 18 Hallen, 5 Brunnen und 12 Küchen. Aus den Vorratsräumen im zweiten Stockwerk konnte das Getreide durch kleine Löcher in den Bodenplanken nach unten ablaufen. In den Abwasser*(yin)*-kanälen saßen Schildkröten, die durch ihre Schwimmbewegungen ein Verschlammen verhinderten. Auf den massiven Mauern führt ein Korridor um den Hof. 96 Fenster und 196 Schießscharten sind zur Bewachung und Verteidigung in die Mauer eingelassen. Das Haupttor ist 2,7 Meter hoch, die Türflügel sind mit doppelter Lage Holz gezimmert. Über dem Tor steht der Name Anzhenbao, die Seiten dekoriert das Spruchpaar: „Bei Regen friedvoll vereint, bei Wind durch Beständigkeit geborgen."

Oben: Eingangstor mit der Inschrift „Langwährendes Glück" repräsentiert von Torhütern *(menshen)* in Zivil
Rechts oben: Blick vom Tianma-Berg auf das Anzhenbao
Rechts unten: Blick von der Ostseite auf das 安貞堡

The earth castle named Anzhenbao

The castle of peace and loyalty (Anzhenbao) gave shelter to a clan. It took fifteen years to build, and the castle was completed in 1885 AD. In the north the Tianma Mountain, its *fengshui* mountain, and in the west the Qihu Mountain offer shelter. The front faces the south and the main gate of the yard in front of the castle opens to the south-east. Colossal walls seven to eight meters in height and with a base four meters in diameter surround the yards. The castle is set on a square, measuring 10000 square meters to confirm that the castle will last forever.

The castle is laid out as a courtyard in the *siheyuan* style. The transverse buildings of the courtyard rise in three steps, as they do in the Five-Phoenix-Buildings. The roofs of the central hall tower above the whole castle. The tiled roofs of the two-storeyed wings overlap each other, step by step, to leave space for air to circulate. Pictures, wooden carvings and ceramics in the style of the Qing Dynasty decorate the buildings. The castle has 320 rooms, 18 halls, 5 wells and 12 kitchens. The base planks of the store rooms on the second floor are perforated with little holes, to let the corn run down when needed. In the drainage *(yin)* channels turtles swam, to prevent them from silting up. On the massive wall a guard corridor was let in for defense, from there 96 windows look out, and 196 embrasures are let in the wall. The main door is 2.7 meters high and double layered. The entrance is framed by the antithetical couplet: "Joined in peace in the time of rain, secured by steadiness in the time of wind. *(An yu wei yu chou mou gu, zhen guan xiu feng mijing duo.)*"

Above: Main door with the inscription "Lasting happiness" represented by door guards *(menshen)* in civil style
Right above: View of the Anzhenbao from the Tianma mountain
Right below: Overall view from the east side

Oben: Galerie des oberen Stockwerks
Unten: Blick auf die Pferdewandelgalerie *(zoumalang)*

Above: Gallery of the second floor with overlapping roofs
Below: The so called walking horse gallery *(zoumalang)*

Oben: Holzgitterfenster, darunter narrative Malereien und Keramik
Unten: Fensterflügel mit Schnitzerei von Phönixen und Drachen das Doppelzeichen *xi* (Glückssymbol der Eheschließung) bildend; an der linken Seite eine Spinne am Faden, die Ankunft eines Sohnes symbolisierend, und ein Unsterblicher einen Fächer haltend, um Unglück abzuwehren

Above: Wooden lattice windows, below decorations of narrative paintings and ceramics
Below: Window wings with wooden carvings, dragons and phoenixes formed as the double character *xi* (symbol of luck in marriage); to the left an immortal holding a fan to drive away evil and a spider hanging on a thread symbolizing the arrival of a son

Oben: Zentraler *tianjing* mit Aufgang in die Ahnenhalle
Rechts: Innen- und Außenansicht der Fenster über der Ahnenhalle; zentrale glockenförmige Öffnung umrahmt von Drachenornamenten; in den Fenstern zu beiden Seiten Embleme zweier Drachen mit Juwel, geformt zu einer Vase; darüber Schnitzereien von Blumen und Vögeln

Above: *Tianjing* in front of the central hall
Right: Window above the ancestor hall from outside and from inside; the central aperture shaped as a bell and framed with wooden lattices made up by carvings of flowers and birds and two dragons forming a vase

Festungen (diaofang) 碉房 und Wachtürme (diaolou) 碉樓 in Sichuan 四川

Die trockenen Gebirgslandschaften in Tibet (Xizang), Qinghai, Gansu und Sichuan sind die Heimat der Zang-Völker. Ihre Häuser sind sichere Festungsgebäude (diaofang), deren Struktur die schroffen Berge imitiert, und sie bilden terrassenförmig an den Hängen liegende, wie Gebirgsminiaturen wirkende Dörfer, die sich harmonisch in das Landschaftsbild einfügen.

In Städten auf Ebenen werden Häuser dieses Stils, genannt pingdinglou (Haus mit Flachdach), mit zentralen Brunnenhöfen angelegt. An den Gebirgshängen müssen die Häuser auf so schmaler Grundfläche gebaut werden, daß sie nur selten einen Brunnenhof umschließen. Die Häuser dort haben zwei bis drei Stockwerke. Sie sind aus Holzgerüsten konstruiert und von hohen festen Mauern umschlossen. Im Parterre führt der Weg über den Hof in die Ställe, im zweiten Stockwerk liegen Küche, Schlafraum und Vorratsraum, im dritten Stockwerk führt der Weg über ein offenes Flachdach in eine Halle. Zum Schutz gegen Unwetter sind auf dem Holzboden des Daches Kieselsteine verlegt, die mit gestampfter Erde gefestigt sind. In den oberen Stockwerken werden die Holzgerüste von der Außenmauer getragen und stehen an einer Seite über. In der Halle im oberen Stockwerk, die nach der Tradition Buddha geweiht war, finden offizielle Zeremonien und Familienfeste statt.

Fortresses (diaofang) and Watchtowers (diaolou) in Sichuan

The mountain ranges in Tibet (Xizang), Qinghai, Gansu and Sichuan where the Zang people live are very dry and stony. Their houses are secure fortresses (diaofang), designed to imitatate the shape of steep mountains, and they form villages in rising terraces which harmonize beautifully with the scenery.

In the cities on the plains their houses are flat roofed and called pingdinglou (flat-roofed houses). They frame well yards, while on the mountain slopes, where the surfaces are very narrow, they usually do not have these. They have two or three floors, which are built with timber frames supported by wooden pillars and enclosed by high, solid walls. On the ground floor the path through the entrance crosses the yard to the shed. On the second floor there is the kitchen, and on the third floor are the bedrooms. The top floor is kept partly open for drying the grain, and to protect against storms and rain the wooden planks of the floor are covered with pebbles compressed with rammed earth. The framework of the upper floors is supported by the outer walls and usually projects over the street on one side. Traditionally Buddha is worshipped, and family festivities take place in the hall of the upper floors, which therefore used to be beautifully decorated.

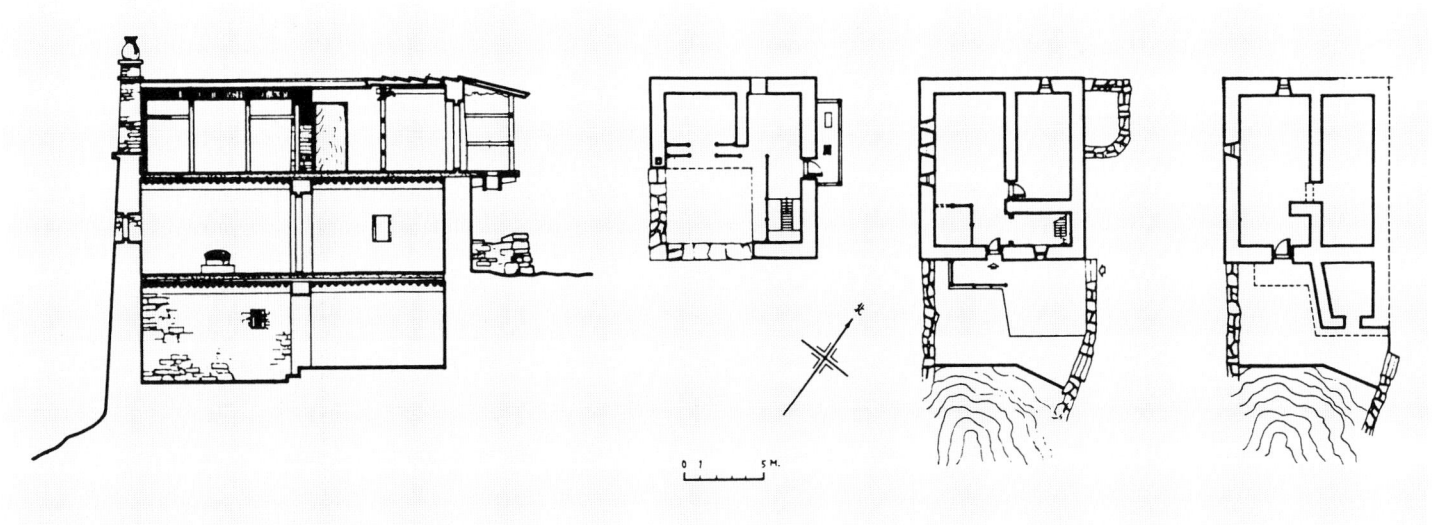

Skizze eines Hauses der Zang-Völker in Sichuan
Outline of a Zang people's house in Sichuan

Festungsgebäude des Dorfes Zhoukeji in Maerkang, Sichuan
Fortresses in the village of Zhoukeji in Maerkang, Sichuan

Festungsgebäude eines hohen Beamten in Songgang in Maerkang, Sichuan
Fortress of a high offical in the village of Songgang in Maerkang, Sichuan

Festungsgebäude und Wachtürme
Fortresses and watchtowers
Sichuan, Maerkang, Songgang

Bruchstück der Bergfeste
Dilapidated recruiting headquarters
Sichuan, Maerkang, Zhoukeji

Seitenansicht eines Festungsgebäudes
Side view of a fortress
Maerkang, Sichuan

Die Rote Backsteinbaukunst in Fujian 福建

Die Rote Backsteinbaukunst Süd-Chinas hat ihren Ursprung in Fujian. Sie ist von den Sippen entwickelt worden, die nach den Kriegswirren der Dynastie der drei Reiche und der Jin-Dynastien übergesiedelt waren. Von Fuzhou nach Yongding verlaufend, unterteilt eine gedachte Grenzlinie die Provinz in den westlichen Bezirk der Grauen und in den östlichen Bezirk der Roten Backsteinbaukunst, der sich über ein Fünftel der Provinz ausbreitet. Da in China graue Ziegel Tradition hatten, stellt sich wiederholt die Frage, warum die Sippen zuerst in Nord- und Ost-Fujian die Graue und nach Übersiedlung in den Süden Fujians die Rote Backsteinbaukunst entwickelt haben. Quanzhou war der größte Hafen Asiens und Ausgangspunkt der Seidenstraße, in dem Kulturströmungen aus Ost und West zusammenflossen. So sind Häuser im Stil der Romanischen Baukunst entstanden. Vorderasiatische Einflüsse kamen vornehmlich an Sakralbauten zum Ausdruck. Die Höfe wurden meist im *siheyuan*-Stil angelegt, und es ist zu vermuten, daß auch ästhetische Aspekte, hervorgerufen durch das Spiel der Farben in der subtropischen Landschaft mit ihrer roten Erde, zu diesem Stil führten. In der Tönung zwischen löß- und blutrot, harmonieren die Häuser mit dem üppigen Grün der Pflanzenwelt.

The Red-Brick-Architecture in Fujian

The Red-Brick-Architecture of South-China originated in Fujian. The style was invented by the eight clans, who, after the war in the Dynasty of The Three Kingdoms and the two Jin Dynasties, migrated to Fujian. A line could be drawn, running from Fuzhou to Yongding, which divides the province into the Grey and Red-Brick-Districts. To the west the Grey-Brick-District covers four fifth, to the east the Red-Brick-District covers one fifth of the Province. Since in China only grey bricks were used in architecture, we still do not know why these clans first built houses in the Grey-Brick-Style, and later, after settling in the south of Fujian, created Red-Brick-Architecture. Quanzhou was the most important harbor in Asia and the starting point for the silk road, where streams of cultures from east and west crossed. The influence of Roman architecture is recognizable in the style of the Red-Brick-Architecture in Fujian. Near Eastern influences appeared mainly in sacred buildings. Usually the courtyards were built in the *siheyuan* style. Most obvious is the aesthetic aspiration inspired by the subtropical landscape with its red earth, which led to this style. The color of the earth is retained in the bricks, modified in the process of baking, varying from loess red to intensive blood red.

Giebel verziert mit Ornamenten von Glück symbolisierenden in Wolken schwebenden Drachen. Fujian, Quanzhou
Gables decorated with ornaments of dragons floating in clouds, symbolizing good fortune. Fujian, Quanzhou

Giebel einer Ahnenhalle in Qingyang, Jinjiang, Fujian   Gables of an ancestor hall in Qingyang, Jinjiang, Fujian

Ein schöner Hof in diesem Stil ist die Yang Amiao Residenz südlich des Yangtse-Unterlaufes. Sie wurde Ende des 19. Jahrhunderts von Yang Jiazhong gebaut. Der Hof ist symmetrisch mit einem zentralen und vier seitlichen *tianjing* auf einer Fläche von 1200 qm angelegt. Die Dächer sind konkav geneigt. Ihre Firste schwingen sanft zu den sogenannten Schwalbenschwanz-Giebeln auf. Rot und schiefergrau getönte Backsteine, in verschiedenen Mustern gelegt und verziert mit Glück und langes Leben symbolisierenden Schriftzeichen, prägen das Bild der Fassade. Die auf Schiefersockeln ruhenden Vorsprünge der Trennwände von Haupt- und Seitengebäuden unterteilen die Front. Dazwischen sind Fenster eingelassen, deren Steingitterstäbe Schnitzereien von Blumen verzieren. Gravierte Schieferplatten schmücken die Seiten des Haupttores. Die Gerüste sind im *tailiang*-Stil gebaut. Schlanke, runde Holzsäulen stützen die zum *tianjing* geneigten Dächer, deren Gewölbe frei einsehbar sind. Die Längsträger sind schlicht, während die mondsichelförmigen Querbalken unterhalb mit Schnitzereien von Blumen und Vögeln verziert sind. Schnitzereien von Jahreszeiten symbolisierenden Blumen schmücken die Innenfenster. Die Residenz entspricht den Ästhetikprinzipien der Baukunst, und ist zudem ein Meisterwerk der Einheit der Kontraste des chinesischen Imperiums jener Zeit.

The residence of Yang Jiazhong in Amiao, south of the lower course of the Yangtze, is a beautiful courtyard in this style. The courtyard, covering an area of 1200 square meters, was built in the late 19th century. The design is symmetrical about the central axis crossing the main *tianjing*. Four narrow *tianjing* are laid out along the wings. The roofs are decorated with ridges, rising concavely upwards to the so-called swallow tail gables. Slate slabs with engravings are let into the wall beside the main entrance for decoration. The projections of the walls, which divide the main building from the wings, are placed on slate pedestals engraved with ornaments. Slate window bars, carved with flower patterns, decorate the front windows. The bricks are laid in different patterns and carved ornaments, signifying fortune and long life, decorate the front. The roofs sloping towards the *tianjing* are supported by fine, round wooden columns The vaulting is constructed in the fully-open style, the cross beams imitate the shape of a crescent moon. Wooden carvings of flowers and birds, colored with gold leaf, are added below. Carvings of flowers symbolizing the seasons decorate the windows of the inner yard. The residence is in accordance with the aesthetic principles of traditional architecture and reflects the unity of contrasts of the Chinese Empire at this particular time.

楊阿苗宅
Die Yang Amiao Residenz
The Yang Amiao Residence in Tingdian, Quanzhou, Fujian

Freistehendes Eingangstor der Yang Amiao Residenz mit grauem Steinlager, umsäumt von im 工字 *(gongzi)*-Muster versetzten Ziegeln

Independent entrance of the Yang Amiao Residence, the grey-stone work framed with red bricks tiled in the 工字 *(gongzi)* style

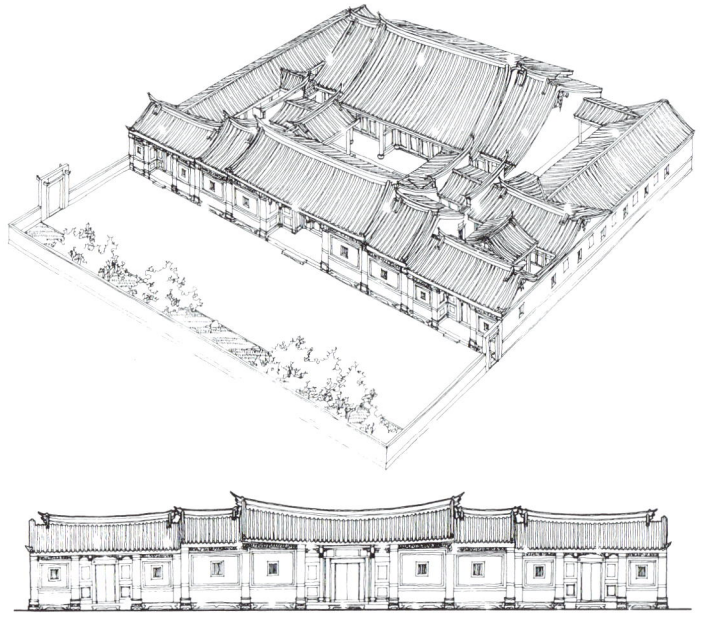

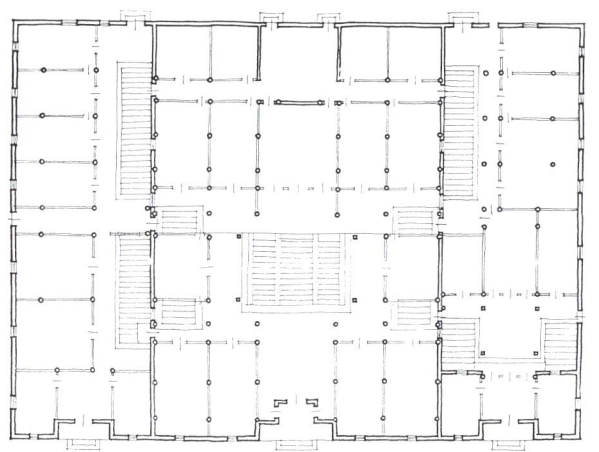

Skizzen der Yang Amiao Residenz
Scetches of the Yang Amiao Residence

Schiefertafel neben dem Haupteingang. Verzierung mit *shou*-Symbolen, Pflanzen und narrativen Schnitzereien
Slab-stone plate with engravings of plants and ornaments, signifying long life, above the plate: carved narrative

Frontansicht der Yang Amiao Residenz. Tingdian, Quanzhou, Fujian

Front view of the Yang Amiao Residence. Tingdian, Quanzhou, Fujian

Blick von einem seitlichen *tianjing* in den zentralen *tianjing*
View from a side *tianjing* into the central *tianjing*

Ahnenhalle der Yang Amiao Residenz
Oben: Vorfahren des Gründers
Links unten: Das Gründerpaar auf der Ahnentafel
Rechts unten: Kleiner Bewohner des Hofes auf einem Plastikstuhl in der Eingangshalle *(menting)*

Ancestor hall of the Yang Amiao Residence
Above: Ancestors of the founder
Left below: The founder and his wife on the ancestor wall
Right below: Little inhabitant of the courtyard sitting on a plastic chair in the entrance hall *(menting)*

Vollständig offenes Dachgewölbe *(toukong xingshi)* in der Vorhalle des Hofes; mondsichelförmige Querbalken des im *tailiang*-Stil konstruierten Holzgerüstes verziert mit mit Blattgold bemalten Holzschnitzereien von Vögeln und Blumen

Vaulting in the fully open style *(toukong xingshi)* in the entrance hall supported by the framework built in the *tailiang* style with cross beams formed like a crescent moon decorated with wooden carvings of flowers and birds painted with gold leaf

Anhang
Appendix

Register

Anzhenbao (tubao)	216 ff.
ba gua – Acht Trigramme	88
Ba-Völker	40, 60
Baiyue-Völker	40
Bailianchao-Rebellion	132
baogushi – Trommelstein	104 f., 153
ba xian – Die acht Unsterblichen	94 f.
bofeng bantou – Giebelbrett	99
Chengyang-Brücke	62, 72 f.
Chengzhi-Halle	172, 176
Chu-Völker	40
chuandou – Fachwerk	112, 116, 117
chuihuamen – Tor der hängenden Blumen	133
Cixi – Kaiserwitwe	22, 137
cuojikou – Hofanlagestil	42
Dai-Volk	34 ff.
Di-Völker	40
diaojiaolou – überhängende Häuser	40
Dong-Volk	56 ff.
dougong – sogenannte Ochsenkopfkapitelle	118, 196
doumao – ein Stil der Schutzmauern	74
dulishi yaodong – Stil der freistehenden Höhlen	20 ff.
duijing – gegenüber der Szenerie	110
dunmen – Steinblöcke an Haustoren	126
Eryilou *(tulou)*	206
fantiaofang – überhängender Giebel	44
fengshui – Wind-Wasser	156
fu – fu – Fledermaus – Glück	94 ff.
fudeci – Schrein des Wohlstands und der Ethik	150
fusi – Wachturm mit Giebel-Walmdach	44 f., 51
Fuyulou – (Fünf-Phönix-Gebäude)	210 f.
ganlan – Pfahlbauten	34 ff., 40 ff., 62 ff.
Gong Fu – Palast in Beijing	133
gongting – Palasthalle	129
gongzi – Hofanlagestil und Mauermuster	130, 228
guangliang – ein Stil der Hoftore in Beijing	127
guanyindou – ein Stil der Schutzmauern	74
Guanyin (Boddhisatva)	101
gulou – Trommelturm	57, 62, 69 f.
Han Fei	190
Hehe er xian – Thema einer narrativen Schnitzerei	94
He Shen	132
Hou Dianyuan	22
Huguajing – Brunnen	115
hui – ein Stil für Hofanlagen und Arabesken	97, 170, 187
huopu – Feuerplatz	46
huotang – Feuerstelle	60
jian – Raumeinheit	20, 118
jiangjinzhu – ein Stil der Hoftore in Beijing	44
jiating – Familienhalle	34 ff.
jiejing – Borgen der Szenerie	196
jinggan – Brunnenpfahl(haus)	116 f.
Jingpo-Volk	34
jintiaoge – Fußbodenmuster	195
jinzhu – ein Stil der Hoftore in Beijing	127 f.

Index

Anzhenbao (tubao)	216 ff.
ba gua – Eight Trigrams	88
Ba people	40, 60
Baiyue people	40
Bailianchao rebellion	132
baogushi – drum stone	104 f., 153
ba xian – The eight Immortals	94 f.
bofeng bantou – gable board	99
Chengyang Bridge	62, 72 f.
Chengzhi Hall	172, 176
Chu people	40
chuandou – framework	112, 116, 117
chuihuamen – hanging flower gate	133
Cixi Dowager	22, 137
cuojikou – courtyard layout style	42
Dai people	34 ff.
Di people	40
diaojiaolou – overhanging houses	40
Dong people	56 ff.
dougong – so-called ox-head capitals	118, 196
doumao – style of fire proof walls	74
dulishi yaodong – standalone style caves	20 ff.
duijing – opposite the scenery	110
dunmen – stone blocks framing house doors	127
Eryilou *(tulou)*	206
fantiaofang – turned overhanging gable	45
fengshui – wind-water	156
fu – fu – bat – happiness	95 ff.
fudeci – shrine of wealth and ethic	150
fusi – watchtower with gabled and hipped roof	44 f., 51
Fuyulou (Five Phoenix Building)	210 f.
ganlan – stilt houses	34 ff., 40 ff., 62 ff.
Gong Fu – Palace in Beijing	133
gongting – palace hall	129
gongzi – style of courtyard layout and of brickwork	130, 228
guangliang – style of courtyard gates in Beijing	127
guanyindou – style of fire proof walls	74
Guanyin (Boddhisatva)	101
gulou – drum tower	57, 62, 69 f.
Han Fei	190
Hehe er xian – topic of a narrative carving	94
He Shen	132
Hou Dianyuan	22
Huguajing – well	115
hui – style of courtyard layout and arabesques	97, 170, 187
huopu – fire place	46
huotang – fire place	60
jian – house unit	20, 118
jiangjinzhu – style of courtyard gates in Beijing	45
jiating – family hall	34 ff.
jiejing – borrowing of the scenery	196
jinggan – well-stilt (house)	116 f.
Jingpo people	34
jintiaoge – floor pattern	195
jinzhu – style of courtyard gates in Beijing	127 f.

kaijian – Buchten der Häuser	20, 118	*kaijian* – bays of dwellings	20
kang – Ofenbett	20, 46	*kang* – oven bed	20, 46
kanyu – Begriff der Erforschung von Territorien	88	*kanyu* – term of Chinese exploration of territories	89
kanzi – Schrein für Idole	44, 48 f.	*kanzi* – shrine of idols	45, 48 f.
kaoanshi yaodong – an das Ufer gelehnte Höhlen	12, 18 f.	*kaoanshi yaodong* – draw alongside caves	12, 18 f.
Konfuzius	199	Confucius	199
Laozi	190	Laozi	190
li wu wai san, chuan xin louyuan – Hofanlagestil	136, 138	*li wu wai san, chuan xin louyuan* – courtyard style	136, 138
Lisu-Volk	36	Lisu people	37
Liu Bowen	122	Liu Bowen	122
Luban-Tempel	112 f.	Luban Temple	112 f.
lu – lu – Hirsch – Beamtengehalt	95, 97, 150	*lu – lu* – deer – wealth symbol	95, 97, 150
manzi – ein Stil der Hoftore in Beijing		*manzi* – a style of courtyard gates in Beijing	
matou – ein Stil der Schutzmauern	74	*matou* – a style of fire proof walls	74
meirenkao – Lehnen der schönen Menschen	44	*meirenkao* – leaning of the beautiful human beings	45
minju – Volkshäuser	130	*minju* – folk house	130
Mu Wang	108	Mu Wang	108
Necha	122	Necha	122
Niuxingcun – Ochsendorf	192 f.	Niuxingcun – Ox village	192 f.
Pu-Volk	36	Pu people	37
Qijian Qilin Baoxiating – Hofanlage	22 f.	Qijian Qilin Baoxiating – courtyard	22 f.
qilou – reitendes Stockwerk	74	*qilou* – riding storey	74
Qiang-Volk	40	Qiang people	40
Qiao-Großhof	134 ff.	Qiao great court	134 ff.
queweishi matouqiang – Schutzmauerstil	120 f., 178	*queweishi matouqiang* – fire proof wall	120 f., 178
ren – ein Zeichenstil der Schutzmauern	74, 180	*ren* – a character style of fire proof walls	74, 180
Rishengchang	22	Rishenchang	22
Rushenglou	207	Rushenglou (*tulou*)	207
ruyi – Gückssymbol	95, 97, 127, 187	*ruyi* – symbol of luck	95, 97, 127, 187
sanheshui – Hofanlagestil	42	*sanheshui* – courtyard layout style	42
Sanyuan-Tempel	46, 52 f.	Sanyuan temple	46, 52 f.
Satianba-Geist	56, 62	Satianba spirit	58, 62
Shanyue – Landschaft und Volk	165	Shanyue – landscape and people	165
She-Volk	111	She people	111
Shunyulou (*tulou*)	204	Shunyulou (*tulou*)	204
shou – Zeichen des langen Lebens	135 ff., 157	*shou* – character of long life	135 ff., 157
sihedouyuan – Hofanlagestil	138	*sihedouyuan* – courtyard layout style	138
siheyuan – Hofanlagestil	22 ff.	*siheyuan* – courtyard layout style	22 ff.
siheshui – Hofanlagestil	42	*siheshui* – courtyard layout style	42
siyan – Schutzgiebel	44	*siyan* – protecting gable	45
Songfeng Shuiyue (Hof)	112 f.	Songfeng Shuiyue (courtyard)	112 f.
sui han san you – Thema einer narrativen Schnitzerei	106	*sui han san you* – topic of a narrative carving	106
Su Wu mu yang – Thema einer narrativen Schnitzerei	199	*Su Wu mu yang* – topic of a narrative carving	199
taishibi – Ahnentafel	172	*taishibi* – ancestor wall	172
taishiyi – Ahnensessel	172	*taishiyi* – ancestor chair	172
tantou – Späherkopf	99	*tantou* – spy head	99
tailiang – Holzbaustil	112, 116	*tailiang* – style of wood construction	112, 116
taishan – Dachstil	44	*taishan* – roofing style	46
Taishanshi gandang	99 f., 139	Taishanshi gandang	99 f., 139
tianjing – Himmel-Brunnen	43 ff.	*tianjing* – heaven-well	43 ff.
Tianluokeng (*tulou*)	203	Tianluokeng (*tulou*)	203
tiantingyuan – Himmel-Halle-Hof	160	*tiantingyuan* – heaven-hall-courtyard	160
toukong xingshi – Dachgewölbestil	180, 185 f., 234	*toukong xingshi* – vaulting style	180, 185 f., 234
Tudi – Erdherrscher	15, 56 ff., 150	Tudi – Earth Ruler	15, 56 ff., 150
Tujia – Volk	40 ff.	Tujia people	40 ff.

tubao – Erdschlösser	212 ff.		*tubao* – earth rammed castles	212 ff.
tulou – aus Erde gestampfte Häuser	202 ff.		*tulou* – earth rammed houses	202 ff.
Wa-Volk	36		Wa people	36
wan – Zeichen für 10000, Symbol der Unendlichkeit	95		*wan* – character of 10000, symbol of eternity	95
Wudaoci – Ahnenhallel	135, 149		Wudaoci – ancestor hall	135, 149
wufenglou – Fünf-Phönix-Gebäude	210 ff.		*wufenglou* – Five-Phoenix-Buildings	210 ff.
Wu Hu Luan Hua (Rebellion)	40		*Wu Hu Luan Hua* – rebellion	40
xi – Glückssymbol	43, 219		*xi* – symbol of happiness	43, 219
xiachenshi yaodong – Stil der versenkten Höhlen	12 f.		*xiachenshi yaodong* – sunken cave style	12 f.
xieshan – Dachstil	44		*xieshan* – roof style	45
xuanshan – Dachstil	44		*xuanshan* – sloping mountain	45
Yang Amiao Residenz	228 ff.		Yang Amiao Residence	228 ff.
Yang Jiazhong	228		Yang Jiazhong	228
yaoshi – Hofanlagestil	42		*yaoshi* – courtyard layout style	42
yi ban yi ci – Wandtäfelungstil	165, 195		*yi ban yi ci* – wainscoting style	165, 195
yiming liangan – Hofanlagestil	20, 118, 170		*yiming liangan* – courtyard layout style	20, 119, 170
yiming ernei – Hofanlagestil	118		*yiming ernei* – courtyard layout style	119
yi zhu shier liang – Holzkonstruktion	44, 45		*yi zhu shier liang* – wood construction	44, 45
yiziwu – Hofanlagestil	42, 44		*yiziwu* – one-character house	42, 44
yinzi – Hofanlagestil	62		*yinzi* – courtyard layout style	62
yuedongmen – Mondhöhlentor	93		*yuedongmen* – moon cave gate	93
Yuemu ci zi – Thema einer narrativen Schnitzerei	199		Yuemu ci zi – topic of a narrative carving	199
Yusanlou *(tulou)*	205		Yusanlou *(tulou)*	205
Zao Fu	108		Zao Fu	108
Zhuang Chou	108		Zhuang Chou	108
Zhu Xi	191		Zhu Xi	191
zicheng – Kaiserstadt	85 f.		*zicheng* – emperor's city	85 f.
zoumalang – Pferdewandelkorridor	218		*zoumalang* – horse walking corridor	218

Verwendete Quellen:

Die nachfolgend angeführten Textpassagen beziehen sich auf die in Klammern gesetzten bibliografischen Angaben. Für ihre Übersetzung und Interpretation zeichnet die Autorin verantwortlich.

Kapitel:
- S. 12 – 33 (1, 21, 26)
- S. 34 – 39 (3, 21)
- S. 40 – 57 (1, 32)
- S. 58 – 75 (3)
- S. 76 – 83 (5)
- S. 84 – 121 (2, 7, 8, 10, 11, 12, 13, 14, 16, 19, 20, 22, 23, 25, 29, 30)
- S. 122 – 128 (13, 16, 18, 20, 27, 33)
- S. 129 – 133 (1, 26)
- S. 134 – 159 (13, 26, 34)
- S. 160 – 201 (1, 25, 31)
- S. 202 – 221 (6, 9, 17, 18)
- S. 222 – 225 (20, 21)
- S. 226 – 235 (17, 28)

Sources consulted:

The text passages listed below refer to the bibliographical details given in brackets. The author is responsable for her translation and interpretation.

Chapter:
- pp. 12 – 33 (1, 21, 26)
- pp. 34 – 39 (3, 21)
- pp. 40 – 57 (1, 32)
- pp. 58 – 75 (3)
- pp. 76 – 83 (5)
- pp. 84 – 121 (2, 7, 8, 10, 11, 12, 13, 14, 16, 19, 20, 22, 23, 25, 29, 30)
- pp. 122 – 128 (13, 16, 18, 20, 27, 33)
- pp. 129 – 133 (1, 26)
- pp. 134 – 159 (13, 26, 34)
- pp. 160 – 201 (1, 25, 31)
- pp. 202 – 221 (6, 9, 17, 18)
- pp. 222 – 225 (20, 21)
- pp. 226 – 235 (17, 28)

Bibliographie/Bibliography

1. Bai Shouyi: Précis d'histoire de Chine, Zhongguo Waiwen Chubanshi chuban, Beijing 1988

2. Ch'en Kenneth: Buddhism in China, Princeton University Press, 1964

3. Chen Moude & Wang Cuilan: Zhengui de Minzu Jianzhu Wenhua, Jiangsu Meishu Chubanshi, Nanjing 2000

4. Chen Shouxiang: Duojin Xiaolou Cheng Yitong, Dongzu Mulou Sanyi. Lao Fangzi, Jiangsu Meishu Chubanshi, Nanjing 1996

5. Chen Ping: Zhongguo Juzhu Wenhua, Zhonghua Shuju, Xianggang 1992

6. Chen Shumin: Lidai Tulou de Yanbian Licheng. Da Di, Taiwan 1993

7. Chen Zhihua: Nanxijiang Zhongyou Gucunlou, Shenghuo·Dushu·Xinzhi·Sanlian Shudian, Beijing 1999

8. Cheng Jianjun: Fengshuixie Jianzhu, Jiangsu Kexue Jishu Chubanshi, Nanchang 1992

9. Dai Zhijian: Zhaoan Minju Yuwenhua. Kejia Congress, Hongkong 1990

10. Eberhard Wolfram: A Dictionary of Chinese Symbols. Taiwan, Edition SMC Publishing Inc., 1994

11. Feuchtwang Stephan D. R.: An Anthropological Analysis of Chinese Geomancy, Nantian Shujuyou Xiangongsi, Taipei 1971

12. Fung Yulan: A History of Chinese Philosophy, Princeton University Press, 1983

13. Granet Marcel: Das chinesische Denken, Suhrkamp Taschenbuch Wissenschaft, Frankfurt 1985

14. Granet Marcel: Die chinesische Zivilisation, Suhrkamp Taschenbuch Wissenschaft, Frankfurt 1988

15. Grenet Jaques: Die chinesische Welt, Suhrkamp Taschenbuch 1505, Erste Auflage 1988

16. Hou Youbing: Zhongguo Jianzhu Meixue, Heilongjiang Kexue Jishu Chubanshi, Beijing 1997

17. Huang Hanmin: Fujian Minju, Jiangsu Meishu Chubanshi, Nanjing 1994

18. Kongzi: Lunyu Biecai, Liji Jijie (xia), Wenshi · Zhishi · Chubanqu Yinxing, Taipei 1992

19. Kwok Man-ho with O'Brien Joanne: The Elements of Fengshui, Element Books Limited, Great Britain 1991

20. Liu Dunzhen: Zhongguo Gudai Jianzhu Meixue, Zhongguo Jianzhu Gongye Chubanshi, Beijing 1978

21. Long Bingyi: Zhongguo Chuantong Minju Jianzhu, Regional Council, Hongkong 1995

22. Münke Wolfgang: Die klassische chinesische Mythologie. Ernst Klett Verlag, Stuttgart 1976

23. Needham Joseph: Science and Civilisation in China, Cambridge University Press, 1956, Vol. IV, 1959

24. Sullivan Michael: The Arts of China, SMC Publishing Inc., Taipei 1979

25. Speiser Werner: China, Spirit and Society, Mcthuan London, 1960, Reprint 1966

26. Wang Qijun: Shanxi Minju Daolun. Lao Fangzi, Jiangsu Meishu Chubanshi, Nanjing 1993

27. Wang Qijun: Beijing Siheyuan, Lao Fangzi, Jiangsu Meishu Chubanshi, Nanjing 1995

28. Wang Zhili, Wang Qijun: Zhongguo Chuangtong Minju Jianzhu, Taipei Nantian Shuju Chubanju, 1993,

29. Wilhelm Richard: I Ging, Text und Materialien, Eugen Diedrichs Verlag, München 1973

30. Williams C. A. S.: Outlines of Chinese Symbolism and Art Motives, Dover Publications Inc., New York 1976

31. Yu Hongli: Zhongguo Chuantong Minjian Jianzhu de Jingcai Huazhang – Huizhou Minju. Jiangsu Meishu Chubanshi, Nanjing 1993

32. Zhang Zonggao: Tujia Diaojiaolou – Jingyuanshi Ganlan de Qu, Lai, Jin. Lao Fangzi, Jiangsu Meishu Chubanshi, Nanjing 1994

33. Zhou Shachen: Beijing Old and New, A Historical Guide to Places of Interest, New World Press, Beijing 1984

34. Zhengxie Shanxisheng Yixian Weiyuangong Bianyin Shanxisheng Yixian Minsu Bowuguan: Da Qiao Yuanjia, Shanxi 1995

Abbildungsnachweise:	Illustration acknowledgements

Alle Fotos, mit Ausnahme der unten aufgeführten, wurden von dem Fotografen Li Yuxiang aufgenommen

Chen Jianxing: S. 82
Gao Peng: S. 92
Zhang Yonggao: S. 48, 50
Zhu Chengliang: S. 77, 78, 80/81/83, 114
Almut E. I. Bettels: S. 84 links, 228 – 232

Die Aufnahmen der Seite 36 unten und Mitte entstammen den Administrationsbüros der Bezirke Fugong und Mengjiao; die Aufnahmen der Seiten 78, 79 entstammen den Administrationsbüros der Bezirke Yinxian und Zhaoyu

Alle Skizzen, mit Ausnahme der unten aufgeführten, wurden der Buchreihe „Lao Fangzi" entnommen und mit Genehmigung des Jiangsu-Kunstverlages abgebildet

S. 12, 51, 88
Hou Youbing: Zhongguo Jianzhu Meixue,
S. 18, 86, 87, 126
Liu Dunzhen: Zhongguo Gudai Jianzhu Meixue
S. 48, 162, 163
Long Bingyi: Zhongguo Chuantong Minju Jianzhu,
S. 58
Chen Ping: Zhongguo Juzhu Wenhua
S. 124
Hou Youbing: Zhongguo Jianzhu Meixue
S. 190, 191
Gugong Bowuyuan, Taipei

All the photographs with the exception of those listed below were taken by Li Yuxiang

Chen Jianxing: p. 82
Gao Peng: p. 92
Zhang Yonggao: pp. 48, 50
Zhu Chengliang: pp. 77, 78, 80/81/83, 114
Almut E. I. Bettels: p. 84 left, pp. 228 – 232

The photograph on page 36 (bottom and centre) were loaned by the administrative offices of the Fugong and Mengjiao districts, the photographs on page 78, 79 by the administrative offices of the districts Yinxian and Zhaoyu

All sketches and pictures with the exception of those listed below are taken from the "Lao Fangzi" book series and reproduced by permission of the Jiangsu Art Press

pp. 12, 51, 88
Hou Youbing: Zhongguo Jianzhu Meixue,
pp. 18, 86, 87, 126
Liu Dunzhen: Zhongguo Gudai Jianzhu Meixue
pp. 48, 162, 163
Long Bingyi: Zhongguo Chuantong Minju Jianzhu,
p. 58
Chen Ping: Zhongguo Juzhu Wenhua
p. 124
Hou Youbing: Zhongguo Jianzhu Meixue
pp. 190, 191
Gugong Bowuyuan, Taipei